CHAPTERS ON

ENGLISH METRE

BY

JOSEPH B. MAYOR, M.A.

HONORARY FELLOW OF ST JOHN'S COLLEGE, CAMBRIDGE.

SECOND EDITION

REVISED AND ENLARGED.

CAMBRIDGE:

AT THE UNIVERSITY PRESS.

1901

CAMBRIDGE
UNIVERSITY PRESS

University Printing House, Cambridge CB2 8BS, United Kingdom

Cambridge University Press is part of the University of Cambridge.

It furthers the University's mission by disseminating knowledge in the pursuit of education, learning and research at the highest international levels of excellence.

www.cambridge.org
Information on this title: www.cambridge.org/9781107445819

© Cambridge University Press 1901

First published 1901
First paperback edition 2014

A catalogue record for this publication is available from the British Library

ISBN 978-1-107-44581-9 Paperback

PREFACE TO THE FIRST EDITION.

My attention was first drawn to the exact study of English prosody many years ago in lecturing on Shakespeare to classes both male and female. As a rule I found those who attended the classes devoid of any but the vaguest idea of metre; and I knew of no book which I could recommend to them as giving an entirely satisfactory account of the matter, the books of the highest authority seeming to me to start from assumptions which were inconsistent with the practice of English poets from the time of Shakespeare downwards. I endeavoured to point out these inconsistencies and, at the same time, to give the outline of what I thought to be a truer system, in three papers, which were read before the London Philological Society between the years 1874 and 1877. The substance of those papers, greatly modified and expanded, appears in the chapters which follow, numbered I. to V. VIII. XI.; the remaining chapters are altogether new.

My own views have naturally undergone some change in the interval which has elapsed since the first paper was written. For instance, I have now no doubt (see examples from Shelley in p. 242) that we must recognize the substitution of tribrachs for iambs in English blank verse, a point which was still an open question to me when pp. 71 and 75 were written. I am now less disposed to agree with Dr Abbott in his attempt to explain away Shakespeare's trisyllabic feet by the process of slurring, than I was when I wrote my paper on *Macbeth* (pp. 174 foll.). On the other hand, I have given in p. 200 the reasons which have finally decided me to adopt Dr Abbott's, rather than Mr A. J. Ellis's view, in reference to the feminine caesura, of which I had spoken doubtfully in my earlier paper. As far as I know, these are the only points in which any difference of view will be found; should there be any others, a reference to the Index will at once enable the reader to compare together all that is said on any given subject.

There is another matter on which I should like to add a word to what is stated in the text. Prof. H. Sidgwick, who has most kindly looked over some of the proof-sheets, suggests, in reference to the chapter on Metrical Metamorphosis, that it would be well to make it more clear to the reader, that it is not a mere verbal question, whether, for instance, a line should be called an iambic with initial truncation or a trochaic with final truncation; and asks me how I would propose to answer "the real and interesting aesthetic question, whether the type (i.e. the normal line) so far predominates in the reader's mind, that he feels the particular line (which departs from the normal line) rather as a variant than as a distinct change of type." To this I would reply (1) that my chief aim will be accomplished, if I can get my readers to observe the different metrical effects of the lines which they read, and to describe them in clear and definite terms, and that this will not be interfered with, even though we should allow of alternative expressions for the same fact; (2) that a certain number of variants have now become established, as it were, by universal consent, such as the feminine iambic and truncated

trochaic; (3) that when a question arises about the scansion of
a line which cannot be referred to any such recognized sub-
class, it is not ordinarily a matter of indifference which of two
possible explanations we shall adopt, but that we have first
to compare such a line with the other lines of the poem in
which it occurs, and see whether we can discover any similar
irregularities, as for instance in regard to Milton's use of the
double trochee (p. 38); and must reject any theory which will
not suit all such irregular lines. (See the discussion in pp. 86,
87, 92 on the metre of *Christabel.*) (4) that in cases where
nothing can be absolutely decided from a comparison of the
rest of the poem or of other similar poems, the choice between
two possible explanations of a verse must in the last resort rest
with the educated taste of the reader. It is not enough simply
that the ear should be naturally sensitive to the harmonies of
sound; the ear must have been accustomed to the particular
metre or rhythm, or it will not be able to appreciate it rightly.
No doubt it is possible that, even so, differently constituted
minds and ears may be differently affected by the same break or
change in the rhythm. In such a case I should be inclined to
say with Horne Tooke 'truth is what each man troweth'; the
accurate explanation will be that which accurately expresses
each man's own feeling of the rhythm of the line.

I have given my book the title of *Chapters on Metre* in
order to show that it makes no pretence to completeness. I have
not attempted to deal, otherwise than incidentally, either with the
aesthetic or the historic side of metrical investigation. I have
barely touched on such matters as alliteration and rhyme: I
have not ventured to pronounce an opinion as to the origin and
early history of our metres. What I have endeavoured to do is
to ascertain by a process of induction the more general laws of

our modern metre, and to test the results on a variety of instances. I wish very much that some competent scholar would take up that historical side of the question which I have left untouched. To mention only one part of it, I do not know where to find a really careful investigation of the growth of accentual Latin verse. It would have been admirably done by the ever-to-be-lamented Munro, if he had chosen to turn his attention to it. I remember hearing long ago a paper read by him before the Cambridge Philosophical Society, in which he drew attention to the importance of the accent as colouring the rhythm even of the quantitative verse of the Augustan age. Thus he contrasted the rude sing-song of the soldiers at Caesar's triumph,

Ecce Caesar nunc triumphat qui subegit Gallias,

where the verbal accent corresponds throughout with the stress of the quantitative metre, and such a line as that of Virgil,

Itáliam fáto prófugus Lavinia venit,

where the poet studiously opposes the accent to the metre.

What may be the earliest specimen of pure accentual verse in Latin I am unable to say. We are told by Christ (*Metrik der Griechen und Römer*, p. 402) that Ritschl considered the mill-song of the Lesbian women (ἄλει, μύλα, ἄλει) to be an early example of accentual metre in Greek. In Latin the *Instructiones* of the barbarous Com modianus (flourished about the middle of the third century) is usually named as the first specimen of accentual verse, but his metre is almost as indifferent to accent as it is to quantity. The example quoted by Dr Donaldson in his Latin Grammar is a poem on two of the Diocletian martyrs commencing

Dúae quaedam réferuntur Rómae natae féminae.

Whatever may be the date of the earliest existing specimen, there can be no doubt that the feeling for quantity had long before died out among all but the learned few, and that such verses for instance as the irregular Phalaecians addressed to Alexander Severus (Lamprid. c. 38) would be ordinarily read as accentual iambics corresponding to the hendecasyllabic of modern Italian, our own 5-foot feminine.

> *Pulchrum | quod vi|des es|se nos|trum re|gem*
> *Quem Sy|rum te|tulit | propa|go pul|chrum,*
> *Vena|tus fa|cit et | lepus | come|sus*
> *De quo | contin|uum | capit | lepo|rem.*

Hence I am unable to place implicit confidence in the assertion of Zarncke, that the origin of this metre cannot be traced further back than the Romance poets[1].

In conclusion I have to return my hearty thanks to Mr A. J. Ellis for allowing me to make free use of various papers on metre, to Dr Furnival and Prof. Paul Meyer of Paris for much helpful information, and to Mr Roby and Prof. Sidgwick for valuable criticisms and suggestions.

October 1886.

---

[1] '*Der fünffüssige Iambus, als Zehnsilbler oder Eilfsilbler erscheinend, ist nicht vom Alterthume uns überliefert...Als selbstständiger Rhythmus erscheint der Vers nirgends* (i.e. neither in Latin nor in Greek),' p. 3.   See below Appendix A.

Note to the Second Edition.

The second Edition has been revised throughout and enlarged by the addition of a Chapter on the Metrical Systems of Dr Skeat and Mr Robert Bridges, originally addressed to the Philological Society; a Chapter on Shelley's Metre, originally read before the Shelley Society; and a Chapter on the English Hexameter, which appears here for the first time.

I cannot send forth this new edition without paying a last tribute to my old friend Prof. Henry Sidgwick, to whom I am deeply indebted not only for the interest which he took in my metrical studies, but also, far more, for the very great assistance I received from him during the last year of his life in preparing for the Press the Second Part of the Exploratio Philosophica of our common friend, John Grote, who was also his own predecessor in the Chair of Moral Philosophy at Cambridge.

Hort gone, Seeley gone, Sidgwick gone—to me and to many others, how dimmed is the glory of the Cambridge that we knew!

οἵη περ φύλλων γενεή τοιήδε καὶ ἀνδρῶν.

October 1901.

TABLE OF CONTENTS.

CHAPTER IV.

Aesthetic Intuitivism.

CHAPTER V.

Natural or A-posteriori System.

CHAPTER VI.

Metrical Metamorphosis.

CHAPTER VII.

Two recent Metrical Systems.

CHAPTER VIII.

Naming and Classification of Metres. Illustrations from Tennyson.

CHAPTER IX.

Naming and Classification of Metres. Illustrations from the Hymn-book.

CHAPTER XIII.

Modern Blank Verse. Tennyson and Browning.

CHAPTER XIV.

Shelley's Metre.

CHAPTER XV.

The English Hexameter.

APPENDIX A.

APPENDIX B.

Corrigenda.

p. 71, ll. 21, 22, transfer 'bacchius' and 'anti-bacchius'.
p. 157, l. 14, for 'p. 53' read 'p. 51'.
p. 191, l. 23, omit bracket after 'dev'lish'.
p. 228, l. 4 up, for 'iambic' read 'iamb'.

CHAPTER I.

INTRODUCTORY.

THERE are persons to whom system generally is a bugbear, and to whom systems of prosody are especially distasteful. 'The object of rhythm and metre,' they argue, 'is to please the ear. If they fail to do this, they fail of their object, and nothing is gained by showing that they are conformable to certain rules of grammarians. The final authority rests, not with the grammarian, but with those for whom the poet sings.' It may be answered that, just in the same way, the primary object of the musician and painter is to afford pleasure to the eye and ear. If they fail in this, they too fail in their object. But none will deny the importance of theory and rules in these branches of art, both for training the artist in the means by which he may attain his end, and for educating the hearer and spectator to appreciate a higher and more refined order of beauty. Or we might take our illustration not from an art, but from a science, such as botany. The use of botany is to enable us to describe in exact and definite terms the different characteristics of plants, to arrange and classify all that is known about them, and to reduce the various phenomena to their simplest types and laws. So the use of prosody is to supply a technical language by which to describe each specimen of verse brought before us; to distinguish the different kinds of verse, to establish a type of each, by reference to which existing varieties may be compared, and finally to state the laws of composition which have been observed by those whom the world recognizes as poets. Then from this we may draw practical rules of art for the poet or the reader.

No doubt, when the subject matter of the science or art is one with which our affections are more or less intimately connected, there is a natural shrinking from what may appear to be a cold-blooded analysis of that which excites our admiration or love. At best, we think we can gain nothing by it. Like the speaker in 'Maud' we are inclined to say

    a learned man
May give it a clumsy name,
  Let him name it who can,
Its beauty would be the same.

But we are moreover suspicious of any attempt to explain how it is that a poet produces his results. We prefer to accept the poem as a pure inspiration wakening up an answering inspiration in our own minds. We regard the use of analysis as a perfidious attempt to rob us of inspiration and leave us in its stead a studied expertness in certain tricks of art. But this is really a total misconception of what is aimed at in metrical analysis. It only deals with the outer vesture of poetry; it teaches us to look more closely at this, to notice its forms and colours and ornaments, just in the same way as a very slight knowledge of botany enables us to observe the distinguishing beauties of ferns or other plants. It may also go on to show how the inner spirit of poetry reveals itself in its outer vesture, how rhythm and metre correspond to varying moods of feeling and so on, but it makes no pretence to explain the creative inspiration of the poet; on the contrary it enlarges our idea of its operation and thus tends to enhance our admiration and delight, just as the teaching of botany or drawing not only quickens the eye for the external features of a landscape, but vastly increases the imaginative and emotional enjoyment of natural scenery.

Connected with this dislike to the application of scientific terms and methods to poetry, as injurious to its spirit and feeling, there is the dislike sometimes felt by persons of fine ear to the mechanical process of scanning. Partly they despair of explaining by rule, or representing by a scheme, the rich undulation of sound of which the ear is cognizant. This is an objection to which all science is liable. As Bacon says, "subtilitas

naturae subtilitatem argumentandi multis partibus superat."
And partly there is an aristocratic confidence in their own
poetic instinct, and a suspicion and contempt for knowledge
slowly gained by training and effort. Yet, we all know, science
the tortoise quickly outstrips the hare intuition. Singing by
ear is no match for singing from notes. Refined aesthetic
sense or tact may judge instinctively of the quality of this
or that verse, as melodious or the opposite, but this tact passes
away with the individual who possessed it. Science translates
quality into a quantitative scale; rudely, it is true, at first;
but each step gained is a gain for mankind at large, and forms
an ever new vantage-ground for the investigations of each
succeeding generation.

We may assume then that a scientific treatment of the
subject of metre is possible and is desirable. The next question
is, how far has this desirable end been already achieved?
I shall endeavour to answer this in the following chapters by
a careful examination of the metrical systems which possess
the highest authority and are most in esteem at the present
day; and in order to make my criticisms more generally intelligible, I shall commence with a brief sketch of what I hold
to be the natural or truly scientific system.

A subject like prosody lends itself to three different kinds of
treatment in consequence of its connexion with history on the
one side and aesthetics on the other. One of the dangers which
the prosodian or metrist has to guard against is the mixing
up of these different methods of treatment. Thus Dr Guest
in his *History of English Rhythms* sets before himself as his
main object, to trace out the development of one rhythm or
metre from another, and to exhibit the varieties of rhythm
which characterize each poet and each period, a very interesting and important branch of inquiry. But this simple inquiry
into matter of fact is rendered almost valueless by the arbitrary
assumption that the greater part of the development of English
metre has been illegitimate. The rule of verse laid down by
our Anglo-Saxon ancestors is treated as a rule of faith, binding
on their unfortunate successors to the end of time. No right
of private judgment is allowed either to poets or to readers.

Verses, however pleasing to the modern ear, are denied to be metrical at all, or else twisted and mangled to suit the usage of five centuries ago; just as a modern sentence might be condemned as ungrammatical, because it could not be explained on antiquarian views of syntax. A confusion of a different kind is found in other writers on metre (of whom Mr J. A. Symonds may be taken as an example), who deprecate any attempt to name or count the feet in a verse, provided its rhythm satisfies their ear and is in harmony with their idea of the poet's feeling. No good can be done until we clear ourselves of these confusions. The first thing which the metrist should set himself to ascertain in regard to any verses submitted to him is the existing τί, the actual phenomenon; what is the normal line of the metre? how does each particular verse depart from this type? Then he may go on to investigate the ποῖον, the melody and expressiveness of the verse, and the means by which these qualities are attained. And lastly he may investigate the πῶς, observe how any particular metre has come into existence, what metrical effects each poet has borrowed from others, and what he has added for himself.

Treating the subject thus from the purely scientific side, and deferring for the present all reference to historical or aesthetical considerations, I start with the two fundamental questions, What is the distinction between prose and verse? How are the different kinds of verse to be classified?

As regards the first, I suppose all would agree in saying that, in English, verse differed from prose in the regular sequence of the accent or stress. Where the stress recurs in obedience to a definite law, there we have verse. And the kinds of verse are classified according to the intervals which separate the accents, whether an interval of one syllable or of two syllables, and according as the rhythm is ascending, i.e. passing from an unaccented to an accented syllable, or descending, i.e. passing from an accented to an unaccented syllable. We thus get the four simplest kinds of metres, ascending disyllabic, descending disyllabic, ascending trisyllabic, and descending trisyllabic: the metres commonly known as iambic, trochaic, anapaestic, dactylic.

Here I am aware that I enter on debated ground. Mr A. J. Ellis, in the course of his great work on English pronunciation, proposes to consider what light is thrown upon the pronunciation of Shakespeare's time by an examination of the rhymes, the accents, and the number of syllables admitted in his verse. He asserts that "the whole subject of English metres requires re-investigation on the basis of accent." "The old names of measures borrowed from Latin prosodists are entirely misleading, and the routine scansion with the accent on alternate syllables is known only to grammarians, having never been practised by poets."

There are three points here for discussion : Are the classical names to be given up ? Is the routine scansion unknown to poets ? Is it, in any case, of use in the interests of education and science ?

I cannot myself see that the use of the terms 'iambic,' etc., is misleading. No one imagines them to imply that English metre rests on a quantitative basis. The notion of quantity altogether seems to me rather a puzzle to English people; they know what a long vowel is, but I doubt whether they would recognize a long syllable such as 'strength' where the vowel was short. Again, it cannot be denied that there is to the ear a strong resemblance between the rhythm of the English accentual, and the Greek quantitative iambic and trochaic, and it is certainly more convenient to speak of iambic than of ascending disyllabic. The only other way in which I could imagine the term misleading, would be if anyone were to suppose that the rules of the Greek metre were applicable in the English; but this is so easily corrected that it hardly seems worth notice[1].

As to the second point, whether the routine scansion has

---

[1] I find that Mr Ellis objects to the Classical nomenclature, rather in the interests of Classical, than of English metre. His remarks on the above passage are as follows. "It seems to me that the use of the classical names has arisen from our not understanding them, that is, not having the feeling for what they expressed, and that it is essential to our comprehension of the classical metres to dissociate their terminology from that of modern metres which have nothing in common with them." For a fuller discussion he refers to his *Practical Hints on the Quantitative Pronunciation of Latin.*

ever been known to poets, i.e. whether poets have ever kept strictly to the metre in their practice, it surely cannot be denied that some of our poets (Chaucer among them) have in some respects approached the routine scansion; but I am not concerned here either to maintain or to deny that they have done so. What I would affirm is that it is impossible for the routine scansion to die out, as long as there are children and common people, and poetry which commends itself to them. And I would also venture to say that it *ought* not to die out as long as there are scientific men who will endeavour to bring clearness and precision into our notions about poetry as about other things. Routine scansion is the natural form of poetry to a child, as natural to it as the love of sweet things or bright colours: it is only through the routine scansion that its ear can be educated to appreciate in time a more varied and complex rhythm. No one who knows children can doubt this. If example is wanted, it may be found in Ruskin's *Praeterita*, p. 55, where the author speaks of a prolonged struggle between his childish self and his mother "concerning the accent of the "*of* in the lines

> Shall any following spring revive
> The ashes of the urn?

"I insisting partly in childish obstinacy, and partly in true "instinct for rhythm (being wholly careless on the subject both "of urns and their contents) on reciting it with an accented *of*. "It was not till after three weeks' labour that my mother got the "accent lightened on the *of* and laid on the *ashes*, to her mind." But any parent may test it for himself in children who have a taste for poetry. Whatever effort may be made to teach them to observe the true verbal accents and the stops, and attend to the meaning and logic of the line, they will insist on singing it to a chant of their own, disregarding everything but the metrical accent, and are made quite unhappy if compelled to say or read it like prose. And, after all, is this not the right sense of the μῆνιν ἄειδε, and 'arma cano'? is it not the fact that the earliest recitation of poetry was really what we should consider a childish sing-song? This becomes still more probable when we remember that music and dancing were frequent accompaniments of the earliest kinds of poetry, the effect of which would undoubtedly be to emphasize and regulate the beats or accents of the line; just as in church-singing now the verbal accent is ignored, if it is opposed to the general rhythmical character of the verse.

But independently of the natural instinct of children to scan, it seems to me that we need the division of the line into metrical feet as the simple basis of all description and comparison of metres. The foot is the unit which by repetition constitutes the line; the syllable is a mere fraction, and no index to the metre. On the other hand, to assume a larger unit, such as Dr Guest's *section* spoken of in the next chapter, or the double foot, the μέτρον, implied by the terms trimeter and tetrameter, is contrary to the feeling of English verse, and the latter is altogether unsuitable for the description of our heroic metre, which in its simplest form has five equal beats, and in no way suggests two wholes and a half. As regards the name 'foot,' for which Mr Ellis would substitute 'measure,' it seems to me a matter of little importance; 'measure' no doubt expresses its meaning more clearly than the metaphorical 'foot,' but the latter is in possession, while the former is generally understood in a wider and more abstract sense.

I am in favour then of the scanning by feet, on the ground that it is both natural and necessary, and also that it is scientific. I should further urge it in the interests of practical education. One good effect of the old plan of making all boys write Latin verses was to give men some idea of versification and rhythm, which women seldom have, unless gifted with specially good ears. It is probable that in time to come Latin verse writing will be less and less required, and it is at all events desirable that a purely English education should enable people to enter into and appreciate the beauties of English verse. For this purpose, boys and girls should be practised in observing how the mechanical pendulum swing of scansion is developed into the magnificent harmonies of Milton; they should be taught to notice and explain the difference in rhythm of Dryden and Pope, of Cowper and Wordsworth, of Keats, and Shelley, and Tennyson, and Browning.

Having thus stated how far I disagree with what I believe to be Mr Ellis's meaning, I will state where I should go along with him. I altogether object to putting a poet into the bed of Procrustes. If the foundation of Milton's verse is, as I believe, the regular five-foot iambic, yet it seems to me absurd to say that we must therefore expect to find five regular iambics in every line. Again, I can sympathize with Mr Ellis in his objection to the classicists who would force upon us such terms as choriambic and proceleusmatic to explain the rhythm of Milton. I do not deny that the effect of his rhythm might sometimes be represented by such terms; but if we really imagine that by their use we shall be able to explain the music of his poetry, we are attempting an impossibility, to express in technical language the infinite variety of measured sound which a genius like Milton could draw out of the little five-stringed instrument on which he chose to play.

Returning now to our simplest genera, the disyllabic and trisyllabic ascending and descending metres, how are we to classify the varieties of these? First we have the unmixed species of each differing in the number of feet alone; and of these we have two subspecies, one in which the normal line consists of so many perfect feet and nothing more, the other where the law of the metre requires either the addition or the omission of a short unaccented syllable at the beginning or the end of the line. Of addition we have an example in what is called the 'anacrusis' (back stroke), what Dr Abbott has called the 'catch,' a name given to an unaccented hyper-metrical syllable preceding the first foot of the line, as in the old Latin Saturnian or its English equivalent the six-foot trochaic,

[1]The) Queen was | in her | parlour | eating | bread and | honey|;

and again in the so-called feminine ending, by which is meant

---

[1] This might be otherwise explained as made up of a three-foot iambic line with feminine ending, followed by a three-foot trochaic. However, it may serve for illustration. Other examples of anacrusis will be found in the chapter on Classification of Metres under the head Trochaic.

an unaccented hypermetrical syllable following the last foot of the line, as in

Let's dry | our eyes | and thus | far hear | me Crom(well.

The omission of short syllables at the beginning or end of a line is known as 'truncation.' It occurs most frequently in trisyllabic metres. Thus in

Slow|ly and sad|ly we laid | him down |,

the first anapaest is represented by a monosyllable; and in like manner in

Merrily | merrily | shall I live | now |

the last dactyl is represented by a monosyllable.

Then we have the mixed species, in which the law of the verse requires (not merely permits) the mixture either of the ascending and descending, or of the disyllabic and trisyllabic metres.

In the chapter on the metres of Tennyson I have endeavoured to arrange all the varieties of his verse under the above heads; I will here only add a word as to the means by which one particular kind of iambic verse, the heroic, is varied. The normal rhythm is most clearly seen where the accents are perfectly regular in number and in position, where the end of each foot coincides with the end of a word, and the end of the line coincides with a pause in the sense, especially if there is no clashing between the length of the syllable and the position of the accent. Such a normal line is

And swims | or sinks | or wades | or creeps | or flies |.

Of course a series of such lines would be intolerably monotonous to all who have passed out of the stage in which sugar is the most exquisite of tastes, and the most beautiful of faces that which presents the sharpest contrast of red and white. It was to avoid such monotony that the rule of the caesura was introduced in Greek and Latin verse; that we find great masters of rhythm, such as Virgil and Milton, so careful to vary the position of their stops; that the accents are multiplied, diminished, or inverted, and the number of syllables lessened or increased. Later on I propose to discuss the limits of such variation.

The business then of the metrist in regard to any set of verses submitted to him is, first, to ascertain the general type of the verse, five-foot iambic, or whatever it may be, and further to state whether it is metrically *complete*, or *incomplete*, owing to final or initial truncation, or *more than complete*, owing to *anacrusis* or feminine ending; in technical language, whether it is *acatalectic, catalectic,* or *hypercatalectic.* He has then to point out in each particular line, how far there has been a departure from this general type in respect to the position of the accents or the number of syllables, as by the substitution of a trochee or an anapaest for an iamb, or, say, by the insertion of an extra-metrical syllable in the middle of the line. He has to notice the continuity or discontinuity of the rhythm as determined by grammatical stops or other pauses; and the smoothness or roughness of the rhythm as determined not only by the smoothness or roughness of the separate syllables, the crowding of consonants and so on, but by the relation of the long and short syllables to the normal metrical accents, the grouping of syllables into words, or phrases equivalent to a word, and the division of the words into feet. He has also to notice any special artifices employed by the poet to give harmony to his verses, such as alliteration and rhyme. Lastly, in reading the poem, the metrist has to pay due regard to the rhetorical importance of each word or phrase without allowing this to obscure the more properly metrical effects above described. It may be well to illustrate my meaning, so far as it can be done at this stage of our analysis, by examining the following line of Marlowe's,

See where | Christ's blood | streams in | the fir|mament |.

This is a five-foot iambic with trochaic substitution in the 1st and 3rd feet, and spondaic substitution in the 2nd. There is a rhythmical pause after the 1st, 4th, and 5th syllables, and strong rhetorical emphasis is laid on the 3rd and 5th syllables, *Christ's* and *streams*, which are also very long and connected by alliteration. In compensation the 6th and 7th syllables are as short and weak as possible, and form one phrase with the last word.

Having thus briefly stated what are my own views on the subject of metre, I shall proceed in the chapters which follow to examine the metrical systems of others, especially those of Dr Guest and Dr Abbott.

CHAPTER II.

ANTIQUARIAN A-PRIORISM.

DR GUEST ON ENGLISH METRE.

DR GUEST'S learned work on the *History of English Rhythms* was published in 1838. Though the book had become very scarce, it was not reprinted during the author's lifetime; and it is therefore uncertain how far it can be considered to represent his final view on the subject of which it treats. Since his death a new edition has appeared (in the year 1882) under the very competent supervision of the Cambridge Professor of Anglo-Saxon, who has made many corrections in detail, but who probably did not feel himself at liberty to do what, I think, was required, and recast it throughout. If the book was to be reprinted, and no doubt it possesses permanent value in its copious illustrations, it appears to me that it would have been better to throw it into two separate treatises, one on the history of the Early-English Language and Literature, and the other on the history of English Metre down to the 16th century, omitting altogether the reference to later metres. I will not take upon me to say that, even as to our earlier metres, Dr Guest would always have been a trustworthy guide. I observe that in many instances his scanning of Anglo-Saxon or Early-English metres is objected to by Professor Skeat, and Dr Guest himself owns (p. 525) that he is unable to understand the nature of Chaucer's versification, as to which the editor says in a note 'thanks to the patient researches of Professor Child and Mr Ellis and the grammatical rules of Dr Morris, the scansion of Chaucer is now a tolerably easy matter.'

My object, however, in these chapters, is not to trace the historical development of English metres from their first beginning, but to ascertain the laws of versification which have been observed by the English poets generally during the last three hundred years, and to lay down a simple and natural system of scansion. It is from this point of view that I find Dr Guest's book so entirely misleading and unsatisfactory; and as it comes out now under the apparent sanction of one of our chief authorities, and is also referred to in the Cambridge Shakespeare (vol. I. p. XVII.) as the best guide to the understanding of Shakespearian versification, I feel bound to state plainly my reasons against it. I shall therefore endeavour to show that the system there laid down is not only most perplexing for the ordinary reader, but that it insists on a rule which has been obsolete for centuries, that it condemns, as unrhythmical, verses which, I will venture to say, the great majority of educated men find perfectly satisfying to their ear, that it approves what to them appears mere discord, and throws together lines regular and irregular, possible and impossible, in the most bewildering confusion[1].

Dr Guest holds that our modern English metres should conform in the main to the rules of the Anglo-Saxon verse; his account of which may be thus summarized. "Our Anglo-Saxon poems consist of certain sections bound together in pairs by alliteration. The pure elementary section cannot have more than three, or less than two, accents. Each couple of adjacent accents must be separated by not more than two unaccented syllables; but two accents may come together, if the place of the intervening syllable is supplied by a pause,

---

[1] The view stated in the text is shared by Dr Schipper (*Englische Metrik* p. 2): "Dr Guest macht die älteste Form englischer Poesie, nämlich die alliterierende Langzeile, oder vielmehr die rhythmische Section derselben, zur Basis auch der späteren unter ganz anderen Einflüssen sich entwickelnden englischen Verskunst und zieht aus dieser Voraussetzung dann natürlich ganz falsche Schlüsse. Eine weitere Folge davon ist, dass es so verworren angelegt und durchgeführt ist, dass man sich nur mit grosser Mühe, selbst wenn man von seinem Gedankengange sich leiten lässt, hindurchfinden kann, und so ist denn das Werk, trotz der grossen Fülle von Material, die es bietet, als gänzlich veraltet und unbrauchbar zu bezeichnen."

called the sectional pause. When the accent is separated by one syllable, the rhythm is called *common measure;* when by two, *triple measure.* A section may begin (and similarly it may end) with an accented syllable or with not more than two unaccented syllables. There are three pauses which serve for the regulation of the rhythm, *final, middle* and *sectional.* The two former are necessary and essential, the third is exceptional. The final pause occurs at the end of a verse, the middle pause divides it into two sections, the sectional pause is found in the middle of one of these sections. As a general rule we may lay it down that the final and middle pauses ought always to coincide with the close of a sentence or clause. We never meet with a grammatical stop in the middle of a section. The sectional pause seems to have been only used before words on which it was intended to throw a powerful emphasis " pp. 144—161.

I proceed to test this doctrine of the sections, and I will begin first with the final pause. Is this observed by our best poets? Dr Guest himself confesses that it is not (p. 145). "There never was a greater violation of those first principles, "on which all rhythm must depend, than placing the final "pause in the middle of a word. Yet of this gross fault Milton "has been guilty more than once." And he cites *P. L.* 10. 580, as an example,

> Ophion, with Eurynome, the wide-
> Encroaching Eve perhaps, had first the rule
> Of high Olympus.

"Another serious fault is committed when the final pause separates a qualifying word from the word qualified, e.g.

> And God created the great whales, and *each*
> *Soul* living, each that crept. *P. L.* 7. 391.
> To judgment he proceeded on the *accursed*
> *Serpent,* though brute. *P. L.* 10. 163.

"Or when it separates the preposition from the words governed by it, or the personal pronoun from the governing verb, as :

> Read o'er this,
> And after this, and then to breakfast *with*
> *What appetite* you have. *H. VIII.* 3. 2. 201.

> Let it suffice thee that thou *know'st*
> *Us* happy, and without love no happiness." *P. L.* 8. 620.

This "serious fault," it may be observed, is one to which Shakespeare became more and more prone in his later years. In the earliest plays the sense very commonly closes at the end of the line; in the later his structure is more broken, and his lines frequently close with unaccented syllables connected in sense with what follows.

As to the rule that the end of the verse, the 'final pause,' shall always coincide with the end of a sentence or clause, I find on looking through the first fifty lines of the *P. L.*, that, in Pickering's edition, 34 out of the whole number have no final stop, while 10 close with a comma, and only 6 with a more important stop. So again as regards the rule of the 'middle pause. Put in more familiar language, this means that there should be a stop, or at all events a break in the line, at the end of the second or third foot, or in the middle of the third or fourth. This is at any rate a rule easy of observance; if it is really essential to the rhythm, there is no excuse to be made for the poet who neglects it. And so in fact Dr Guest feels. He quotes (p. 149) with reprobation the lines

> Unbrid|led sen|sual|ity | begat |.
> Thy an|ger un|appeas|able | still ra(ges.

And in p. 185, after granting that "the adoption of foreign metre brought into our language many verses which neither had, nor were intended to have, the middle pause," he goes on to say that "our poetry quickly worked itself free from such admixture," and therefore, "when we meet (four-accent) verses "such as the following:

> Guiding | the fi|ery-wheel|ed throne |,
> The cher|ub Con|templa|tion |,

"I do not see how we can treat them otherwise than as false "rhythm; or, if the middle pause be disowned, at least require "that they should not intrude among verses of a different "character and origin. If the poet make no account of "the pause, let him be consistent and reject its aid altogether. "If he prefer the rhythm of the foreigner, let him show his

"ingenuity in a correct imitation, and not fall back upon our
" English verse when his skill is exhausted.   Both foreign and
" English rhythms are injured by being jumbled together in this
" slovenly and inartificial manner."   Again, in p. 560, speaking
of Milton's use of the heroic verse, it is said, " He varied the
" flow of the rhythm and lengthened the sections; these were
" legitimate alterations; he split the sections and overlaid the
" pauses, and the law of his metre was broken, the science of his
" versification gone."

It may be worth while to add a few more examples of the
non-observance of this middle pause, by way of showing how
little it has been regarded by our best poets, and how far it is
from being essential to the beauty of the rhythm.   Thus in
Ben Jonson's famous lines we have

> That makes | simpli|city | a grace |
> Than all | the adul|teries | of art |

I should have added Milton's line

> And ev|er a|gainst ea|ting cares |

but I observe that Dr Guest marks it as having a pause after
against (p. 101).   It is at any rate an instance in point, as
showing that Milton did not think himself bound to break the
sense in the middle, any more than at the end of the line.
In the first fifty lines of *P. L.*, I find that 22 are printed
without a stop in the central portion of the line, embracing
all the syllables at which the middle pause might occur.   In
the first fifty lines of Pope's *Essay on Man*, there are 23 lines,
and in Tennyson's *Morte d'Arthur* 26 out of 50, without a
central stop.   I do not mean to say that in all these lines
there is precisely the same pause after each of the central
syllables or words, but there are many of them in which
the poet seems to have aimed at a uniform unbroken rhythm,
perhaps by way of contrast to the broken rhythm of preceding
lines.

Such are :

> I may assert eternal Providence,
> And justify the ways of God to man.   *P. L.* 1. 25.

> Or ask of yonder argent fields above.   Pope, *Ess.* i 41.
> A little thing may harm a wounded man.
> Rose up from out the bosom of the lake.   *Morte d'Arthur.*

So much for the rule that there must be a stop in the middle, and at the end, of a line. I now proceed to consider the converse rule, that there must be no sectional stop, i.e. no stop except at the middle and the end. Here too Dr Guest has to confess that the practice of the poets is against him. "A very favourite stop with Shakespeare was the one before the last accented syllable of the verse. Under his sanction it has become familiar, though opposed to every principle of accentual rhythm." Among the examples quoted of this objectionable rhythm is one certainly of the most exquisite lines in the English language,

> Loud, as from numbers without number, sweet
> As from blest voices uttering joy.   *P. L.* 3. 345.

Even the correct Pope sins in the same fashion, e.g.

> And, to their proper operation, still
> Ascribe all good, to their improper, ill.   *Essay,* ii 58.
> Force first made conquest, and that conquest, law.   iii 245.

And Dryden in *Abs. and Ach.*

> Thee, Saviour, thee the nation's vows confess,
> And, never satisfied with blessing, bless.

and Tennyson in the *Gardener's Daughter,*

> Divided in a graceful quiet, paused,
> And dropt the branch she held, and turning, wound
> Her looser hair in braid.

Dr Guest, in spite of his theory, does not seem to object much to the stop following the 8th syllable of the heroic line, as in Milton *P. L.* 1. 10.

> Or, if Sion hill
> Delight thee more, and Siloa's brook, that flowed
> Fast by the oracle of God ; I thence
> Invoke thy aid.

Nor to the stop after the first accent, when it falls on the 2nd syllable, as in Pope's

> Say first, of God above, or man below,
> What can we reason, but from what we know ?

But he speaks of the stop after an accented first syllable, or an unaccented second, following an accented first syllable, as being alike inadmissible.

Of the former we have not only the magnificent examples in Milton;

> Death his dart
> Shook, but delayed to strike, though oft invoked. *P. L.* 11. 491.
>
> Grasping ten thousand thunders, which he sent
> Before him, such as in their souls infused
> Plagues; *P. L.* 6. 830.

but even in Pope it is not uncommon, e.g.

> Know, nature's children all divide her care. *Essay*, III 43.
> Where, but among the heroes and the wise? *Essay*, IV 218.

Of the latter Milton makes a scarcely inferior use in the lines

> And now his heart
> Distends with pride, and, hardening in his strength,
> Glories. *P. L.* 1. 571.
>
> On Lemnos, th' Aegean isle: thus they relate
> Erring: *P. L.* 1. 746.

but Pope too admits this stop without scruple, provided the pause is not so great as to complete the sense.

> Passions, though selfish, if their means be fair,
> List under reason and deserve her care. *Essay*, II 96.

In showing what Draconian justice Dr Guest deals out to the poets who offend against his *à priori* rules, I do not mean to deny that, in general, a more pleasing rhythm is obtained by a pause in the middle or at the end of a verse, than by one immediately after the first or before the last syllable; but the very fact that such a rhythm is usually avoided makes it all the more effective, when the word thus isolated is felt to be weighty enough to justify its position, as in the examples from Milton. I hardly think the rhythm is justified in the lines which follow, taken from Mr Swinburne's *Marino Faliero*:

Dedication St. II,

> Pride, from profoundest humbleness of heart
> Born, self-uplift at once and self-subdued
> Glowed, seeing his face whose hand had borne such part.

p. 18,

> It does not please thee then, if silence have
> Speech, and if thine speak true, to hear me praise
> Bertuccio? Has my boy deserved of thee
> Ill?

p. 98,

> How these knaves,
> Whose life is service or rebellion, fear
> Death! and a child high-born would shame them.
> If
> Death seems so gracious in a great man's eyes,
> Die, my Lord:

p. 117,

> Let there be night, and there was night—who says
> That?
> Nor now, nor then, nor ever now need that
> Be.

Dr Guest continues (p. 156) "our poets sometimes place a stop after the third syllable, but never I think happily." As an instance he quotes

> What in me is dark
> Illumine, what is low raise and support. *P. L.* 1. 22.

Milton has this three times in his first ten lines, and even Pope has it four times in ten lines (*Essay*, I 66—74). It is also common with Tennyson.

I have thought it worth while to add these instances from Pope, because Dr Guest is accustomed to refer to him as a model of correct versification. Thus he ends his chapter on the *stops* with the words "When we see how nearly the freedom of "our elder poets approached to license, we may appreciate, in "some measure the obligations we are under to the school of "Pope and Dryden. The attempts to revive the abuses, which "they reformed, have happily, as yet, met with only partial "success" (p. 157). We may compare with this what is said in p. 529, the meaning of which will become apparent as we proceed: "The rhythm of Pope and Dryden differed from "Milton's in three particulars. It always counted the lengthen-"ing syllable of the first section; it admitted three syllables

"only in the *second* foot of the abrupt section ; and it rejected
"the sectional pause."   Milton's practice is stated just before:
"he did not always count the lengthening syllable of the first
"section.   An abrupt section was furnished with a foot of three
"syllables—the first section always, the second in all cases but
"those in which the first section had a lengthening syllable
"which was counted in the verse.   The pausing section 7 p.
"was sometimes admitted as his first section, and is some-
"times found lengthened."   [The Cimmerian darkness of the
last sentence had better be cleared up at once; the rest will
explain itself as we go on.   By 'pausing section' Dr Guest
means a section in which a pause takes the place of an unaccented syllable.   His 'section 7' is of the form *bAbAbbA*
(*A* standing for accented, *b* for unaccented syllables).   Hence
'7 p.' means that the second unaccented syllable is represented
by a pause (giving the form *bA-AbbA*), as in Milton *P. L.* 1.
253, which Dr Guest scans

A mind | *not* | to be changed | : by place | or time |

the pause after *mind*, together with the monosyllable *not*, representing the 2nd foot.

A pausing section is lengthened when an unaccented syllable
is added at the end, as in *P. L.* 10. 71.

On earth | *these* | thy transgres|*sors* : *but* | thou knowst |

According to Dr Guest's system the monosyllables *these* and
but, with the preceding pauses, stand for the 2nd and 4th feet;
and the last syllable of *transgressors* is superfluous, a feminine
ending of the first section.]

In p. 531 other faults of Milton's verse are pointed out.
"The verbal accent is often disregarded and the same word
"variously accented even within the compass of a few lines."
"Milton's passion for variety too often endangers his metre.
"Not only do his pauses" (i.e. the places where Dr Guest thinks
there ought to be pauses, at the middle and end of the line)
"divide portions of the sentence, most intimately connected
"together, but frequently we have periods ending in the midst
"of a section, and sometimes immediately after the first, or
"before the last syllable of the verse."   If beauty is thus

procured, "it is a beauty beyond the reach of Milton's metre, "a beauty therefore which he had no right to meddle with. "Versification ceases to be a science, if its laws may be thus "lightly broken."

We have already found that, in regard to the position of stops, even our least adventurous poets have asserted the right, which Dr Guest would deny them, of breaking the sense at any point in the line. We proceed to examine the other alleged divergences between the metres of Milton and Pope. The former, it is said, did "not always count the lengthening syllable of the first section." By this it is meant that Milton, as he occasionally introduces a feminine ending of the line, e.g.

That durst | dislike | his reign | and me | prefer(ring,

so he admits a superfluous syllable after the section or half-line. I have no wish to deny that lines may be found even in our latest poets, which are evidently composed of two sections, and in which the first and last foot of either section are allowed all the privileges of the first and last foot of the line. Such lines are Tennyson's long trochaics treated of in another chapter. Whether Milton ever regarded his heroic verse as made up of two sections may be doubted. Shakespeare was, I think, so far conscious of the section, as occasionally to make it a pretext for introducing an extra syllable. Mr A. J. Ellis does not grant even this. He considers that all cases which have been explained on this principle, are really examples of trisyllabic feet. And no doubt, such an explanation is possible in by far the largest number of instances. The question is really complicated with two others, in which I think Dr Guest takes an erroneous view. He regards it, not as a rare exception (such as we find in Chaucer) but as a recognized and established variety of the heroic line for a single accented syllable to take the place of the iambic foot at the beginning of a section, or after what he calls the 'sectional pause.' To a section which thus commences with an accent he gives the name of the 'abrupt section'; and he thinks that it makes no difference to the regularity and correctness of the verse, whether this first accent is separated from the second by one unaccented syllable or by two. The other question is as to the admissibility of trisyllabic feet. As Dr Guest distinctly recognizes the 'triple measure,' one would have thought there could have been no doubt on this subject, but it would seem from several passages that, except in what he calls the tumbling metre, he would desire to confine it to his 'abrupt section.' If he is forced to admit its use elsewhere, he indemnifies himself by denouncing it as licentious; but in general he seeks to explain away such examples on the principle of elision. Thus in p. 37 he supposes *believe, betray, belike,* to lose their first syllable in the lines

Let pi|ty not | be *belie|ved* there | she shook | *Lear,* 4. 3. 31.

To *betray* | the head|y hus|bands rob | the ea(sy

B. Jons. *Cat.* 3. 3.

O *belike* | his maj|esty | hath some | intent | *R. III.* 1. 1. 49.

Instances of two vowels compressed into one are given in p. 41.

Knowing who | I am | as I | know who | thou art | *P. R.* 1. 355.

Half *flying* | behoves | him now | both oar | and sail |

P. L. 2. 941.

Of *riot* | ascends | above | their loft|iest tow'rs | *P. L.* 1. 498.

Without | *media|tor* whose | high of|fice now | *P. L.* 12. 239.

Instances of short vowel elided before *m*, in p. 47.

Legit|imate Ed|gar I | must have | your land | *Lear,* 1. 2. 15.

His mind | so *ven|omously* | that burn|ing shame | *Lear,* 4. 3. 47.

before *ng* p. 52.

With *telling* | me of | the mold|warp and | the ant |

1 *H. IV.* 3. 1. 148.

This oath | I *willing|ly* take | and will | perform |

3 *H. VI.* 1. 1. 201.

before *l* or *r* pp. 55, 57.

A third | more *op|ulent* than | your sis|ters? Speak | *Lear,* 1. 1. 87.

Will but | *remember* | me what | a deal | of world | *R. II.* 1. 3. 268.

Other examples of elision are

Her *del|icate* cheek | it seemed | she was | a queen | *Lear,* 4. 3. 13.

Needs must | the ser|pent now | his *cap|ital* bruise | *P. L.* 12. 383.

Your *hor|rible* plea|sure here | I stand | your slave | *Lear,* 3. 2. 18.

Of the last line it is said (p. 63), "It is clear that *horrible* is a disyllable but whether it should be pronounced *horr'ble* or *horribl'* may be doubted: the latter is perhaps the safer."

Recourse is also had to 'synalœpha,' as in the following:

[1]Pas|sion and ap|athy : and *glo|ry and* shame | *P. L.* 2. 564.

An|guish and doubt | and fear| : and *sor|row and* pain | *P. L.* 1. 558.

No ungrate|ful food| : and food | alike | those pure | *P. L.* 5. 407.

The three following were quoted by Tyrwhitt to show that the heroic verse admitted three syllables in any one of the first three feet.

Ominous | conjec|ture on | the whole | success | *P. L.* 2. 123.

A pil|lar of state | deep | in his front | engrav|en   *P. L.* 2. 301.

Celest|ial *spi|rits* in bond|age nor | the abyss | *P. L.* 1. 658.

Dr Guest says on this (p. 175), "if a critic of Tyrwhitt's "reputation did not know that *ominous, pillar,* and *spirit* were to "be pronounced *om'nous, pill'r,* and *sp'rit,* can we fairly expect "such knowledge to flash, as it were by intuition, on the unin-"structed reader? Of late years, however, the fashionable "opinion has been that in such cases the vowel may be pro-"nounced without injury to the rhythm. Thelwall discovered "in Milton an *appoggiatura* or syllable more than is counted in "the bar, and was of opinion that such syllables constitute an "essential part of the expressive harmony of the best writers "and should never be superseded by the barbarous expedient "of elision. He reads the following verses one with twelve and "the other with thirteen syllables!

Covĕring the beach and blackĕning the strand.   Dryden.

Ungrateful offĕring to the immortal powĕrs.   Pope.

"There *are* men entitled to our respect whose writings "have, to a certain extent, countenanced this error. Both

---

[1] I give Dr Guest's division of the three lines. By the colon he marks what he considers to be the middle pause; by the bar he denotes that the preceding syllable bears the accent.

"Wordsworth and Coleridge use certain words, as though they "still contained the same number of syllables, as in the time "of Shakespeare. Thus they make *delicate* a dissyllable, yet "would certainly shrink from pronouncing it *del'cate*." He adds that the pettiness of the delinquency cannot be pleaded in defence of this sacrifice of rhythm, for "if a short and evanescent syllable may be obtruded, so may a long one." It is with pleasure we read Prof. Skeat's note on the above: "On the 'contrary I think that the pettiness of the delinquency *may* "be pleaded....The true rule concerning trisyllabic feet is "simply this, that the intrusive syllable should be as short and "light as possible. A good example is Pope's favourite line

The free|zing Tan|ais through | a waste | of snows |

"Here the intrusive syllable is the short *a* in *Tanais* and "is very light and short, as it should be. It adds a great beauty "to the verse, as may easily be perceived by reading *Tannis* and "comparing the results[1]." Prof. Skeat thinks the author must have subsequently abandoned his theory, 'because,' he says, 'examples of trisyllabic feet abound in the later part of the book.' And he cites from p. 217

Write | them togeth|er : yours | is as fair | a name |
Jul. Caes. 1. 2. 144.

Me | from attemp|ting : where|fore do I | assume | *P. L.* 2. 450.

Let | me not think | on't: frail|ty thy name | is wom(an
Hamlet, 1. 2. 146.

But these all come under the category of the abrupt section, in which Dr Guest has always admitted the triple measure. Thus in the very line, in which he denies Tyrwhitt's right to find a trisyllabic second foot, he has himself no difficulty in recognizing a trisyllabic fourth foot, because it follows an initial accent, i.e. a monosyllabic foot commencing a section:

A pillar | of state, : deep | in his front | engra(ven.

We do however find some instances which cannot be thus explained as in pp. 166, 225, 239 and 240:

That | invin|cible Sam|son : far | renowned |
Like | the first | of a thun|der : show'r | and now |

[1] Cf. also the editor's note on p. 51.

In | their trip|le degrees| : re|gions to which |
Shoots | invis|ible vir|tue : e'en | to the deep |
With | impet|uous recoil| : and jar|ring sound |
We may bold|ly spend| : upon | the hope | of what |
In elect|ion for| : the Ro|man emp ery | [1]

Then comes the question, whether the evidence adduced in
support of a superfluous syllable at the end of the first section,
may not be explained on the hypothesis of such a trisyllabic
foot in the middle of the line; whether in fact there is anything more to be said in its favour than for the extra syllable
which Dr Abbott admits before a pause in any part of the
Shakespearian line (*S. G.* § 454), or the superfluous unemphatic syllable which he allows in any foot (*S. G.* § 456). I
have treated of Shakespearian usage in another chapter. As
to Milton, I venture to say that, of all the numerous instances
cited by Dr Guest of an extra syllable before the middle pause,
there is not one which may not be more easily explained as a
trisyllabic foot. And the great advantage of such an explanation is that it enables us to get rid of the monosyllabic foot
and all the exceptional rules which this necessitates. For instance Dr Guest's complicated rule, "An abrupt section was
(by Milton) furnished with a foot of three syllables, the first
section always, the second in all cases but those in which the
first section had a lengthening syllable which was counted in
the verse," is exemplified in the lines

Oth|ers apart| : sat | on a hill | retired |
A|ges of hope|less end| : this | would be worse |
Write | them togeth|er : yours | is as fair | a name |
Confound|ed though | immor|tal : but | his doom | .

How far more simple does the metrical analysis become, as
soon as we recognize that the accentual trochee and anapaest
are permitted alternatives for the iamb, and that the middle
pause has no metrical effect. Marking the *feet* by bars, I find
in the line

---

[1] I do not of course agree with Dr
Guest's scansion of these lines, except-
ing the last two. The first four commence with a double trochee, of which
more hereafter : the third has also a
trochee in the last foot but one. The
fifth line may be read as beginning
with trochee followed by dactyl, or
the first foot is an anapaest, the remaining feet iambs.

    Óthers | apárt | sát on | a híll | retíred |

a trochee in the first and third feet; and in

    Wríte them | togéth|er, yoúrs | is as fáir | a náme |

a trochee in the first foot and an anapaest in the fourth.

    But Dr Guest not only admits a monosyllabic foot, when it is followed by two unaccented syllables (which we have seen to be his way of describing trochee followed by iamb), but also when it is separated by one unaccented syllable from the next accent. This is in fact his first rhythm (p. XVII.), which he denotes by the formula AbA, and of which he cites as examples:

    Ja|el who | with hos|pita|ble guile | .   p. 210.
    Which | by God's | will : kind | and calm|ly blows | .   p. 211.
    With | the love | juice : as | I bid | thee do | .   p. 215.
    For | the cool shade| : thith|er has|tily got | .   p. 215.
    As | throw out | our eyes| : for brave | Othel|lo.   p. 232.
    So | by for|mer lec|ture : and | advice | .   p. 233.

It is scarcely credible that any educated person could have read these lines without suspecting some error; but such is the force of erroneous theory, that Dr Guest could actually thus *misread* lines which are correctly given as follows, both in Professor Skeat's notes, and in any editions which I have been able to consult.

    Jael | who with | *in*hos|pitab|le guile | *Sams. Ag.* 989.
    Which by | God's will | *full* kynd | and calm|ly blows | .   Gascoyne.
    With the | love juice | as I | *did* bid | thee do |
                                 M. N. D. 3. 2. 36.
    For the | cool shade | *him* thith|er hast|ily got | *F. Q.* I 2. 29.
    As *to* | throw out | our eyes | for brave | Othel(lo   *Oth.* 2. 1. 36.
    So by | *my* for|mer lec|ture and | advice | *Hamlet,* 2. 1. 64.

    These are not by any means all the misquotations noticed by the editor. Where the lines are rightly given, they are frequently misscanned; or else they are mispronounced or misdivided or were never meant to be complete verses. A very small fraction remain which are probably corrupt, or in any case are so exceptional, that it is absurd to base a theory of metre upon them. I give examples of each class, with Dr G.'s scansion.

p. 209,

> vive | le roi|: as | I have banked | their towers|.

Here *vive* ought to be read as a disyllable, as is shown by Dr Abbott, *S. G.* § 489.

Several of the instances given contain exclamations, which may be either extra-metrical, as p. 250,

> O) ye Gods | ye Gods | must I | endure | all this |

or may be lengthened or repeated at pleasure, as in p. 211,

> Tut! | when struck'st | thou: one | blow in | the field
> O | this learn|ing: what | a thing | it is | .

Others are intended to be fragmentary, as in 211,

> Nev|er! nev|er!: come | away | away | .

The scanning is in fault in pp. 234, 235,

> See | him pluck | Aufid|ius: down | by the hair |

which properly begins with a trisyllabic foot,

> See him pluck | Aufid|ius | down by | the hair |

and

> What | an al|tera|tion of hon|our has |

where *alteration* has really five syllables and the line should be divided

> What an alt|era|tion | of ho nour has | .

The same unfortunate theory has converted five-foot iambics into Alexandrines, as in p. 249,

> Hath | he asked | for me|: know | you not | he has |

p. 292,

> I knew | not which | to take|: and what | to leave,| ha|!
> Bound | to keep life | in drones|: and id|le moths|? No|!

The first of these lines should be divided

> Hath he | asked for | me know | you not | he has |

In the 2nd and 3rd we have extra-metrical exclamations ab-
surdly forced into the lines; indeed the 2nd is printed as
prose in the Globe edition.

p. 250

> We'll | along | ourselves|: and meet | them at | Philip|pi
> Vir|tue as | I thought|: truth du|ty so | enjoin|ing.

The former verse may either be read with an initial anapaest, or the first syllable of *along* disappears (see Abbott § 460).
The latter commences with a trochee and anapaest, unless we
suppose with Dr Abbott that the 2nd and 3rd syllables run into
one.

We have thus seen that Milton knows nothing of abrupt
section and middle pause, and that the rhythmical effects,
described by Dr Guest under these names, are easily explained
by the fact that he admits freely trochaic and trisyllabic feet.
We will next enquire whether he admits a monosyllabic foot
under the guise of the 'sectional pause.'   Before we can answer
this, we must examine Dr Guest's view of the concurrence of
accented syllables.   He finds great fault with Dr Johnson for
suggesting that sometimes the accent is equally strong upon
two adjoining syllables, as (p. 75)

> Thus at their shady lodge arrived, *bóth stoód,*
> *Bóth túrned.*

" Here," it is said, " every reader of taste would pronounce
" the words *stood, turned,* with a greater stress than that which
" falls on the word preceding.   But these words are at least
" equal in quantity, and Johnson fell into the mistake of con-
" sidering quantity identical with accent."   On the contrary I
should say that every reader of common sense would feel that
the repeated *both* was strongly emphatic and that Johnson was
quite right in laying at least equal stress on the two words.
I am glad to find the editor in his note on p. 416 refusing his
assent to Dr Guest's dictum, that two accented syllables cannot
come together.   I think however that he is mistaken in speaking
of the examples given in p. 281 as inconsistent with Dr Guest's
theory, because in those examples a pause is supposed to inter-

vene between the accented syllables and to be equivalent to an omitted syllable. The fact is Dr Guest, finding he could not get rid of all cases of adjacent accents either by the numerous exceptions admitted in Bk I. ch. 4, or by his theory of abrupt sections, bethought him of the sectional pause, as a further means of explaining all cases in which trochee followed on iamb. Thus in the line quoted on p. 295

A mind | nót to | be changed| by place | or time |

he makes the accented *not* a monosyllabic foot, and considers that it may follow accented *mind* because there is an intervening pause occupying the time of an unaccented syllable. Similarly the line

He speáks | lét us | dráw néar | mátchless | in might |

takes with him the form

He speaks | let | us draw near|: match|less in might | .

We are now in a position to understand Dr Guest's remarks quoted above on p. 19 as to the difference between the rhythm of Pope and Milton. Pope, it is there said, always counted the lengthening syllable of the first section (i.e. ignored Dr Guest's sections); but so, as we have seen, did Milton. Pope rejected the sectional pause (i.e. did not follow up iamb with trochee). This, I grant, is much rarer in Pope than Milton, but still we find such a line as

Is the | gréat cháin | that dráws | áll to | agree | *Essay*, I 33.

which on Dr Guest's system would require a sectional pause between *draws* and *all*, and must be divided as follows :

Is | the great chain|: that draws | all | to agree |

The third distinction is, that Pope admits three syllables only in the 2nd foot, but the line just quoted would be an example of a final trisyllabic, if read with the sectional pause ; and in the 'favorite line'

The freez|ing Tan|ais through | a waste | of snows |

we have three syllables in the 3rd foot.   Compare also the following[1]:

> *Annual* | for me | the grape | the rose | renew |
> The juice | necta|*reous and* | the bal|my dew | *Essay*, I 134.
> Then na|ture de|*viates and* | can man | do less | *ib.* 150.
> Account | for mor|al as | for nat|*ural things* | *ib.* 162.
> *To inspect* | a mite | not com|prehend | the heaven | *ib.* 197.
> From the | green my|*riads in* | the peo|pled grass | *ib.* 210.
> For ev|er sep|*arate yet* | for ev|er near | *ib.* 224.

If it be said, these should be slurred, so as to make them di-syllables, it may be replied that, that is just what Dr Guest said of Milton's trisyllabic feet in the first part of his book, though here at the end (p. 529) he has to confess that the common view is the right one.

The remaining charge brought against Milton is that he disregards the verbal accent.   This is merely Dr Guest's admission that his system, with all its cycles and epicycles, does not really accord with the facts, οὐ σώζει τὰ φαινόμενα.   He assumes that (except where the normal rhythm is broken through by the law of sections and pauses) every foot in the heroic measure is bound to be strictly iambic.   But he laments that here, as elsewhere, the poets will persist in disobeying his laws.   Their iambs are such as to defy all rules of accentuation. They accent the article and the preposition more strongly than the noun as in (p. 81 foll.)

> A third | thought wise | and lear|ned *a* | fourth rich | B. Jonson.
> She was | not *the* | prime cause | but I | myself | Milton, *S. A.* 234.
> Profaned | first by | the ser|pent *by* | him first | *P. L.* 9. 929.

["Here," it is said, "the pronoun requires an emphasis which makes the false accentuation still more glaring."]

They give a stronger accent to the possessive pronoun than to the following adjective, to the personal and relative pronoun than to the verb, as in Fletcher's

> That I | may sit | and pour | out *my* | sad sprite.

---

[1] Some might prefer to divide some of the lines differently, e.g.

> The juice | necta|reous | and the bal|my dew |

["This verse of Fletcher has even more than his usual proportion of blunders. With proper accents it would belong to the triple measure,

> That | I may sit | and pour out | my sad sprite | "

I do not know how others may feel, but to me this utter misconception of a most beautiful line is a conclusive proof of Dr Guest's unfitness to write on the subject of metre.]

So in Milton's

> Crea|ted hu|gest *that* | swim th' o|cean stream. *P. L.* 1. 200.

The most cruel blow is, that even Pope should be an offender in these respects, e.g.

> The treach|erous col|ours *the* | fair art | betray | *Criticism*, 492.
>
> In words | as fash|ions *the* | same rule | will hold | *do.* 333.
>
> Against | the po|et *their* | own arms | they turned | *do.* 106.

Now what is the real state of the case? Do we really suppose that the poets were so foolish as to lay an unnatural stress on the most unimportant word in the line, and so destroy the force and meaning of the line? Is it not plain that they intended to vary the ordinary rhythm by introducing an accentual pyrrhic followed by an accentual spondee (*e.g.* the treach|erous col|oŭrs thĕ | faīr ārt | betray!) and that the result produced by this means is most satisfactory to the educated ear?

I think that I have said enough to show that Dr Guest, with all his learning, is not a safe guide to the study of metre. There is hardly a single rule which he has laid down, which is not in flat opposition to the practice of the poets of the last three centuries. Tried by his code, they are all miserable sinners, they have left undone what they ought to have done, and done what they ought not to have done. They know nothing of that which he makes the foundation of his system, the doctrine of the sections and pauses; they put their stops wherever it pleases them; they substitute freely trochees, pyrrhics, spondees and trisyllabic feet for the iamb. But Dr Guest's theory not only condemns as unmetrical what is proved to be metrical by the consistent practice of the poets;

he is, as we have seen, equally unfortunate in admitting what is palpably impossible. He mistakes a verse belonging to one metre for a verse belonging to another metre, e.g. the five-foot, for the six-foot iambic, and puts under the same head verses belonging to different metrical systems, as in p. 198, where he gives, as examples of the formula *bAbA : AbbAb*, two lines, one iambic, the other anapaestic.

Well struck | in years|: fair | and not jea|lous   *R. III.* 1. 1. 90.

Forthwith | how thou | oughtst | to receive | him   *S. Agon.* 328.

The former is no doubt difficult, but it occurs in the middle of a speech of the ordinary heroic verse, and unless there is very strong reason to the contrary, it should be treated as such itself. Dr Abbott (*S. G.* § 480) says "it might be possible to scan as "follows:

Well struck | in years, fa|ir and | not jeal(ous

"but the Folio has *jealious* and the word is often thus written "and pronounced by Elizabethan authors." If *jealious*, which may be compared with the archaic *stupendious*, is rejected, I should myself prefer to make the last foot a trochee, as in *Macbeth*, 5. 5. 32.

But know | not how | to do | it. Well, | sáy, sir |

It would then be divided as follows

Well struck | in ye|ars fair | and not | jeálous |

The line from *Samson Agonistes* should be compared with other examples of anapaestic metre in the same poem, e.g.

Or the sphere | of for|tune rai(ses.   l. 172.

Univer|sally crowned | with high|est prai(ses.   l. 175.

So this should be divided

Forthwíth | how thou oúghtst | to receíve (him

Milton probably intended it to correspond to the *versus paroemiacus*, or *anapaestic dimeter catalectic*, which formed the closing line of the anapaestic system in Greek.

The points named above, as condemnatory of Dr Guest's system, are selected from a very much larger number which

I had noted down in three distinct perusals of his book. I have thought it right to give my criticisms a permanent form, not in the least from a wish to depreciate the value of the author's work in this and other departments of English history and literature. On the contrary I have a most sincere respect for his industry and independence. I think later writers might have avoided some errors into which they have fallen if they had considered more carefully the evidence which he has accumulated. But in my opinion the book is entirely unfitted to be, what is still a desideratum in English education, a practical guide to the study of metre.

CHAPTER III.

LOGICAL A-PRIORISM.

Dr Abbott on English Metre.

Dr Guest's system of prosody is, as far as I know, original; that which comes next for consideration, Dr Abbott's, is a modification of what may be called the traditional system. In its general outline, I believe this to be also the true and natural system, giving technical expression to the practice of the best writers and readers of poetry, and not setting up an antiquarian standard to which they are required to conform. In the particular form, however, which Dr Abbott has given to this system, he seems to me to have gone wrong in the same way as Dr Guest, by insisting on certain *a priori* rules, which it is not always easy to reconcile with the practice of the poets. He has the advantage over Dr Guest in starting with the true normal line, instead of the fictitious sections, but he is too much enamoured with a mechanical regularity, and makes too little allowance for the freedom of English versification.

The general theory is given in the *Shakespearian Grammar*, 2nd ed. 1870, §§ 452—515, and in the Third Part of Abbott and Seeley's *English Lessons for English People*, 1871, §§ 97—150[1].

The *foot*, not the section, is there assumed as the basis of metre. It is defined as the smallest recurring combination of syllables. In English the names of feet, trochee, iambus, &c.

---

[1] The metrical rules laid down in the older book, for which Dr Abbott is solely responsible, seem to be somewhat less sweeping than those in the later book, in which he is a co-worker with Prof. Seeley.

denote groups of accented and non-accented syllables without regard to quantity. *Accent* means a loud stress of voice. A distinction is made between *word-accent* and *metrical accent.* Every polysyllable has at least one word-accent. The accent of monosyllables depends upon their collocation. The metrical accent, if it falls on a word at all, must fall on its principal word-accent, but it may also fall on a syllable which has no word-accent (e.g. on a monosyllable or on the last syllable of a tri-syllabic word such as *merrily*). We can never have three consecutive clearly pronounced syllables without a metrical accent. Emphasis is a stress laid on monosyllables or the word-accent of polysyllables, for the purpose of calling attention to the meaning. In poetry an emphatic syllable generally receives the metrical accent, but we sometimes find the metrical accent falling on an unemphatic syllable, and followed by an emphatic non-accented syllable. It is rarely that all the metrical accents of a line are also emphatic. In reading we should allow emphasis as well as accent to exert its influence. Any mono-syllable, however unemphatic, that comes between two un-accented monosyllables (this should be *syllables*) must receive a metrical accent in disyllabic metre. As examples we have (*Eng. Less.* p. 155 foll.)

> Oh, weep for Adonais. *Thé* quick dreams.
> Then tore with bloody talon *thé* rent plain.
> Spreads his light wings and *in* a moment flies.
> Make satire *a* lampoon and fiction lie.

The difficulty which occurs to us on reading these lines is, how we are to make the metrical accent on the italicized syllables correspond to the definition of accent, "a loud stress of the voice." It is plain that *the, in* and *a* are about the least im-portant words in the lines in which they occur, and that in the first two lines *the* is intentionally prefixed to the important words *quick* and *rent* in order to give them additional emphasis. In technical language *the* is here a 'proclitic'; so far from laying any stress upon it, a good reader would pass it over more lightly than any other word in the lines. I am unable therefore to see the propriety of describing these as accented syllables, unless, when we use the term metrical accent, we simply mean that

the syllables, which are said to be metrically accented, are those
which, if the verse were mechanically regular, would have had a
word-accent, and to which therefore the general influence of
the rhythm may seem to impart a sort of shadow of the word-
accent. As far as the reading goes, accentuation on this principle
becomes unmeaning, and the only thing to regard is emphasis,
or the distinction between the emphatic and unemphatic syllables. All verses will be perfectly regular as regards accents
(or feet), but variety will be produced by the over-riding
emphasis. This is a simple and logical view, but, as we shall
see, it is not consistently adhered to.

Thus in *S. G.* § 457, where the question is raised, whether
'an unemphatic monosyllable is allowed to stand in an emphatic place and receive the accent,' it is stated that the
article seems to have been regarded as capable of more emphasis in Shakespeare's time than it is now ; but still attempts
are made to explain away several of the instances in which *the*
and still more *a* are found in the even syllables of the verse,
and would therefore, on the mechanical principle, receive the
accent. Thus in the line which Dr Abbott scans

> a devil | a bor|n dev|il on | whose na(ture,

but which I should scan

> a dev|il a | born dev|il on | whose na(ture,

the accent on *a* is avoided by assigning two syllables to *born*
and one syllable to the first *devil ;* and, in the following lines,
it is suggested that an accented *the* may be avoided by the free
admission of trisyllabic feet (both anapaest and amphibrach),
and by giving two syllables to *dead*, three syllables to *lightenings*,
and four to *physician*.

> Your breath | first kindled | the de|ad coal | of war |
> Than meet | and join | Jove's light|enings | the precúr(sors
> More neéds she | the divíne | thán the | physíc|ián |

I do not deny that monosyllables, in which *r* follows a vowel,
are often disyllabized in Shakespeare (cf. *S. G.* §§ 480, 485, and
my chapter on the Metre of Shakespeare), but I have great
doubts as to some other monosyllables treated of in §§ 481—484,

and 486; and I think that, in the instances which follow, it was the desire for regularity of accentuation which prompted the scansion adopted, or at any rate allowed, by Dr Abbott; e.g. in the line

> How in | my strength | you please | for yo|u Ed(mund,

you is divided unnecessarily to escape a final trochee.

> To fa il in the | dispo|sing of | these chan(ces.

Here, in order to avoid an unaccented second foot, *fail* is made disyllabic, and a supernumerary unaccented syllable is assigned to the second foot.

> Doth com|fort thée in | thy sle|ep live | and flou(rish.

The second foot should end with *thee*, *thy* is emphatic, contrasting the sleep of Henry with the troubled dreams of Richard.

> Full fif|teen hundred | besi|des com|mon men |.

Besides is made trisyllabic to avoid an unaccented third foot.

> Go tó the | creáting | a whó|le tríbe | of fóps |.

Here the third foot is properly unaccented, the second is an anapaest ending with the second syllable of *creating*.

> But could | be willing | to ma|rch on | to Cal(ais.

March made disyllabic, to avoid unaccented third foot.

> Of Lion|el Duke | of Clarence | the thi|rd son |.

Third made disyllabic, to avoid unaccented fourth foot.

> Yóu and | your crá|fts yóu | have craft|ed fair.

[The line (*Cor.* IV. 6. 118) is incomplete; it should run:

> You and | your crafts | you've craft|ed fair | you've brought.]

> The Go|ds not | the patric|ians make | it and |

Gods made disyllabic, to avoid the trochee in the second place.

> With Ti|tus Larcius | a mo|st val|iant Ro(man.

Most made disyllabic, to avoid an unaccented third foot.

It is needless to point out the extreme harshness of rhythm which follows from this attempt to ignore the simple fact that it is not necessary for all the feet to have what is called in the *Lessons* the emphatic accent, what I should rather call simply the accent or stress, on the second syllable of the foot. But it will be noticed that in some of the lines quoted, the fiction of the regular metrical accent is abandoned : thus in

<blockquote>More needs she | the divine | thán the | physic|ian|,</blockquote>

the accent of the fourth foot is placed on the former syllable *than* instead of on *the*. This irregularity comes under the head of Dr Abbott's *License of trochee*, of which he gives the following account (*Lessons*, § 138). "In the initial foot and after a pause, " in iambic metre, a trochee instead of an iamb is allowed. A " very slight pause in the dramatic and free iambic metres "justifies a trochee ; even a long syllable, with the slight pause " necessary for its distinct pronunciation, is sufficient. But some " slight pause is necessary, and hence it may be laid down as a " rule in iambic metre that one trochee cannot follow another. " Milton's line

<blockquote>*Únivérsal* reproách far wórse to beár,</blockquote>

" would be a monstrosity if read with the usual accents. It is " far more likely that Milton pronounced the word *univérsál*, " perhaps influenced by the fact that the *i* is long in Latin[1]."

---

[1] As Milton uses the word 'universal' in twenty other passages and always with the present pronunciation, I cannot think it at all likely that he follows the Latin quantity in this passage. There is only one verse (in *S. Ag.* 175), which, if taken by itself, might tolerate the long *i*, but taken in connexion with the preceding lines, it is evident that the metre is anapaestic, requiring short *i*,

For him | I reck|on not | in high | estate |	iamb. 5
Whom long | descent | of birth |	iamb. 3
Or the sphere | of for|tune rais(es;	anap. 3
But thee | whose strength | while vir.tue was | her mate |	iamb. 5
Might have | subdued | the earth |	iamb. 3
Univer|sally· crowned | with high|est prai(ses.	anap. 4

As I have shown below, the double trochee is a known peculiarity of Milton's verse, borrowed by him from the Italian. If however anyone finds it intolerable, I have no objection to treat it as a case of initial truncation. Thus scanned the line would run

<blockquote>U|niver|sal reproach |</blockquote>

the 3rd foot being an anapaest. But, after all, it makes no difference in the reading. Whether we call the 1st foot a trochee or not, we can only make it rhythmical by pausing on the 1st syllable and giving a very strong emphasis to the 3rd.

Another rule is that "a trochee in the middle of a verse must not follow an unemphatic accent," as it does in Milton's lines

> Burned af|ter them | to the | bottom|less pit |.
> Light from | above | from the | fountain | of light |.

The first remark which suggests itself on this, is that the principle of fictitious accentuation is here abandoned. The accent of the foot is declared to be reversed when the emphasis falls on the first instead of the second syllable. But if the metrical accent is to be determined by the real or natural stress given to each syllable by a good reader, it will be found necessary to admit other licenses besides that of the trochee. The so-called unemphatic accent is no accent at all in this sense of the term, so that we shall find ourselves compelled to admit pyrrhics on the one hand, and on the other hand, since two emphatic syllables may come together in verse as well as prose, we shall find that there are natural spondees just as there are natural trochees[1]. It may be granted that the use of the trochee is generally confined within the limits specified, though I should have worded

---

[1] To test the frequency of these irregular feet in Shakespeare, I have been carefully through *Macbeth*, and I find there 175 spondees in all, distributed as follows: 20 in the first foot, 60 in the second, 19 in the third, 23 in the fourth, and 53 in the fifth. Of these 31 follow trochees, 75 follow pyrrhics, 40 come after a pause, and 29 are continuous after a long syllable. As examples of what I call spondees, I would mention the foot made up of the last syllable of an iamb and the first of a trochee, e.g.

> Would cre|*ate* sol|diers make | our wom|en fight |

that made up of an emphatic monosyllable and the first syllable of a trochee, e.g.

> *Sit, wor*|thy friends | ; my lord | is of|ten thus |
> Promised | no less | to them|. *That trust*|ed home

or of two emphatic monosyllables,

> Why do | you show | me this? | a fourth! *Start, eyes!* |

especially where the emphasis is required to give the right sense, as

> *But screw* | your cou|rage to | the stick|ing place |
> *Who wrought* | with them | and all | things else | that might |
> Making | the green | *one red,*

or for the sake of antithesis, e.g.

> That which | hath made | *them drunk* | hath made | *me bold* |
> Lest our | *old robes* | sit eas|ier than | our new |.

the rule about the pause differently, and said that the trochee was admissible everywhere, but was naturally preceded by a little pause to take breath before pronouncing a strongly emphatic syllable ; but there is no such stringent and absolute law as to constitute any exception a ' monstrosity.'   Indeed the double trochee can scarcely be called a rarity in Milton, cf.

> Présent | thús to | his Son | aúdi|bly spake | *P. L.* VII. 518.
> Óver | físh of | the sea | and fowl | of the air | *P. L.* VII. 533.
> Bý the | wáters | of life | where'er | they sat | *P. L.* XI. 77.

It is also found in Spenser, as in the beautiful line praised by Leigh Hunt,

> Ás the | gód of | my life |. Why hath | he me | abhorred|?
> *F. Q.* I. 3. 7.

So Tennyson in the *Coming of Arthur:*

> Félt the | líght of | her eyes | ínto | his life |.

For other instances I may refer to Dr Abbott himself (*S. G.* § 453) and to Dr Guest's *English Rhythms*, pp. 238, 240.   Dr Guest even treats the verse commencing with the double trochee as a recognized variety of the ten-syllable iambic[1].   Authority apart, it seems to me that the rhythm of such lines as the following is satisfactory to the ear, and would not be improved by the alternative given in italics :

> brávest, gréatest, and best ; a king of men.
> *the brave, the great, the good; a king of men.*
> éndless sórrow, eternity of woe.
> *undying pain, eternity of woe.*

Besides the theoretical objections which have been stated to Dr Abbott's view of accentuation, a practical difficulty arises in applying it to educational purposes.   In the Preface to *English Lessons* it is said that the object of the chapters on Metre is practical utility, to teach the pupil how to read a verse so as to mark the metre, without converting the metrical line into monotonous doggrel.   If the pupil's metrical exercise were confined to dividing a line into feet and marking the emphatic and unemphatic syllables, neglecting the metrical accent altogether,

---

[1] See also below, ch. v. p. 76.

the task is simple. But the admission of the trochee complicates matters. Even Dr Abbott hesitates (*E. L.* p. 159) whether in the line

The lone | couch of | his ev|erlas|ting sleep |

the second foot shall be called a trochee, or an iambus consisting of a long emphatic unaccented syllable followed by a short unemphatic accented syllable. So in p. 150 we have the line,

Proud to | catch cold | at a | Vene|tian door |

in which it is said to be doubtful whether *at a* should be considered a trochee or iambus. And many other instances occur.

The quantity of syllables seems to introduce a still further complication, as we are told (*E. L.* p. 168) that, though it has quite a secondary position in English metre, yet Shakespeare, Milton, &c., are fond of giving a special character to their rhythm by the introduction of long monosyllables without the metrical accent, e.g.

O'er bog or steep, through strait, *rough*, dense, or rare,
With head, *hands*, wings, or feet pursues his way.

Here *rough* and *hands* are treated by Dr Abbott simply as long syllables, but surely it is plain that their rhythmical weight is owing to their emphasis, and to the stop which follows them; otherwise *rough* in itself is no longer than *of.* However, I note this merely to point out that the pupil has here a fourth sort of stress to add to the three (emphasis and the two accents) before considered.

We go on now to the syllabic license in disyllabic verse. The license of defect, monosyllabic for disyllabic foot, is on the whole well treated in *S. G.* § 479 foll., except that, as we have seen, monosyllables are often unnecessarily disyllabized, in order to escape transference or omission of accent.

The syllabic license of excess may consist either in syllables supernumerary, not counted in the feet; or in syllables within the feet, which may be either more or less slurred, or distinctly pronounced. Of the first we read, *S. G.* § 454, " An extra syllable is frequently added before a pause, especially at the end of a line, but also at the end of the second[1], and, less frequently, of the third foot; rarely at the end of the fourth." And § 458, "Two extra syllables are sometimes allowed before a pause, especially at the end of a line."

It will be observed that these rules do not justify such scanning as we have had in the lines

> To fa|*il in the* | dispos|ing of | these chanc(es.
> *Go tó the* | *creáting* | a who|le tribe | of fops |,

where the superfluous syllable appears without a pause, and (in the second line) at the close of the first as well as of the second foot. As to the general principle, while I am disposed to allow that an extra syllable is sometimes found at the close of the first section of a line which naturally divides into two sections, I see no reason for admitting it elsewhere, as for instance after the fourth foot. Dr Abbott gives two examples of the last from the *Tempest,* in which the trisyllabic foot is very common.

> With all | my hon|ours on | my broth*er* | whereon|.
> So dear | the love | my peo|ple bore *me* | nor set|.

Is there any objection to regarding both as final anapaests?

The account of trisyllabic metre in the *Lessons* § 143 foll. seems to me satisfactory so far as it goes, but I think confusion is caused in the *Grammar* by mixing up proper dactyls and

---

[1] The example given seems to me very doubtful,

> But mine | own sáfeties |. You máy | be right|ly júst |.

Read with the context, it is evident that *you* is emphatic, and Mr A. J. Ellis would divide

> But mine | own safe|ties. *You* | may | be right|ly just |
> Whatev|er *I* | shall think |.

It is possible however that the initial *but* ought to be appended to the previous line, thus

> Without | leave ta|king. I | pray you | let not |
> My jeal|ousies | be your | dishon|ours, but |
> Mine own | safeties |. You may | be right|ly just |.

So I had taken it in my paper read before the Philological Society, and I find Mr Roby scans it in the same way. Both the 2nd and 3rd feet would then be trochees.

anapaests with what would commonly be denominated *amphibrachs*, but which Dr Abbott describes as iambs with a superfluous unaccented syllable which has to be dropped or slurred in sound (*S. G.* § 456). I do not deny that words are often so rapidly pronounced in Shakespeare as to lose their full complement of syllables, e.g. the words *Prospero, parallel* and *being* may be so read in the following lines from the *Tempest* I. 2. 72,

> And *Pros|pero* the | príme dúke | *being* so | repu(ted
> In dig|nity | and for | the lib|eral arts |
> Without | a *par|allel*, those | *being* all | my stud(y.

Dr Abbott has given a very full list of words which he thinks were so pronounced. But I do not think such a device helps much in the line already cited

> Go to the | creating | a who|le tribe | of fops |.

So divided, the second foot could be nothing but an amphibrach. On the other hand in the *Tempest* I. 2. 301,

> Go make | thyself | *like a nymph* | o' the sea |; be sub(ject
> *To no sight* | but thine | and mine |,

and in 1 *Henry VI.* I. 1. 95,

> The duke | *of Alen|çon* fli|eth to | his side |,

the italicized feet can only be described as anapaests. In the *Lessons* § 136 Dr Abbott has no difficulty in allowing this in the case of Tennyson's

> The sound | of man|y *a heav|ily gall|oping hoof* |,

and, as he says in the same passage, that modern blank verse is, for the most part, more strict than that of Milton, and Milton is more strict than Shakespeare, in limiting himself to ten syllables in a line, why should he deny to Shakespeare the liberty he allows to the moderns? Why should he take such pains to get rid of anapaests and dactyls in the elder poet by elision, contraction, extra-metrical syllables and other expedients, which are plainly inapplicable in modern poetry? He does indeed, though with a groan, admit one anapaest of portentous harshness, which I think we are not bound to retain.

> *Which most gib|ingly* | ungrave|ly he | did fash(ion   *Cor.* II. 3. 233.

I should prefer to divide this and the preceding line as follows :

> Th' apprehen|sion of | his pres|ent port|ance which |
> Most gi|bingly | ungrave|ly he | did fash(ion.

The sequence dactyl-iamb (and *a fortiori* dactyl-anapaest) which Dr Guest, as we have seen, repudiates in Milton's line

> *Ominous* | conjec|ture on | the whole | success |

is equally opposed to Dr Abbott's rule that " we cannot have three consecutive clearly pronounced syllables without a metrical accent." Yet it is by no means uncommon in Tennyson, cf.

> *Galloping* | *of hor*|ses o|ver the gras|sy plain |.
> *Petulant* | *she spoke* | and at | herself | she laughed |.
> *Modulate* | *me soul* | of min|cing mi|micry '.
> *Hammering* | *and clink*|ing chat|tering sto|ny names |.
> *Glorify*|*ing clown* | and sat|yr whence | they need |.
> *Timorous*|*ly and as* | the lea|der of | the herd '.

Perhaps the principle of slurring is carried a little too far, especially in the attempt to get rid of Alexandrines (*S. G.* § 495 ff.). No doubt Dr Abbott has succeeded in showing that many apparent Alexandrines are to be read as ten-syllable iambics, but I see no reason for objecting to the following, for instance :

> That seem|ing to | be most | which we | indeed | least are |
> Acquire | too high | a fame | when him | we serve's | away |
> Besides | I like | you not |. If you | will know | my house |

Nor do I quite understand why such a line as the following should be called a trimeter couplet, rather than an Alexandrine,

> Why ring | not out | the bells | aloud | throughout | the town '.

I shall not carry further my examination of Dr Abbott's system. As a critic of Shakespeare he seems to me to be too anxious to reduce every line to the normal shape. No doubt he allows many broken lines; but I think he goes too far in endeavouring to raise the following, for instance, to the full number of syllables by disyllabizing *will* and *fare* :

> Why then | I wi|ll. Fa|rewell | old Gaunt '.

Surely it is better to suppose the actor to supply the want of the missing syllable, or syllables, by the pause which marks the change of subject, than to dwell on such a monosyllable as *will*.

Again, as regards the heroic verse generally, I think Dr Abbott is too anxious to limit and regulate any departure from the normal accentuation, and that, in treating of syllabic license, he is too much disposed to disguise or explain away examples of trisyllabic feet by the various devices already referred to, and especially by, what seems to me, the somewhat desperate remedy of allowing extra-metrical syllables in any part of the line. If the superfluous syllable is ever allowed within the line, it must be after the section or hemistich, because we know that it was the law of the Old English and French poetry, with which our modern heroic is historically connected, to admit the feminine ending in the middle, as well as at the end of the line[1]. Yet even in Shakespeare it is very difficult to find an indisputable instance of this. Dr Abbott sends me the following, but it is quite possible to divide them so as to ignore the section altogether, giving an anapaest in the 3rd foot of the former and the 4th foot of the latter, thus

To lack | discret|ion. Come, go | we to | the King |
$$\hspace{6cm} Hamlet \text{ II. 1. 117.}$$

To feed | and clothe | thee. Why | should the poor | be flat|tered?
$$\hspace{6cm} Hamlet \text{ III. 1. 64.}$$

My own feeling is that, dactyls and anapaests being recognized English feet, and both undoubtedly employed in the place of iambs by our poets of all ages, it is wiser to use them, where they will serve, to explain the metre of a verse, rather than to have recourse to extra-metrical syllables, a license which, except at the end of the line, is now unknown, and is not recognized by all even in Shakespeare. On the same ground I should be more chary of admitting the amphibrach, as the substitute for an iamb, because it is never, as far as I know, made the basis of any English poem, and, though I see no objection to its use, I cannot call to mind any instance of a heroic line which may not be explained without it.

---

[1] See Appendix at the end of the volume.

I must not however close my remarks on Dr Abbott without bearing my witness to the great services which he has rendered to all students of English poetry. There is plenty of room for diversity of opinion in dealing with the refinements and subtleties of a subject so hard to fix as metre, but none can dispute the judgment, the acuteness and the laborious industry exhibited in the two volumes on which I have been commenting.

[Dr Abbott has kindly looked through this chapter and authorizes me to say that, while retaining his old view as to the not unfrequent disyllabization of such words as *year, fire, say, pale,* in Shakespeare, he finds himself in general agreement with me as to the scansion of the particular lines quoted. The scansions given were in some cases suggested by him as possibilities which he is now disposed to reject. In regard to an accented ' the,' he would wish to limit himself to the statement, that the metrically accented ' the' usually precedes a monosyllable which is long, in other words, precedes a spondee. He has no objection to recognize dactyls and anapaests, but considers that they are for the most part restricted to certain collocations of syllables, or pauses.]

CHAPTER IV.

AESTHETIC INTUITIVISM.

MR J. A. SYMONDS.

I HAVE spoken of the mischief arising from the confusion between the aesthetic and the scientific views of metre. Each is good in its place, but they should be kept distinct, and the scientific examination should come first. Otherwise metrical analysis shares in all the difficulties of aesthetic analysis, and is in danger of becoming to a great extent a matter of individual feeling. As an example of this aesthetic or intuitivist way of regarding metrical questions, I will take an article on the Blank Verse of Milton written by Mr J. A. Symonds, which appeared in the *Fortnightly* for Dec. 1874. I give his system in his own words slightly condensed. " English blank verse consists of " periods of lines, each one of which is made up normally of ten " syllables, so disposed that five beats occur at regular intervals, " giving the effect of an iambic rhythm. Johnson was wrong " in condemning deviation from this ideal structure as inhar- " monious. It is precisely such deviation that constitutes the " beauty of blank verse. A verse may often have more than ten " syllables, and more or less than five accents, but it must carry " so much sound as shall be a satisfactory equivalent for ten " syllables, and must have its accents arranged so as to content " an ear prepared for five."

So far we may say all metrists, with perhaps the single exception of Dr Guest, would be agreed: the question is how we are to interpret the vague phrase " satisfactory equivalent," but we shall seek in vain for anything more definite in the

course of Mr Symonds' article. We have a good deal of
eloquent declamation about the "balance and proportion of
syllables," "the massing of sounds so as to produce a whole
harmonious to the ear, but beyond the reach of analysis by
feet." We are told that in order to understand the rhythm of
the line—

> 'Tis true, I am that spirit unfortunate—

"it was necessary to have heard and seen the fiend as Milton
"heard and saw him. Johnson, with eyes fixed on the ground,
"searching for iambs, had not gazed on the fallen archangel's
"face, nor heard the low slow accents of the first two syllables,
"the proud emphasis upon the fourth, the stately and melancholy
"music-roll which closed the line." [With equal justice Mr
Symonds might protest against the profanation of attempting to give a grammatical or rhetorical analysis of a speech
of Demosthenes.] Again, "spasms of intense emotion have
"to be imagined in order to give its metrical value to the
"verse,—

> Me, me only, just object of his ire,"

and so on.

In fact Mr Symonds distinctly asserts what I should call
the principle of aesthetic intuitivism in the words "the one
"sound rule for readers is—Attend strictly to the sense and the
"pauses: the lines will then be perfectly melodious; but if you
"attempt to scan the lines on any preconceived metrical system,
"you will violate the sense and vitiate the music." I need
not repeat the objections to this view, which have been already
fully stated in my introductory chapter. Suffice it to say that
it renders impossible the classification and comparison of metrical
effects, and encourages the delusion that verse is subject to no
rules and admits of no science. If nothing more were wanted
than that the casual reader should be satisfied or gratified by
his own recitation of a poem, what security should we have
against misprints and false readings being treated as rhythmical,
as in the instances quoted from Dr Guest's book in a former
chapter? What is there to prevent Milton's heroic

> Universal reproach far worse to bear

from being read as a four-foot iambic commencing with two anapaests? Or why should Mr Symonds take the trouble to argue that certain lines containing twelve syllables ought not to be regarded as Alexandrines, if the line will be perfectly melodious when read according to the sense and the pauses without any preconceived metrical system? The same confusion between the scientific and the aesthetic view appears in the assumption that those who maintain the value of metrical analysis, i.e. of scansion, would also maintain that the reading of the line should be determined merely by its scansion, and not by its meaning. And apparently the writer thinks that this was the case with classical versification. He allows that "such terms as trochee and amphibrach may be usefully employed between students employed in metrical analysis," that "our daily speech is larded with trochees and cretics and so forth": on the other hand, "since quantity forms no part of our prosody, and since the licenses of quantity in blank verse can never have been determined, it is plainly not much to the purpose to talk about choriambs in Milton—though they are undoubtedly to be found there—but these names of classic feet do not explain the secret of the varied melody of Milton"; "they do not solve the problem of blank verse."

It is difficult to deal with the mass of inconsistencies in these lines: first it is stated that trochees, etc., exist in English, and that the terms may be usefully employed by students for the purpose of analyzing English metre, and then again we are told that since quantity does not enter into our prosody, therefore it is useless to talk of choriambs and classic feet in Milton, though he has them. Not to dwell upon this, the writer is evidently contrasting quantitative and accentual metre, and deprecates the use of classical terms as not explaining the secret of the varied melody of the latter. But who ever asserted or supposed that Virgil's melody was *explained* by the mere naming of the feet or the scanning of the lines? Even a schoolboy in saying his lines is corrected if he scans them instead of reciting them with the proper accent and emphasis; even a schoolboy in writing his Latin verses knows that it is only a small portion of his task to produce lines that will construe and scan. Lines may construe and scan, and yet be utterly inadmissible, and even when he has learnt to produce a decent line, he is told that he is to notice how Virgil varies his rhythm by the position of the caesura, by the prevalence of spondees or dactyls, by the length of the clauses and periods. Mr Symonds seems to think it an objection to the scanning of English verse, that the metrical feet will not always coincide with the natural pauses in the sense, but so far from this being an objection in Latin poetry, it is the actual rule that they should not in general coincide. No doubt the scanning of Virgil is an easy thing, and the scanning of Shakespeare and Milton is a hard thing, but I see no reason for saying that scanning is more necessary or useful in the case of the one than of the other, unless we are prepared to maintain that there is absolutely no rule at all observed in the English heroic. The scanning of Plautus is just as hard as that of Virgil is easy, and hard for the same reason as the scanning of English verse is hard, because syllables may be slurred in rapid pronunciation, because the metrical value of many of the syllables is not fixed, as it was in later Latin, and because the alternative feet are so numerous. Thus the place of an iambus may be taken by a trochee, a tribrach, a spondee, an anapaest, a dactyl, Wagner would say, even a proceleusmatic (see his Introduction to the *Aulularia*). But no one on this account thinks scanning superfluous in Plautus. On the contrary, whilst the scanning of Virgil is left to those who are commencing their studies in Latin verse, the scansion of Plautus has occupied the attention of the ablest scholars from Bentley to Ritschl; and the result is that a metre, of which even Cicero confessed that he could make nothing, is now intelligible to any ordinary reader. This is a case in which the scientific metrical analysis preceded and rendered possible the aesthetic analysis, and so I believe it has been and will be in other cases.

We found an inconsistency just now between the statement that the classical terminology might be usefully employed in reference to English metre by students accustomed to metrical analysis, and the subsequent statement that, since quantity formed no part of our prosody, these classical names were only misleading. Further on we are told that, in English blank verse, "scansion by time takes the place of scansion by metrical feet; the bars of the musical composer, where different values from the breve to the demi-semi-quaver find their place, suggest a truer basis of measurement than the longs and shorts of classic feet." If this is to be taken literally, while every foot should occupy the same time to pronounce, it may consist of any number of syllables from one to thirty-two. Getting rid of hyperbole, let us say, from one to four, and consider what degree of truth there is in the statement. It is difficult to see what connexion there can be between such a metre as this and those with which Milton's verse is historically connected, the later metre of Dryden, and the earlier metre of Surrey, Sackville, Greene, and Peele, who are said to have shown "great hesitation as to any departure from iambic regularity[1]." It is difficult also to see how such terms as "trochee and amphibrach can be usefully employed by students engaged in the analysis" of such a metre. But leaving this, is it true that each foot occupies the same time; e.g. in what Mr Symonds calls the ponderous

Showers, hails, snows, frosts, and two-edged winds that prime

and in what he calls the light and rapid

Athens, the eye of Greece, mother of arts

is it not palpable that the spondee 'showers, hails,' takes longer to pronounce than the trochee 'Athens'? Is it true that there may be more than three syllables in a foot? This too I should deny. If there is any apparent case of such a thing, I should say that one or more syllables have suffered elision or slurring, the apoggiatura of music. And lastly is it, as seems to be implied, a matter of indifference on which syllable in the bar or foot the accent falls? If there are three syllables, is it the same thing whether the accent falls on the first, second, or third of these? I cannot think we shall gain much from 'this scansion by time.'

There still remain two points for consideration, the one the inconsistent results obtained by the old metrists, the other the

---

[1] How little this is true of Surrey will appear below in ch. x.

challenge offered to explain certain lines of Milton by the ordinary scanning. To shew the inconsistencies of the old metrists we are told that in the line

> Partakers, and uncropt falls to the ground

the last four syllables were made a choriambic by Todd and a dactyl with a demifoot by Brydges. I am not concerned to defend either, and in fact both have gone beyond the limits of scientific metrical analysis, through a wish to suggest the general rhythmical effect. The first business of the metrist is to give the bare fact that we have in this line an accented seventh followed by an unaccented eighth syllable, making what is commonly called a trochee, and again an unaccented ninth followed by an accented tenth, commonly called an iamb. Todd is not wrong in saying that the two together constitute a choriamb, only that, to be consistent, he should very much enlarge his terminology and have a name ready for any possible collocation of two feet. Brydges, on the other hand, is altogether on the wrong tack, and opens the door to any sort of license.

We come now to the lines which are said to be beyond the reach of analysis by feet. I give what I consider the true scanning of each.

> Ruining | along | the illim|itab|le inane |

First dactyl, second iamb, third slurred iamb, or anapaest, according to the pleasure of the reader, fourth iamb, fifth same as the third.

> The one wind|ing the oth|er straight | and left | between |

First slurred spondee, second slurred iamb, the rest iambs.

> See where | Christ's blood | streams in | the fir|mament |

First trochee, second spondee, third trochee, fourth and fifth iambs. The third foot is said to be "illegitimate according to iambic scansion," but this is so only according to narrow *a priori* systems such as Johnson's. The limit of trochaic variation will be discussed further on.

> 'Tis true | I am | that spirit | unfor|tunate |

First, second, fourth, fifth iambs, third slurred iamb, or if the reader pleases to pronounce both syllables of 'spirit' distinctly, the last syllable would make the fourth foot an anapaest.

Me me | only | just object of | his ire |

First spondee, second trochee, third spondee, fourth pyrrhic, fifth iamb. Of this line it is said, "it is obvious here that scansion by feet will be of little use, but the line is understood as soon as we allow the time of two whole syllables to the first emphatic 'me,' and bring over the next words 'me only' in the time of another two syllables." If it is meant that scansion by feet will not of itself tell us how to read the line, of course I agree; but if it is implied that whenever the second syllable of the line is joined closely in sense with what follows it is to be reckoned as forming part of the second foot, then I say that we destroy the foundation of metre. Nor do I recognize any given time for two syllables. I do not see why a reader should not give as much time to the first 'me' as to the four last syllables of the line.

Mr Symonds continues, "The truth of this method is still more evident when we take for analysis a line at first singularly inharmonious.

Submiss | he reared | me and whom | thou soughtest | I am |

Try to scan this line, and it seems a confusion of uncertain feet." The feet are all iambs but the third, which may be read either as slurred iamb or as anapaest.

To avoid any possible misconception, I repeat again that I find no fault with Mr Symonds for what he has done, but for what he has failed to do, and condemned others for doing. His aesthetic analysis may be excellent in itself, but it cannot take the place of the scientific analysis, nor is there the least inconsistency between them. By all means let Mr Symonds 'gaze on the archangel's face and hear his stately and melancholy music-roll,' but why should that interfere with Johnson's humble search for iambs? I venture to say that, as a rule, the ear which has been first purged by listening for iambs will be better prepared to receive those higher aesthetic pleasures on which Mr Symonds discourses so eloquently.

CHAPTER V.

NATURAL OR A-POSTERIORI SYSTEM.

MR A. J. ELLIS. MR MASSON. MR KEIGHTLEY.

INTERMEDIATE between the rigid *a priori* systems of Dr Guest and Dr Abbott, and the anarchical no-system of the Intuitivists, comes what I should call the natural or *a posteriori* system of which Mr A. J. Ellis may be regarded as a representative. I am glad to be able to give Mr Ellis' theory of the heroic verse in his own words slightly abbreviated from a paper read before the Philological Society in June 1876. He commences with a quotation from the *Essentials of Phonetics*, p. 76, published by him in 1848 but long out of print.

"An English heroic verse is usually stated to consist of ten syllables. It is better divided into five groups [what we commonly call *feet*, what Mr Ellis prefers to call measures], each of which theoretically consists of two syllables, of which the second only is accented. The theoretical English verse is therefore 01, 01, 01, 01, 01 (0 = absence, 1 = presence of stress); but this normal form is very seldom found. Practically, many of the groups are allowed to consist of three syllables, two of them being unaccented; but in these cases the syllable immediately preceding is very strongly accented. The number of syllables may therefore be greater than ten, while the accents may be, and most generally are, less than five. It is necessary for an English verse of this description, that there should be an accent at the end of the third and fifth group, or at the end of the second and fourth; and if either of these requisites is complied with, other accents may be distributed almost at pleasure.

The last group may also have one or two unaccented syllables after its last accent.   Much of the beauty of a verse arises from the proper distribution of the pauses between the words, and also of the groups of accents among the groups of words.   Thus the second or third group, or measure, must in general be divided, that is, must be distributed between two words, or the effect on the ear will not be harmonious."

Mr Ellis then gives the first sixteen lines of *Paradise Lost*, denoting the degree of stress laid on each syllable by the figures 2, 1, 0 written underneath, the divisions of the feet being marked by commas.

1.   Of man's first disobedience, and the fruit
   . 0   2,   1   0, 0 2, 0 0   0,   0   2

2.   Of that forbidden tree, whose mortal taste
      0   1,   0   2, 0   1,   0   2, 0   2

3.   Brought death into the world, and all our woe
      1   2,   0 0, 0   2,   0   1,   0   2

4.   With loss of Eden, till one greater man
      0   1,   0   2, 0   0,   0   2, 0   2

5.   Restore us, and regain the blissful seat,
      0   2,   0   0,   0   2,   0   2,   0   2

6.   Sing, heavenly Muse, that, on the secret top
      2   2, 0 0   2,   1   0,   0 2, 0   1

7.   Of Horeb or of Sinai, didst inspire
      0   2, 0   0, 0   2, 0 0   1,   0   2

8.   That shepherd, who first taught the chosen seed
      1   2,   0   0,   2   2,   0   2, 0   2

9.   In the beginning, how the heavens and earth
      0   0,   0 2,   0   1,   0   2,   0   0   2

10.   Rose out of chaos. Or, if Zion hill
      2   0,   0   2, 0   1, 0 2, 0   2

11.   Delight thee more; and Siloa's brook that flows
      0   2,   0   2,   0   2, 0 0   2,   0   2

12.   Fast by the oracles of God, I thence
      2   0,   0   2, 0 0,   0   2,   1   2

13.   Invoke thy aid to my adventurous song:
      0   2,   0   2, 0   0,   0 2, 0   0   2

14.   That with no middle flight intends to soar
      0   0,   2   2,   0   2   0 2,   0   2

15.   Above the Aonian mount, while it pursues
      0   1,   0   0 2, 0 0   2,   2   0,   0 2

16.   Things unattempted yet, in prose or rhyme
      2   0, 0   2,   0   1,   0   2,   0   2

" In these sixteen lines, there is not one with a superfluous syllable at the end of the line, but lines 1, 6, 7, 9, 11 and 13 have eleven syllables, and line 15 has as many as twelve syllables. There are several groups, therefore, of more than two syllables, some groups of two, and one (in the first line) of three unaccented syllables. Sometimes a group has two accents, as in lines 6, 8, 14. Lines 1, 3, 5, 7, 8, 15, owe their rhythm to accents at the end of the third and fifth groups; lines 2, 4, 6, 9, 10, 12, 13, 16, to accents at the end of the second and fourth groups; and both characteristics are united in lines 11, 14. The mode in which these necessary conditions are diversified, by the introduction of other and unexpected accents, or by the omission of accents, is very remarkable, and shews the art and rhythmical feeling of the poet. So far from the theoretical standard, 01, 01, 01, 01, 01, being of constant recurrence, we only find one line (the second) in which it is strictly observed; and even then we have to assume that sub-accents have the same effect on the ear as primary accents, which is far from being the case. Line 11, in spite of the three syllables in the fourth group, approaches the theoretical standard nearer than any other verse, and it is immediately succeeded by line 12, which, as a contrast, goes miles away from the standard form.

"At a later period, in my *Early English Pronunciation*, Part I., 1869, pp. 333—5, I made some passing remarks on Chaucer's rhythm as different from the modern, and I laid down my modern tests with a few variations, thus:

"In the modern verse of five measures, there must be a principal stress on the last syllable of the second and fourth measures; or of the first and fourth measures; or of the third and some other measure. There is also generally a stress upon the last syllable of the fifth measure; but if any one of the three conditions above stated is satisfied, the verse, so far as stress is concerned, is complete, no matter what other syllables have a greater or less stress or length. The length of syllables has much to do with the force and character of a verse, but does not form part of its rhythmical laws. It is a mistake to suppose that there are commonly or regularly five stresses, one to each measure. Take, for example, the first six lines of Lord Byron's *Corsair*, marking the even measures by italics, and the relative amount of stress by 0, 1, 2, we have—

1. O'er the *glad waters* of *the dark* blue sea
   1   0,   1   2, 0   0, 0   2,   1   2

2. Our thoughts *as boundl*ess and *our souls* as free,
   1   1,   0   2,   0   0,   0   2, 0 2

3. Far as *the breeze* can bear, *the bil*lows foam,
  2   0, 0   1,   0   2,   0   1, 0   2

4. Survey *our em*pire, and *behold* our home!
   0 1,   0   2,   0   0,   0 2,   0   2

5. These are *our realms*, no lim*its to* their sway—
  2   0,   0   1,   2 1, 0 0,   0   2

6. Our flag *the scep*tre all *who meet* obey
  1   2,   0   2, 0 1,   0   2, 0 2

" The distribution of stress is seen to be very varied, but the action of the rules given in the text is well marked. Different readers would probably differ in the ratios 1 and 2, in some lines, and others might think that it would be sufficient to mark stress and no-stress. The last line most nearly approaches to having five principal stresses.

" Our English verse, though based on alternations of force, is materially governed by length and pause, is seldom or never unaccompanied by variety of pitch unknown in prose, and is more than all perhaps governed by weight, which is due to expression and mental conceptions of importance, and is distinct from force, length, pitch, and pause or silence ; but results partly from expression in delivery (a very different thing from mere emphasis), produced by quality of tone and gliding pitch, with often actual weakness of tone, and partly from the mental effect of the constructional predominance of conceptions, as of substantives over adjectives, and verbs over adverbs, even when the greater force or emphasis is given to the lighter words. Weight is a very complex phenomenon, therefore, which certainly affects English rhythm in a remarkable manner at times, entirely crossing the rules of force or strength. We want, therefore, a nomenclature which shall distinguish degrees of force, length, pitch, and weight in syllables, and in groups of syllables so affected, and of degrees of duration of silence. Our rhythms are thus greatly more complicated than the classical, so far as we can appreciate them, except the dithyrambic and the comic, which, as Cicero felt, required music. (*Orator* §§ 183—4, quōs cum cantū spoliāveris nūda paene remanet ōrātiō.)

"I have elaborated a series of expressions for degrees of force, length, pitch, weight, and silence, which will in some way avoid the great ambiguities, and indeed contradictions, which occur in the use of the words *accent* and *emphasis* among writers on rhythm. These are as follows. Nine degrees are distinguished, representable by the numbers 1, the smallest, to 9, the greatest. But of these three are principal, each having a super- and sub-form.

	FORCE.	LENGTH.	PITCH.	WEIGHT.	SILENCE.
9.	superstrong	superlong	superhigh	superheavy	supergreat
8.	*—strong —*	*long*	*— high*	*— heavy*	*— great*
7.	substrong	sublong	subhigh	subheavy	subgreat
6.	supermean	supermedial	supermiddle	supermoderate	supermedium
5.	*—mean*	*— medial —*	*middle —*	*moderate —*	*medium*
4.	submean	submedial	submiddle	submoderate	submedium
3.	superweak	supershort	superlow	superlight	supersmall
2.	*—weak*	*— short*	*— low*	*— light*	*— small*
1.	subweak	subshort	sublow	sublight	subsmall

" For all practical purposes the three principal degrees suffice, but fewer will not serve. I have found it of great practical advantage to be able to speak of a *strong* syllable, quite independently of the origin of its strength, which may arise from its position as an accented syllable in polysyllables, or from its emphatic pronunciation in a monosyllable. Thus we may say that English rhythm is primarily governed by alternations and groups of strong and weak syllables, and that it is materially influenced by alternations and groups of long and short, high and low, heavy and light syllables, and great and small pauses. The names of these groups would require great care to be sufficiently intelligible, and I have not yet attempted to work them out. As English verse would have, however, to be studied in reference to all of them, it is very easy to express a group of syllables by the initials F, L, P, W, S, and the corresponding figures. Thus what used to be called an accentual iambus will assume any of the forms F 19, 29, 39, 49, 59, 69, 79, 89; or F 18, 28, 38, 48, 58, 68, 78; or F 17, 27, 37, 47, 57, 67; or F 16, 26, 36, 46, 56; or F 15, 25, 35, 45; or F 14, 24, 34; or F 13, 23; or F 12; and very subtle ears might be ready to appreciate all these forms, although the forms F 28, 58, 25 would be all that might be generally reckoned. But in such groups we might also have L 28, 58, 25 ; P 28, 58, 25 ; and W 28, 58, 25. Thus F 28 + W 28, and F 28 + W 58, would have very different effects, and new effects would be introduced by the distribution of the syllables in a group among different words and the length of the corresponding silences, if any, no silence not being marked. It will be found not easy to take note of all these peculiarities in reading a piece of poetry. Joshua Steele and James Rush tried much this way, see my paper on Accent and Emphasis, *Philological Transactions* 1873-4, pp. 129—132. Steele attended to length and silence in one, under the name of time, and distributed them so as to divide speech, in prose or verse, into equal intervals of time, answering to musical *bars ;* he especially noted pitch, and also force, not however as here employed, but as part of expression, and hence forming part of weight, and corresponding to the crescendos and diminuendos of music, and in fact the whole apparatus of oratory. What is here meant by force he calls weight, and makes it agree so completely with the beating of a conductor of music, that he assigns weight to silences.

"When merely two grades are necessary, the long vowel, implying a long syllable, has the long mark, as *sēat ;* the long syllable with a short vowel may have the short mark over the vowel, as *strĕngth ;* short vowels and syllables are unmarked. Strong syllables have a turned period (˙) after a long vowel, as *rē˙gion*, or the consonant following a short vowel, as *wrĕtch˙ed ;* weak syllables are unmarked. High syllables have an acute accent over the short vowel in short syllables, as *cánō*, or after the vowel bearing the long or short mark in long syllables, as *cā´nō, cắ´nto.* The glide down from a high pitch to a low one, always on a long vowel, is marked by the circumflex, as *sûme.* The glide up from a low pitch to a high one, also always on a long vowel, is marked by a grave accent on the vowel followed by an acute accent after it, as Norwegian *dà´g.* The low pitch is unmarked. But a grave accent marks a still lower pitch. Heavy syllables are in italics, light syllables unmarked. Emphasis as affecting a whole word is represented by (˙) placed before the whole word, and will mark any peculiarity of expression by which it is indicated in speech. Silence, when not marked by the usual points or dashes, or in addition to these, is denoted by ($_\circ$), a turned mark of degrees, for small, and (0), a turned zero, for long silences. Odd measures end with | , and even measures with]. By this means all the principal points of rhythm can be easily marked by ordinary types.

"From the above it will be seen how minute are my own notions of rhythm as actually practised by poets in a developed state of literature, not those who had to struggle with singsong doggrel, as in much of our oldest rhymes. This also shews in what sense I consider the old classical terms 'misleading' —principally, as now used, in studying classical metres with modern prepossessions,—and also as utterly insufficient for English purposes.

"I will conclude by appending a few lines which I have put together for the sole purpose of contrasting irregularities with regularities. Lines in strange rhythms would never be so accumulated and contrasted in practice. I mark them for force only below, but roughly for length, pitch, weight, silence, and measure, in the text, and add remarks.

1. In the | blǎck· *skȳ'*$_\circ$] glím·mĕrs | the pā'·le] cō·ld *mōo·n*$_\circ$
     2 2   6   8,   8 2,   2   6   6   8

2. Sǎd· ghŏ·st | of *nǐ·ght,*$_\circ$] aud the stā'·rs | *twǐn·klė*] arŏu·nd
     5   5,   2   5,   2   2   8,   7 2,   2   6
                   or, 2   2,   7   8,   2   2   6

3. Trĕm·bling | *spǎn·glĕs·*$_\circ$] set· in | her dā'·rk] gāu·ze *vēi·l*
     5   2,   5   2,   5 2,   2   5,   7   8

4. Pā·le *quēe·n*, | pū·re *quēe·n*,] dǔ·ll· *quēe·n*, | forlŏ'·rn] quēe·n$_\circ$; ā'·ye$_0$
     5   6,   5   6,   7   5,   5   8   8   9

5. Giv·e me | the sŏ'·]cial *glō·w*, | the brǐ·ght] *cŏá·l*$_\circ$, the$_0$
     7   2,   2, 8, 2   7,   2   7,   8   2

6. Fit·ful·ly gê·]nial *flā·me,*$_0$ | lǐ·ghting] ēa·ch chēe·k,
    6 2, 2   7, 2 2   7,   8 5,   5   8,

7. Gǐl·ding | ēach *smǐ·le*], brǐ'·ghtsome | accŏm·]paniment
     8 5,   5   8,   8   3   2 8   1 2 2

8. Of brǐ·ght|some *mel·*]*ody* rǐng·|ing from brǐ·ght]some hēa·rts.
    2   8,   3   8, 3 2 8,   3   2   8,   3   8

9. The rig· id lǐ'·ne] encā·sed | in rig·]id rū'·les$_\circ$,
    2   7, 2   7,   2 7,   1   7, 2   7

10. As dǔ·ll· | as stág·]nant *wā·|ter,*$_0$ *dǔ·ll·s*] the mǐ·nd
     1   8,   1 8,   1   7, 1   8,   2   7

11. That *lŏng·s* | to frēe·'·] itself·$_\circ$ | from hā'·rsh] *contrŏ·l*$_\circ$
     1   8,   1 8, 2 7,   1   7,   2 8

12. And$_o$ in | the vă·]ried *rhy'th·|m* of hēa'·rt] and sŏu'·l
    3   1,   1 7,   2   7,   1 1   7,   1   8

13. Fēe'·ls the | sŭn·-gŏ'd·,] trūe· *pō·|esў's·*] trūe'· *kĭng·*
    7   1,   8 7,   7   8 1 2   7   8

It will be at once evident that force is here very insufficient
for marking the rhythm, and that length, weight and silence
have much effect. The only regular lines are 9, 10, 11, and
they have a singularly dull effect among the others. Some of
the lines set all ordinary rules at naught, and some readers
may take them, as Goethe's mother took Klopstock's *Messiah*,
for 'prose run mad.' Line 1, an ordinary form, begins with
two short and weak syllables, followed by two strong and long
ones, of which the first, 'blăck·,' has a short vowel and an
ordinary pitch, and the second, 'skȳ·,' has a long diphthong,
and with a higher pitch. The next two measures are of the
form strong-weak weak-strong, very usual at the commencement or on beginning the third or fourth measure. The third
measure, 'glim·mĕrs,' has a short strong high first syllable, and
a long weak low second syllable, which is also very common.
The three long strong syllables which close the line are very
common as an ending, the first is high, and the other two
descend, but the voice must not drop to 'mōo·n,' as the
sentence does not end. The weight of the last words makes the
metre secure. In line 2 there are three long and rather strong
syllables, but the pitch is low, and the weight unimportant.
These are relieved by the trisyllabic third measure, in which
the first two syllables are extremely light, short and weak.
The pitch rises on the long and strong 'stā'·rs,' but higher yet
on its verb (and hence heavy) 'twín·klĕ,' in which the first
syllable is short and strong, but the second long and weak, the
lĕ standing for the long *l* only. Line 3 does not satisfy any
one of my three tests, for it is only the fourth and fifth
measures which end with a strong syllable. On examination it
will be seen that the line consists of two sections; the first,
'trĕm·bling spăn·glĕs,' of two measures with the strong and
long syllable first, and the last ending with a long syllable; and
the second, 'set· in her dā'·rk gau·ze *vēi`l*,' of three measures,
of which the first two are common initial and post-pausal
measures (strong-weak + weak-strong), and it is this arrange-

ment which saves the line; the last three syllables are all
strong, but the last is the *heaviest,* and this makes the line
complete. It would be easy to alter the line to

> Set· in | her dā·′rk] gäu·ze *vēi·l* | like trĕm·]bling *spăn·glĕs,*

or to

> Trĕm·bling | like spă′n·]glĕs in | her dā·rk] gäu·ze *vēi·′l,*

or

> Like spă′n·]gles trĕm·]bling in | her dā·rk] gäu·ze *vēi·′l.*

But all these would be far more commonplace both in rhythm
and poetry. At present, the beginning of the line typifies the
feeling of the trembling starlight, while the three strong final
syllables contrast this with the dark expanse of the heavens.

"Line 4, with its nine strong syllables, is strange. The fifth
syllable, 'dull,' has decidedly more force than the sixth, 'queen,'
because the word forms a climax, but the 'queen' throughout
has much weight from grammatical reasons, which restores the
balance of rhythm. The slight pause in the fifth measure
raises the 'queen' in force, and also requires the pitch to be
sustained, that the ear may be prepared for the 'ā·′ye,' which
not only rises in force, but much more in pitch, and must be
followed by a much longer silence, ready for the burst in the
next line (5), where the first words, 'give me the,' will be very
short, though 'give' will be distinctly emphasised, and with a
much lower pitch than the preceding 'ā·′ye.' The chief force
comes on 'sō·′cial,' which will lengthen its first syllable and
rise in pitch, whereas 'glow' will be nearly as strong, much
heavier, but lower. The last four syllables seem to knock
verse on the head, but the nearly equal force of 'bright' and
'coal,' with heavier weight and higher pitch of 'coal,' allow
the slight pause after it; the weak but lengthened 'the'
(which must have a perceptible pause after it, without dropping
the voice to the lowest pitch, to fill up the last measure) prepares the mind to contrast the steady brightness of the glowing
coal with the jerking darting flame—typified in the whole two
lines 6 and 7, first by the three-fold recurrence of the group
strong-weak + weak-strong (the first united with another of the
form weak-weak-strong, having the weak syllables almost sub-

weak and sub-short, and the two others, complete in themselves, with the weak syllables rising to medium force and medial length), and next in the curious form of the last two measures of line 7, 'accŏm·paniment,' which must retain all its five syllables. The gushing of the 'melody' is indicated in a similar manner by the two trisyllabic measures in line 8; the effect may be readily seen by avoiding them thus—

> Of brī·ghtsome nō·tes, rīng·ing from brī·ghtsome hēa·'rts,

or, worse far, but restoring regularity—

> Of brī·'ghtsome nō·'tes, that rī'ng· from brī·'ghtsome hēa·'rts,

where I have marked the regular singsong pitch. One can fancy Pope 'correcting' to this form!

"After the three very dull regular lines 9, 10, 11, the ear is greatly relieved by the line 12, beginning with three weak syllables, rising to a climax of weight and pitch in 'rhythm,' and introducing a trisyllabic fourth measure, with sustained pitch on the last syllable of the fifth measure to mark the parenthetical clause, and lead on to the last line 13, with its heavy lengthy rhythm, marked especially by the word 'sun-god,' which has most force on the first syllable, 'sun,' but higher pitch and heavier weight on the second, 'god.' The last three measures of this line, with four long, strong, and heavy syllables, is relieved by distributing them into two groups of two, separated by a very light weak measure with a last syllable of medial length, which saves the line from ponderosity without detracting from its majesty.

"These observations on my own lines, patched together for the mere purpose of exemplification, will serve to shew the method in which, if I could bestow the requisite time upon them, I should study the rhythms of real poets, and the great complexity of English rhythms in the state they have reached since the beginning of the seventeenth century, when Shakspeare had learned to be daring in metre as well as poetry. But each poet would have to be considered in relation to his antecedents and his contemporaries, and the state of our language at the time, as shewn by its pronunciation, and its prose manipulation. Each poet, worthy of being so called, bears his own individual rhythmical stamp, as well as that of his age. We must not judge Chaucer's rhythms by Browning's or Swinburne's, any more than we must judge the unison music of the Greeks by the choral music of Handel and Bach."

Mr Ellis remarks subsequently that the above rules are defective in not paying sufficient regard to the fifth measure, which, striking the ear last, like a cadence in music, is often typical. With respect to this fifth measure, the general condition, although circumstances sometimes arise which induce the poet to violate it, is that the last syllable should *not be weaker* than the preceding syllable or syllables, and that, when it is actually weaker, it should be at least longer or heavier. The usual form of the fifth measure is weak-strong.

" In looking through the first book of *Paradise Lost*, I find this usual form in a decided majority of instances. It occurs in fifteen out of the first sixteen lines already quoted (p. 55). Even in the exception (line 12), the fifth measure is at most mean-strong. In a few instances I have noted weak-weak-strong; but then the weak is usually sub-weak, as: ethere-al sky, fie-ry gulf, tempestu-ous fire, mutu-al league, perpetu-al king, sulphu-rous hail, fie-ry waves, Stygi-an flood, oblivi-ous pool, superi-or friend, ponde-rous shield, cho-sen this place, popu-lous North, barba-rous sons, fie-ry couch, tem-ple of God, border-ing flood, gener-al names, Isra-el 'scape, spi-rit more lewd (where the second weak syllable is almost sub-mean, but *sprite* may have been said), counten-ance cast, follow-ers rather (with a superfluous syllable also), spir-it that fell. A very common variety is simply weak-weak, as: ar-gument, prov-idence, vis-ible, en-emy, suprem-acy, es-sences, mis-ery, mis-erable, (with a superfluous syllable, which is not usual after a fifth measure of this kind), calam-ity, circum-ference, chiv-alry. car-casses, invis-ible, etc.

" The most important deviation, however, consists in having fifth measures of the form strong-superstrong, or mean-strong, or even strong-strong or strong-heavy. I subjoin all cases of this kind which occur in the first book of *Paradise Lost*, quoting the whole line, and italicising those other measures, which, instead of being weak-strong, have any other form, as weak-

weak, mean-strong, strong-strong, strong-mean, strong-weak, or trisyllabic. The figures prefixed shew all the measures in which the *last* syllable predominates over the others, and a glance at them will shew that, whatever other measures satisfy this condition, we have always either the third and fifth, or the second and fourth, that most frequently only four measures satisfy this condition, and that when all the five measures have the principal force on the last syllable (which occurs in seven cases), one at least of these measures is varied by strengthening or lengthening the preceding syllable, or trisyllabising a measure, and thus avoiding the monotony—in fact only one ('By ancient. Tarsus') does not treat at least two measures in this way.

1 345	Wast pre|*sent, and*] with might|y wings] out-spread
123 5	*Say first* | for Heav'n] *hides noth|ing from*] thy view
2345	*Nor the* | *deep tract*] of Hell ; | *say first*] what cause
23 5	*Favour'd* | of Heav'n] so high|*ly to*] fall off
123 5	*The infer*|nal ser]pent ; he | *it was,*] whose guile
2345	*Mix'd with* | obdu]rate pride | and stead]fast hate
12 45	A dun|geon hor]*rible* | on all] sides round
123 5	As one | *great fur*]nace flam'd ; | *yet from* those flames
2345	*Regions* | of sor]row, dole|ful shades,] where peace
123 5	That comes | to all;] but tor|*ture with*]out end
2 45	*There the* | compan]*ions of* | his fall] o'erwhelm'd
123 5	And thence | in Heav'n] *call'd Sat|an, with*] bold words
12345	If thou | *beest he;*] but O, | *how fall'n!*] how chang'd
23 5	*Cloth'd with* | transcend]ent bright|*ness, didst* | outshine
12345	*Though chang'd* | in out]ward lus|tre that] fix'd mind
2 45	*Who from* | the ter]*rour of* | this arm] so late
2 45	Irrec|oncile]*able* | to our] grand foe
2345	*Out of* | our e]vil seek | to bring] forth good
12345	By an|cient Tars]us held; | or that] sea-beast
2 45	*Moors by* | his side] *under* | the lee,] while night
12345	*So stretch'd* | *out huge*] in length | the arch-]fiend lay
2 45	*Evil* | to oth]*ers; and* | enrag'd,] might see
123 5	*How all* | his mal]ice serv'd | *but to*] bring forth
123 5	That felt | unu]*sual weight; | till on*] dry land
123 5	Of un|*blest feet.*] *Him fol|low'd his*] next mate
23 5	In this | unhap]py man|*sion; or*] once more
2 45	*Hung on* | his should]*ers like* | the moon, | whose orb
2 45	*Or in* | Valdar]*no to* | descry] new lands
12345	Hath vex'd | the Red] *Sea coast,* | *whose waves*] o'erthrew

2345   *Roaming* | to seek] their prey | on earth,] durst fix
12345   By that | uxo]*rious king,* | *whose heart*] though large
123 5   Of Tham|muz year]ly wound|*ed; the*] love-tale
123 5   Infect|ed Si]on's daught|*ers with*] like heat
1 345   Of a|*liena*]ted Ju|dah. Next] came one
2345   *Maim'd his* | *brute im*|age, head | and hands] lopt off
1 345   From mor|*tal or*] immor|tal minds.] Thus they
123 5   That fought | at Thebes] and Il|*ium, on*] each side
123 5   That all | *these pu*|*issant le*|*gions whose* | exile
1 345   He spake, | *and, to*] confirm] his words | out-flew
1 3 5   In vi|*sion be*]atif|*ic: by*] him first
12345   To man|*y a row*] of pipes | the sound-]board breathes

Nevertheless, even with this supplementary caution respecting
the constitution of the fifth measure, my rules do not form, as
I thought, the sole conditions of rhythmical verse. A really
rhythmical line can be contrived (as line 3 of my own, p. 60),
which does not follow my rules, but owes its rhythmical
character to other considerations, which I have partly noticed
on p. 61."

In the above remarks of Mr Ellis I cordially agree, (1) as to
the general statement of the law of the heroic metre, (2) as to
the greater or less intensity of the metrical stress even in what
would be usually treated as regular iambic feet. I also agree,
to a considerable extent, in what he says (3) as to the limits of
trisyllabic and trochaic substitution. But whilst I admire, I
with difficulty repress a shudder at the elaborate apparatus he
has provided for registering the minutest variations of metrical
stress. Not only does he distinguish nine different degrees of
force, but there are the same number of degrees of length,
pitch, silence, and weight, making altogether forty-five varieties
of stress at the disposal of the metrist. The first observation
which occurs upon this is that, here as elsewhere, the better is
the enemy of the good. If the analysis of rhythm is so terribly
complicated, let us rush into the arms of the intuitivists and
trust to our ears only, for life is not long enough to admit of
characterizing lines when there are forty-five expressions for
each syllable to be considered. But leaving this: there is no
difficulty in understanding what is meant by force, pitch, length
and silence, and I allow that all of them have an influence on

English rhythm, though the first alone determines its general character. But what is meant by "weight"? Mr Ellis calls it "a very complex phenomenon," which "is, more than all, the governing principle of English verse," and "is due to expression and mental conceptions of importance, resulting partly from expression in delivery, produced by quality of tone and gliding pitch, and partly from the mental effect of the constructional predominance of conceptions." I cannot think that what is thus described has any right to be classed along with those very definite accidents or conditions of sound, force, pitch, length and silence. Feeling and thought may be expressed by any one of these, as well as by the regularity or irregularity of successive sounds. Weight therefore cannot be defined as expressiveness; or if it is, it is something which cannot exist separately, but only manifests itself through the medium of one of the others[1]. Nor do I find the difficulty cleared up by looking at Mr Ellis' examples. In his own lines he tells us (p. 61) that "moon," at the end of the first, has weight, but in the second, "sad ghost of night," though "long and strong," is "unimportant in weight": "twinkle" is heavy as being a verb, and also "glow" and "coal" further on. I confess I fail to see any ground for these distinctions; to insist upon them as essential to the appreciation of rhythm seems to me to be putting an unnecessary burden on all students of poetry. The one thing to attend to is the variation of *force*, arising either from emphasis, in the case of monosyllables, or from the word-accent in polysyllables. When this is thoroughly grasped it may be well to notice how the rhythm thus obtained receives a further colouring from pitch, length, or silence, from alliteration, and in various other ways, but all these are secondary.

I proceed now to consider the limitation which Mr Ellis puts upon the general rule that every foot admits of the inversion of the accent. In the remarks above quoted he gives

[1] On this Mr Ellis writes "respecting 'weight,' I am afraid I cannot go into further particulars. I do not insist on the appreciation of weight, or pitch, or quality, or length, or anything but variety of force for the mere discovery of the laws of rhythm. The other considerations are only required for the complete estimation of the poet's march within those laws, and this march differs materially from poet to poet."

two views, not quite consistent with each other, one of which appeared for the first time in 1848, and the other in 1869. According to the former, " it is necessary that there should be an accent on the last syllable, either of the third and fifth measures, or of the second and fourth. If either of these requisites is complied with, other accents may be distributed almost at pleasure." According to the latter view, " there must be a principal stress on the last syllable of the second and fourth measures; or of the first and fourth; or of the third and some other. If any one of these three conditions is satisfied, the verse, so far as stress is concerned, is complete." Yet elsewhere Mr Ellis confesses that even this later and freer view is only applicable in cases in which " the feeling of the rhythm is still preserved, not in a case in which the initial syllables of all the other measures had the stress"; and that "rhythmical lines can be written which do not observe these rules, though their observance creates rhythmical lines." But how can it be said that " their observance creates rhythmical lines," when it has just been acknowledged that it will *not* do so, if the initial syllables of all the other measures have the stress? I am unable to understand the value of a rule, the observance of which does not necessarily make the line rhythmical, and the breach of which does not necessarily make it unrhythmical. Of the latter we have more than one example in the lines quoted by Mr Ellis himself. Thus his own line,

Trémbling spángles sét in her dárk gauze véil,

has the final stress only in the fourth and fifth measures.

We will now try the effect of an accent on the last syllable of the second and fourth feet, which is all that is required, according to both of Mr Ellis' statements, to complete the verse, as far as stress is concerned.

Hárk there | is heard | soúnd as | of man | groaning|.

I cannot say that this rhythm is at all satisfactory to my ear, and I should doubt very much whether a parallel could be found for it from any iambic passage by a recognized poet. It seems to me that a better rhythm is produced by the iamb in the second and the fifth place; e.g.

Soúnd the | alarm | soúnd the | trúmpet | of war |.

In fact, as Mr Ellis acknowledges in his subsequent statement, the final iamb is almost as characteristic in English as in Greek ; if it is inverted, the rest of the line must be strongly iambic, not to lose its proper rhythmical character. I should be inclined to say that the limit of trochaic substitution was three out of five, provided that the final foot remained iambic, otherwise two out of five (see however below on *Hamlet*). We have tried a line with trochees in all but the second and fifth, we will now give specimens of iambs in the other feet.

First and fifth— The din | thickens | sound the | trumpet | of war |.
Third and fifth— Hark the | chorus | is heard | sweetly | they sing |.

Perhaps one should except also the line which has the two iambs close together (fourth and fifth), as

Hark how | loud the | chorus | of joy | they sing |,

unless there is a decided break in the sense so as to make a pause after the first two feet, as in Mr Ellis' line

Trembling | spangles | set in | her dark | gauze veil |.

I think, however, it is a mistake to pick out a certain position of the accents, as Mr Ellis has done in p. 56, and speak of the rhythm of a line as owing to accents so placed, when the line has other accents which are of themselves capable of sustaining the rhythm.

With regard to the other accentual irregularities, excess of accent, i.e. the spondee, is allowable in any position, and I am inclined to think that the limit of this substitution is wider than those which we have been considering, that in fact there might be four spondees in the line, supposing that the fourth or fifth foot remains iambic ; that we might have, for instance,

Rocks caves, | lakes fens, | bogs dens, | shades dire | of death |
death's re|gion all |
where dark | death reigns |[1].

[1] Since the above was written I have had my attention drawn to Milton's line containing four spondees, the solitary iamb occurring in the 2nd foot,

Say Muse | their names | then known | who first | who last |
2   1   0   1   1   1   1   1   1   1

Defect of accent, the pyrrhic, may also be found in any position, but it is rare for two pyrrhics to come together, and perhaps impossible without a secondary accent falling on one of the syllables, e.g. on the last syllable of *mansionry*.

By his | loved man|sionry | that the | heaven's breath |.

Perhaps this line would be better scanned with a trisyllabic fourth foot, but we might replace ' heaven's breath ' by ' sweet south,' without destroying the rhythm. If not more than two pyrrhics can come together, it follows that the limit to this substitution will be three out of five, and as a rule the other feet would be spondees rather than iambs.

As to trisyllabic substitution it is plain that, if we set no limit to this, the character of the metre is changed, and that, if we were to meet, say, such a line as the following in a heroic passage descriptive of the sphinx,

Terrible | her approach | with a hid|eous yel|ling and scream|,

we could only describe it as an intrusion of trisyllabic metre. On the other hand, we might say, without destroying the iambic character of the line

Terrible | their approach | with on|set huge | of war |
(or)   with hi|deous din | of war |
(but not, I think)   with hi|deous yel|ling and scream|.

That is, I think the limit of trisyllabic substitution is three out of five. I should be surprised to find more than this in any serious poetry, and if it did occur, I think the true scientific account (i.e. the scanning) of the line would be, to call it an anapaestic verse inserted by a freak of the poet in the midst of a passage of a different nature[1].

We must distinguish, however, between the different kinds of trisyllabic feet. The anapaest, which may be considered an

---

[1] Mr Swinburne however has a heroic line which contains four anapaests and yet satisfies the ear :

Thou art old|er and cold|er of spi|rit and blood | than I |.

Mar. Fal. A. 3, Sc. 1.

No doubt the syllables run very smoothly, so that the anapaests are not far removed from slurred iambs.

extension of the iamb, is the most common; the dactyl, which is similarly an extension of the trochee, is only allowable, I think, in the first and either the third or fourth foot; e.g. we may say

> Terrible | their approach | terrible | the clash | of war |

or

> Terrible | the clash | of war | terrible | the din |.

Whether amphibrach, i.e. iamb followed by an unaccented syllable, could be allowed in any place, except, of course, in cases of feminine rhythm, is perhaps doubtful. I cannot remember any parallel to a heroic line such as the following, but I see no objection to it:

> Rebounding | from the rock | the an|gry break|ers roared|.

A similar doubt may be raised with regard to the tribrach, i.e. a foot consisting of three unaccented syllables. Mr Ellis finds a tribrach in the fourth place of the following line,

> Of man's | first dis|obe|dience and | the fruit|,
> 0   2 | 1   0 0 2 0 0 | 0   0   2

which some might prefer to scan

> Of man's | first dis|obe|dience | and the fruit|.

Sometimes the dactyl approaches nearly to a bacchius or cretic, and the anapaest to an antibacchius. The essential rule is that the syllable, which by theory bears the stress, should at all events not be overpowered by the secondary stress.

Mr Masson's views on Milton's versification are given in an Essay prefixed to his edition of Milton. The general formula of Milton's blank verse being xa (where x stands for an unaccented, a for an accented syllable), he explains this formula to mean that "each line delivers into the ear a general $5xa$ effect; the ways of producing this effect being various. What the ways are, can only be ascertained by carefully reading and scanning a sufficient number of specimens of approved blank verse." "On the whole it is best to assume that strictly metrical effects are pretty permanent, that what was agreeable to the English metrical sense in former generations, is agreeable now. and that, even in verse as old as Chaucer's, one of the tests of the right metrical reading of any line is that it shall satisfy the present ear." "What combinations of the disyllabic groups xa, ax, xx, aa, can produce a blank verse which shall be good to the ear, is not a matter for arithmetical computation, but for experience[1]." Sometimes a line will be found satisfactory to the ear, though only one, or not even one, of its feet is of the normal type, e.g.

Scanda|lous or | forbid|den in | our law|.
a x x x x a x x a a
Hail! Son | of the | Most High | heir of | both worlds|.
a a x x a a a x a a

"I perpetually find in Milton a foot for which 'spondee' is the best name." "English blank verse admits a trochee, spondee, or tribrach in almost any place in the line." The number of accents in a line varies from three to eight. In seventy lines, containing trisyllabic feet, Mr Masson finds eighteen anapaests, occurring in any place; six dactyls, occurring in the first, second and fourth feet; six tribrachs in the first, second, and third; three antibacchius, occurring in the second and third; two cretics in the first and fourth; thirty-five amphibrachs, occurring in any foot but the last: in some lines there are two trisyllabic feet. He refuses to get rid of syllables by the process of elision or slurring. As the line has frequently more than ten syllables, so it has occasionally less.

Mr Masson quotes largely in proof of his theory, but it seems

---

[1] This is in somewhat amusing contrast with Dr Guest's *a priori* calculation of the possible varieties of the heroic line. Beginning with the section of two accents, he says, "this, when it begins abruptly, is capable only of two forms AbA and $AbbA$; but, as these may be lengthened and doubly lengthened, they produce six varieties. It is capable of six other varieties when it begins with one unaccented syllable, and of the like number when it begins with two. Hence the whole number of possible varieties is 18. The verse of four accents, being made up of two sections of two accents each, will give 18 multiplied by 18 varieties, or 324. The possible varieties of the verse with five accents is 1296, to wit, 648 when the first section has two accents, and the like number when it has three. Of this vast number by far the larger portion has never yet been applied to the purposes of verse. There are doubtless many combinations, as yet untried, which would satisfy the ear, and it is matter of surprise, at a time when novelty has been sought after with so much zeal, and often to the sacrifice of the highest principles, that a path so promising should have been adventured upon so seldom." *English Rhythms*, p. 160.

to me that in many cases the line is wrongly scanned. Thus to shew that a line may have no more than nine syllables he quotes (from *Comus*, 596)

Self-fed and self-consum'd : if this fail.

But though the *e* of 'consumed' is omitted in the standard editions, we are not bound to consider that this represents the pronunciation, any more than that 'rott'ness' in the next line is a disyllable. If we read 'consumed' as a trisyllable the line is perfectly regular. Another instance of a nine-syllable line has still less to say for itself. In Pickering's edition it reads thus (*P. L.* III. 216)—

Dwells in | all hea|ven char|ity | so deare |,

which is of course perfectly regular.

The question of elision and slurring will be considered further on. If, as I believe, Milton practised both, this would very much weaken, if not entirely destroy, the evidence in favour of such feet as the antibacchius, cretic and amphibrach. As examples of the first we find

If true | here only | and of | deli|cious taste |
Not this | rock only | his om|nipres|ence fills |
Thy pun|ishment | then justly | is at | his will |

In these lines the *y* of *only* and *justly* may be either slurred before the following vowel, or it may be taken with the following foot and change that into an anapaest. For cretics we have the lines

Each to oth|er like | more than | on earth | is thought | .
I must | not suf|fer this | yet 'tis but | the lees | *Com.* 809.

In the former I should be disposed to slur *to*, making the first foot a spondee ; compare

The⌒one wind|ing, the⌒oth|er straight | and left | between|.
                                        P. R. III. 256.
The⌒one sweet|ly flat|ters, the⌒oth|er fear|eth harm|.
                                        Rape of Lucrece 172.

In the latter it might be contended, on other than metrical grounds, that *yet* had been foisted into the text by mistake. "'Tis but the lees" would then give the reason for "I must not suffer this." If the 'yet' is genuine, it implies that, though the lady has committed a punishable offence, yet Comus considering it to be merely owing to the "settlings of a melancholy blood," requires nothing more than that she should drink the contents of the magic glass. In this case, 'yet' should be scanned with the preceding foot, which would then be an anapaest.

As regards the examples of amphibrach, many disappear if we allow of slurring and elision, as

> Whom reason | hath e|qualled force | hath made | supreme |

which becomes regular if we read *reas'n* ;

> Of rainbows | and star|ry eyes | the wa|ters thus |

which should be divided as follows, slurring *y* before *eyes*:

> Of rain|bows and | starry⌢eyes | the wa|ters thus |

In the lines which follow, 'pursuers' and 'the highest' may either be taken as slurred iambs or the last syllable in each case should go with the following foot, making it an anapaest.

> Of their | pursuers | and o|vercame | by flight |
> Aim at | the highest | without | the highest | attained |

In other cases the line may be read with an anapaest instead of an amphibrach

> Fled and | pursued | transverse | the reso|nant fugue |

where the last two feet may be divided

> | the res|onant fugue | .

[In the lines which follow I italicize Mr Masson's amphibrachs, but divide, as I should scan them myself, with anapaests.]

> *The in*|tr*i*cate wards | and ev|ery bolt | and bar |
> *In pi*|ety thus | and pure | devo|tion |
> *Ridic*|ulous and | the work | Confu|sion named |
> *Their ci*|ty his tem|ple and | their ho|ly ark |
> *Mirac*|ulous yet | remain|ing in | those locks |
> *This in*|solence oth|er kind | of an|swer fits|.
> Of mas|*sy ir*|on or sol|id rock | with ease |
> Carna|*tion pur*|ple az|ure or speckt | with gold |
> Out, out | *hyae*|na these | are thy won|ted arts |
> Tongue-dough|*ty gi*|ant how | dost thou prove | me these |

To quench | the drought | *of Phoe|bus* which | as they taste |
But for | that damn'd | *magic|ian* let | him be girt |
Crams and | blasphemes | *his fee|der* shall | I go on |
Made god|dess of | *the riv|er* still | she retains |

I need not go through the whole list. All may be treated
in the same way; I can see no reason why Mr Masson should
have found amphibrachs in them any more than in the following line, which he himself reads with an anapaest, not as
might have been expected, with an initial amphibrach.

Afford | me, assas|sina|ted and | betrayed|. *S. Ag.* 1109.

While agreeing with Mr Masson in finding dactyls, anapaests and trochees in Milton's blank verse, I cannot accept his
scanning of the following lines, which I have divided, so as to
shew what I believe to be the real feet, italicizing Mr Masson's
dactyls.

Little | *sus*pic|ious to an|y king | but now |
Shook the‿*ar*|*senal* | and thun|dered o|ver Greece |
From us | his foes | pronounced | *glory* | *he* exacts |

Next comes the question of the tribrach, of which the
following examples are cited. As before, I italicize the supposed
tribrachs, while giving my own scanning.

Epic|*ure*|an and | the Stoic | severe
1 0 0 1 0 0   0 2 0   0 1

Here I think the 4th foot has a better title to be classed as an
amphibrach than any of those so classed by Mr Masson

Curios|*ity* | *in*quis|itive im|portune |

[Mr Masson considers that the last line consists of anapaest,
tribrach, trochee and two iambs. I read it as anapaest, two
iambs, anapaest, iamb, supposing the accent of 'importune' to
be the same as in *P. L.* IX. 610; if it is accented as in *P. R.*
II. 404, the 4th foot would be an iamb, and the line would
have a feminine ending.]

So he | with dif|*ficul*|*ty* and la|bour hard |
To a | fell ad|*versa*|ry his hate | and name |
The throne | hered|*ita ry* and bound | his reign|.

It may be worth while to compare with Mr Masson's account of the Miltonic line the remarks on the same subject

by Mr Keightley in his interesting volume on the *Life,
Opinions and Writings* of Milton. He considers that English
blank verse is derived from the Italian; that it admits hypermetric syllables both after the caesura (or section) and at the
end of the line; that Milton further borrowed from the Italian
poets the double trochee at the beginning of the line as well
as after the caesura, and a freer use of the anapaest, though
abstaining from one peculiarity of Italian verse, viz. the sequence iamb-trochee at the beginning of the line[1]. As to the
last however Mr Keightley himself cites immediately afterwards
two verses in which this sequence occurs

Inclines | here to | contin|ue and build | up here | *P. L.* ii. 313
0   1   1   0   0 1 0   0   1   0   1

Among | daughters | of men | the fai|rest found | *P. R.* ii. 154
0   1   1   0   0   1   0 1   0   1

and we have already noticed other examples in treating of
Dr Guest's 'pausing section.'

Of the initial double trochee Mr Keightley gives twenty
examples from Milton (one or two of which might be differently scanned, but several might be added in their place)
and shews how common the sequence is in Italian by quotations from the beginning of the *Gerusalemme Liberata*. I
have already touched on this in reference to the line

Uni|versal | reproach | far worse | to bear |.

Of double trochee after caesura we have such examples as

Crea|ted thee | in the | image | of God | *P. L.* vii. 427
1   0   2   0

And dust | shalt eat | all the | days of | thy life | *P. L.* x. 178
1   0   1   0

Cast wan|ton eyes | on the | daughters | of men | *P. R.* ii. 180.
1   0   2   0

Dante and Petrarch are cited as using the same sequence
in Italian.

---

[1] Compare R. W. Evans *Versification* p. 84 "the trochee is admitted by
the Italian into every foot but the last, and even two are allowed to stand
together, as in the very first line of Tasso's epic. Milton, who was deeply
imbued with Italian poetry and had a pedantic turn, accordingly admits it
indiscriminately as in *P. L.*

Shoots in|visi|ble vir|tue e'en | to the deep | iii. 587.
In the | visions | of God | . It was | a hill | xi. 377.
Thy ling|ering, or | with one | stroke of | his dart | ii. 702."

Of the hypermetric syllable at the caesura the following examples are given. I do not object to this, but have divided them below so as to shew that it is possible to scan them otherwise.

> Before | thy fel|lows, am|bitious | to win | P. L. VI. 160
>   2   0
>
> With their | bright lu|minaries|, that set | and rose | P. L. VII. 385
>   0   0   1
>
> Thy con|descen|sion, and | shall be hon|oured ev(er. P. L. VIII. 649
>   0   1   0   0   2
>
> That cru|el ser|pent. On me | exer|cise not | P. L. X. 927
>   0   0   2   1 0
>
> Seemed their | petit|ion, than | when th' an|cient pair | P. L. XI. 10
>   0   1   1   2
>
> For in | those days | might on|ly shall be | admired | ib. 689.
>   0   0   1

Mr Keightley even admits a hypermetric syllable at the semicaesura, as

> On Lem|nos | the Aegáe|an isle |. Thus they | relate | P. L. I. 746

which is usually and, I think, correctly scanned

> On Lem|nos th' Ae|gean isle | thus they | relate |.

His second example is even less appropriate. I scan it

> Who sees | thee? and what | is one? | who should'st | be seen | P. L. IX. 546.

CHAPTER VI.

METRICAL METAMORPHOSIS.

THOSE who have paid little attention to the subject of metre will probably think it a very easy matter to settle off-hand the metre of any verse which is submitted to them. Starting with the four simple metres, they are apt to assume that, if a verse commences with an accented followed by an unaccented syllable, it must be trochaic; if it commences with an unaccented followed by an accented syllable, iambic; if with an accented' followed by two unaccented syllables, dactylic; if with two unaccented syllables followed by an accented syllable, anapaestic. But the most cursory examination of any dozen lines of a poem written in some recognized metre, such as *Paradise Lost*, would be sufficient to prove their error. Take for instance such a line as *P. L.* I. 12

> Fast by the oracle of God. I thence

This seems to begin with two dactyls; why should it not be called dactylic? Because we know that the poem from which it is taken is written in five-foot iambic; and therefore this line must be iambic, and must contain five feet. Dividing it into five pairs of syllables, we find that instead of beginning with two dactyls, it begins with a trochee followed by an iamb. And a little further examination will shew that this is no isolated case, that somewhere about one-sixth of Milton's iambic lines commence with a trochee. A smaller number commence with a dactyl, as I. 87

> Myriads | though bright |, if he | whom mu|tual league |

and a still smaller with anapaest as

> *P. L.* iv. 2   The Apoc|alypse | , heard cry | in Heaven | aloud |
> *P. R.* ii. 234   No advan|tage, and | his strength | as oft | assay |
> *P. L.* ii. 880   With impet|uous | recoil | and jar|ring sound | ;

unless we consider this last to begin with a trochee and dactyl, which perhaps gives a more telling rhythm.

It is plain therefore that the position of the accent in the first three syllables is no criterion as to the metre of the line. The inference which might be drawn from the 1st foot has to be corrected by our knowledge of the general metre of the poem. It is not even safe to judge of the metre from the first two feet, for (as we have seen in p. 76), some iambic lines begin with two trochees. Nor again can we rely upon the close of the line as giving an infallible criterion of the metre. The line is not necessarily trochaic because it ends with an accented followed by an unaccented syllable, nor iambic because it ends with an unaccented followed by an accented syllable. On the contrary, one very common species of the iambic line has the feminine ending, that is, closes with a hyper-metrical unaccented syllable. And thus we find iambic lines which might be said both to begin and end with a trochee, as *P. L.* i. 263

> Better to reign in hell than serve in heaven.

Or take such a line as

> Beautiful Paris, evil-hearted Paris.

Here every foot seems to be a trochee except the 1st, which is a dactyl or extended trochee, bearing the same relation to the trochee proper as the anapaest to the iamb. Yet none of us would hesitate to call it iambic and divide accordingly,

> Beauti|ful Par|is, e|vil-hear|ted Par(is,

because it occurs in a well-known heroic poem.

Conversely the commonest species of trochaic drops its final syllable, that is, suffers truncation, as in

> Hark the | herald | angels | sing | .

Beside the feminine iambic, we find specimens of the masculine form closing with a trochee (like the classical scazon)
as in the following from Morris' *Jason*,

III. 54   About | this keel | that ye | are now | lacking |
                                              1 0

III. 292   With whom | Alcme|na played | but nought | witting |
                                            1 0

III. 549   Anoth|er sun | shine on | this fair | city |
                                          1 0

II. 641   Still flew | on toward | the east | no wit | heeding |
                                            1 0

I. 153   And put | the child | before | him but | Cheiron |
                                          1 0

See examples of the same rhythm quoted from Surrey below,
pp. 159, 160. Conversely we find specimens of a trochaic line
beginning with an iamb in Tennyson's *Dirge*,

The frail | bluebell | peereth | over |
 0   1   2 0   1 0   1 0

Shelley's *Euganean Hills*,

The frail | bark of | this lone | being |
 0   1   2   0   1   1   1 0

Skylark,

The blue | deep thou | wingest |
 0   1   2   0   2 0

The pale | purple | even |
 0   1   2 0 2 0

Invocation,

The fresh | earth in | new leaves | drest |
 0   1   2   0   2   1   2

We have seen that an unaccented syllable may be added
at the end of an iambic line or cut off from the end of a
trochaic line. Does the beginning of the line admit of the
same licenses? We are told that it is so in Chaucer. Prof.
Skeat (in his edition of the *Prioress's Tale* etc. p. LXIII) cites
the following example of initial truncation, making a monosyllabic 1st foot:

By | a may|de lyk | to her | statu(rè
Til | wel ny | the day | bigan | to sprin(gè
Light|ly for | to play | and walk | on fo(tè
But | a gov|ernour | wyly | and wys |

And Dr Morris (in his edition of the *Prologue* etc. p. XLIII) cites

> *In* | a gowne | of fal|dyng to | the kne |
> *Now* | it schy|neth now | it rey|neth fast |

Other examples may be found in Schipper's *Englische Metrik*, Vol. I. p. 462.

This license is found in the heroic metre as late as Marlowe, compare *Tamburlaine* (Dyce, Vol. II. p. 48)

> *Bar*|barous | and blood|y Tam|burlaine |
> p. 189 *Con*|quer sack | and ut|terly | consume |

and see below, pp. 162, 163.

The truncation just spoken of is, I think, now obsolete in the five-foot iambic; but it is not uncommon in shorter iambic lines. Take for instance Marlowe's *Come live with me*. This is a poem in four-foot iambic, and regular, with the exception of the second line in the following verse,

> There will | I make | thee beds | of ro(ses
> *And* | a thou|sand fra|grant po(sies
> A cap | of flow|ers and | a kir(tle
> Embroi|dered all | with leaves | of myr(tle.

In *The Passions* of Collins, a four-foot iambic poem of 118 lines, there are 12 which suffer truncation. In Wordsworth's great ode, out of 200 iambic and anapaestic lines of varying length, there are five which are trochaic in form, i.e. which suffer initial truncation.

Tennyson's *Lady Clara Vere de Vere* is in eight-line stanzas of four-foot iambic, perfectly regular with the exception of the first line of the stanza, which only once has the full number of syllables

> I know | you Cla|ra Vere | de Vere | ,

suffering initial truncation in the other stanzas, as

> Trust | me Cla|ra Vere | de Vere | .

The same poet's *Arabian Nights* consists of fourteen stanzas of ten lines in four-foot iambic, followed by a three-foot feminine refrain

> Of good | Haroun | Alras(chid

One line, and I think one line only in the whole, suffers initial truncation

> *Black* | the gar|den bowers | and grots |
> Slumbered | the sol|emn palms | were ranged |
> Above | unwoo'd | of sum|mer wind | .

The *Lay of the Last Minstrel* is in the same metre with frequent anapaestic substitution.   In Canto I. Stanza 5, the 3rd and 5th lines are truncated :

> Ten squires | ten yeo|men mail-|clad men |
> Waited | the beck | of the war|ders ten |
> *Thir*|ty steeds | both fleet | and white |
> Stood sad|dled in sta|ble day | and night |
> *Barbed* | with front|let of steel | I trow |

Also in Stanza 29,

> *Nev*|er heav|ier man | and horse |
> *Stemm'd* | a mid|night tor|rent's force |
> The war|rior's ver|y plume | I say |
> Was dag|gled by | the dash|ing spray |

Milton's *Hymn on the Nativity* is written in iambic lines containing from three to six feet.   Occasionally we find a monosyllabic first-foot.

> Full lit|tle thought | they then |
> *That* | the migh|ty Pan |
> Was kind|ly come | to live | with them | below | .
>
> *When* | such mu|sic sweet |
> Their hearts | and ears | did greet |
> As nev|er was | by mor|tal fin|ger strook | .
>
> And then | at last | our bliss |
> *Full* | and per|fect is | .
>
> Nor all | the Gods | beside |
> *Long*|er dare | abide | .

So Shirley (*Golden Treasury*, p. 59),

> Devour|ing Fam'ine, Plague, | and War |
> Each a|ble to | undo | mankind |
> Death's ser|vile e'missa'ries are |
> *Nor* | to these | alone | confined | .

Fair Helen (*G. T.* p. 87),

> I wish | I were | where Hel|en lies |
> *Night* | and day | on me | she cries |
> O that | I were | where Hel|en lies |
>   On fair | Kirkcon|nel lea | .

Cowper's *Royal George,*

> *Weigh* | the ves|sel up |
> Once dread|ed by | our foes |
> And min|gle with | the cup |
> The tear | that Eng|land owes | .

Christabel is written in four-foot iambic and anapaestic lines, both of which suffer initial truncation. Thus

> Sir Le|oline | the Bar|on rich |
> *Hath* | a tooth|less mas|tiff bitch |
> *From* | her ken|nel beneath | the rock |
> She ma|keth ans|wer to | the clock |
> *Four* | for the quar|ters and twelve | for the hour |
> *Ev*|er and aye | by sun | and shower | .
>
> *Is* | the night | chilly | and dark |
> The night | is chil|ly but | not dark |
> They steal | their way | from stair | to stair |
> *Now* | in glim|mer and now | in gloom | .
>
> The cham|ber carved | so cur|iously |
> *Carved* | with fig|ures strange | and sweet |
> *All* | made out | of the car|ver's brain | .

It may be asked, however, why the lines classed as truncated iambic should not be treated either as anapaestic or as truncated trochaic. If we met with the following lines apart from the context we should naturally scan them as anapaests; why not adhere to this more natural scansion? e.g.

> That the migh|ty Pan | .
> When such mu|sic sweet | .
> Hath a tooth|less mas'tiff bitch |
> From her ken|nel beneath | the rock | .

The answer is (1) that Milton's *Hymn* is not anapaestic nor in any way irregular. It is composed in verses of eight lines, the 1st, 2nd, 4th, and 5th lines consisting of three iambic feet, the 3rd and 6th of five, the 7th of four, and the 8th of six. Even if we called the two lines just cited anapaestic, we should hardly venture to say the same of

> Long|er dare | abide | .

(2) *Christabel* no doubt admits lines of which the rhythm is trisyllabic; but, as Coleridge himself tells us that the accents are four, though the syllables vary from seven to twelve, this

prevents us from scanning the lines quoted as anapaestic. In any case it would be difficult to make an anapaestic line out of

Is | the night | chilly | and dark | .

1   0   1   2   0   0   1

But, if they cannot be treated as anapaestic, why should they not be called truncated trochaics? Why may not the poet have chosen to vary his iambic lines with an occasional trochaic? No doubt this is a possible explanation in some of the instances, such as

And a | thousand | fragrant | posies |

Thirty | steeds both | fleet and | white | .

These read naturally as trochaics. But take

Now in | glimmer and | now in | gloom |

Barbed with | frontlet of | steel I | trow |

Is the night chilly and dark

The two former would give us a dactyl in the 2nd foot, which is rare in trochaic metre, and the last simply refuses to be treated as a trochaic at all.

Far more common however is the omission of one or both of the unaccented syllables of the anapaest. Iamb for anapaest is usual in all the feet of an anapaestic line, but in the 1st foot a monosyllable is also allowed. Thus in the following verses from the *Burial of Sir John Moore*, consisting of four anapaests with alternate masculine and feminine endings, there are two monosyllabic feet and five iambs, which I have printed in italics.

Few | *and short* | were the prayers | *we said* |

And we spoke | not a word | *of sor*(row

But we stead fastly gazed | on the face | of the dead |

And we bit|terly thought | of the mor(row.

Light|ly they'll talk | of the spi|rit that's gone |

And o'er | his cold ash|es upbraid (him,

But lit|tle he'll wreck | if they let | him sleep on |

In the grave | where a Brit|on has laid (him.

So in Byron,

Thou | who art bear|ing my buck|ler and bow |

Should the sol|diers of Saul | look away | from the foe |

Stretch | me that mo|ment in blood | at thy feet |

Mine | be the doom | which they dared | not to meet | .

And Swinburne (*Erechtheus*),

l. 139 Fair fort|ress and fost|ress of sons | born free |
Who stand | in her sight | and in thine | O sun |
Slaves | of no | man sub|ject of none |

l. 95 *Sun* | that has light|ened and loosed | by thy might |
O|cean and earth | from the lord|ship of night |
Quick|ening with vis|ion his eye | that was veiled |
Fresh|ening the force | in her heart | that had failed |
That sis|ter fet,tered and blind|ed broth(er
Should have sight | by thy grace | and delight | of each oth(er.

Matthew Arnold (*Heine's Grave*),

That | was Hei|ne, and we |
Myr|iads who live | who have died |
What | are we all | but a mood |
A sing|le mood | of the life |
Of the Be|ing in whom | we exist ? |

Elliott (*Lament for Flodden*),

I've heard | them lil|ting at our | ewe milk(ing
Lass|es a' lil|ting before | dawn of day |
But now | they are moan|ing on il|ka green loan(ing
The Flowers | of the For|est are a' | wede away | .

Other examples will be found in the chapters on Classification of Metres.

Corresponding to the initial truncation of the anapaestic line is the final truncation of the dactylic line, as in

Take her up | tenderly |
Lift her with | *care*
Fashioned so | slenderly |
Young and so | *fair*.

Pibroch of | Donuil Dhu |
  Pibroch of | *Donuil*
Wake thy wild | voice anew |
  Summon Clan | *Conuil*.

Brightest and | best of the | sons of the | *morning*
Dawn on our | darkness and | lend us thine | *aid*
Star of the | east the hor|izon ad|*orning*
Guide where the | infant Re|deemer is | *laid*.

It may be asked what reason have we for classifying as anapaestic such a line as

Bright | be the place | of thy soul |

and as dactylic

> Lift her with | care |

since it is plain that the former might be regarded as made up of two dactyls and a long syllable (truncated dactylic), and the latter of a long syllable followed by an anapaest (truncated anapaestic). The answer is that these ambiguous or metamorphous lines must be interpreted by others in the same poem, where the strict law of the metre is observed, such as

> In the orbs | of the bles|sed to shine | .
>
> Take her up | tenderly |

There are no doubt poems composed in a mixed metre, in which the rhythmical effect is produced by the juxtaposition of contrasted metres, say, trochaic and anapaestic; but none could say there was this contrasted effect in the poems above cited. The rhythm is felt to be the same throughout.

But truncation is not only practised at the beginning of the iambic and anapaestic line, and at the end of the trochaic and dactylic; it is also found in the interior of the line itself. Thus *Break, Break, Break* is a somewhat irregular poem, the prevailing rhythm of which is three-foot anapaest, but in two verses, the three anapaests are represented by these three long accented syllables.

Kingsley has internal truncation in his 4-foot anapaestic

> *Clear* | and cool | *clear* | and cool |
> By laugh|ing shal|low and dream|ing pool | .
> *Dank* | and foul | *dank* | and foul |
> By the smo|ky town | in its mur|ky cowl | .
> *Strong* | and free | *strong* | and free |
> The flood | gates are o|pen away | to the sea | .

And Shelley in his *Address to Night*, the metre of which is generally anapaestic with iambic substitution, has a monosyllable for the anapaest in the 3rd foot of the 1st and 3rd of the following lines

> And the wea|ry day | *turned* | to his rest |
> Ling|ering like | an un|loved guest |
> Thy broth|er Death | *came* | and cried |
>   Wouldst | thou me | ?
> The sweet | child Sleep | the fil|my-eyed |

I take the three next examples from Dr Guest. The first is truncated trochaic, which undergoes internal, as well as final truncation, in the 2nd and 7th lines.

> On the | ground |
> *Sleep* | sound |
> I'll ap|ply |
> To your | eye |
> Gentle | lover | reme|dy | .
> When thou | wak'st |
> *Thou* | tak'st |
> True de|light |
> In the | sight |
> Of thy | former | lady's | eye |

The second, from Burns, is four-foot iambic; it suffers internal truncation in the 1st and 3rd lines.

> The sun | blinks blithe | on yon | *town* |
> And on | yon bon|nie braes | of Ayr |
> But my | delight | in yon | *town* |
> And dea|rest bliss | is Lu|cy fair | .

The third is from Moore, written in four-foot and two-foot iambic. Internal truncation will be found in the 1st, 3rd, 5th, 6th and 8th lines.

> The day | had sunk | in dim | *showers* |
> But mid|night now | with lus|tre meek |
> Illu|mined all | the pale | *flowers* |
> Like hope | upon | a mour|ner's cheek | .
> I said | *while* |
> The moon's | *smile* |
> Played o'er | a stream | in dimp|ling bliss |
> The moon | *looks* |
> On ma|ny brooks |
> The brook | can see | no moon | but this | .

We may add the following from Shakespeare :

> For love | is crow|ned with | the prime |
> In spring | *time* |
> The on|ly pret|ty ring | *time* |
> When birds | do sing |
> Hey ding | a ding |
> Sweet lov|ers love | the spring | ,

and this from Scott,

> *March,* | *march,* | Ettrick and | Teviotdale, |
> Why the deil | dinna ye march | forward in | order

where the corresponding lines of the next verse

> Come from the | hills where your | hirsels are | grazing |
> Come from the | glen of the | buck and the | roe |

shew that the monosyllables *march march* represent dactyls, and also that *Teviotdale* and *dinna ye march* must be contracted into trisyllables.

But the first foot is not only liable to *truncation* of un-accented syllables, when such precede the accent according to the law of the metre, as in iambic and anapaestic poems; it may also admit *anacrusis,* i.e. have an unaccented syllable pre-fixed to the accent, where that should naturally come first, as in trochaic and dactylic poems. Thus in Keats' *Realm of Fancy,* a four-foot trochaic poem of 94 lines, there are 7 which begin with a hypermetrical unaccented syllable, as

> Thou shalt | at one | glance be|hold |
> *The*) daisy | and the | mary|gold |.

In his *Ode on the Poets* out of 42 lines there are 3 which have the anacrusis.

In Shelley's *Skylark* the prevailing metre is trochaic, but we find

> What thou | art we | know not |
> What is | most like | thee |
> *From*) rainbow | clouds there | flow not |
> Drops so | bright to | see |

So in *Duncan Gray,*

> Something | in her | bosom | wrings |
> For re|lief a | sigh she | brings |
> *And*) O her | een they | spak sic | things | ,

and Tennyson's *Lilian,*

> Praying | all I | can |
> *If*) prayers | will not | hush thee |
> Airy | Lili|an |
> Like a | rose-leaf | I will | crush thee |
> Fairy | Lili|an | .

It is evident that, when the common truncated trochaic has a hypermetrical syllable prefixed, it becomes undistinguishable from a complete iambic line, just as a truncated iambic, particularly if it has a feminine ending, takes the form of a trochaic. Since from either side, then, the one can so easily pass into the other, it is no wonder that we find poems consisting in nearly equal proportions of iambic and trochaic lines, in which probably neither the poet nor the reader is conscious of a change of metre. Such poems are *L'Allegro* and *Il Penseroso*. Starting with the regular metre in line 11 of the former, we have, in the next fifty lines, an equal number of trochaic and iambic lines. It is to be noticed also that the iambic line often either begins with an accented, or ends with an unaccented syllable, as

And at | my win|dow bids | good mor(row
Scatters | the rear | of dark|ness thin | .

The hypermetrical syllable in trochaic metre is thus always capable of being explained away as an intentional change to iambic, but a similar explanation would be very harsh in dactylic metre, such as the following,

Come away | come away |
Hark to the | summons |
Come in your | war array |
Gentles and | commons. |

Come from deep | glen and |
From) mountain so | rocky |
The) war-pipe and | pennon |
Are) at Inver|lochy | .

There are many examples in Kingsley's *Longbeard's Saga*.

White were the | moorlands |
And) frozen be|fore her |
Green were the | moorlands |
And) blooming be|hind her | .

Shaking the | southwind |
A)round in the | birches |
A)waking the | throstles | .

This) day at the | Wendel's hands |
Eagles must | tear them |
Their) mother thrall|-weary |
Must) grind for the | Wendels | .

High in Val|halla |
A) window stands | open |
Its) sill is the | snowpeaks |
Its) posts are the | waterspouts |
Storm wrack its | lintel | .

It will be observed that, where a line begins with the hyper-metrical syllable, the preceding line frequently ends with a trochee for dactyl, so that the effect is simply to complete the dactylic rhythm. This is not however the case in the following passage from *Christabel*, where two dactylic lines are interposed between anapaests,

And foundst | a bright la|dy surpass|ingly fair |
And) didst bring her | home with thee | [1]
In) love and in | charity |
To shield | her and shel|ter her from | the night air |

nor in the following from Hood's *Bridge of Sighs*, where in two of the lines anacrusis follows a complete dactyl at the end of the previous line,

A)las for the | rarity |
Of) Christian | charity |
Under the | sun |
O it was | pitiful |
Near a whole | city full |
Home there was | none |
Dreadfully | staring |
Thro) muddy im|purity |
As) when with the | daring |
Last) look of des|pairing |
Fixed on fu|turity | .

Sometimes we find even two hypermetrical syllables, when the final dactyl of the preceding line is represented by a long syllable, thus passing into anapaestic rhythm, unless we are to regard this as a case of 'scriptorial disguise' treated of below.

The) bleak wind of | March |
Made her) tremble and | shiver |
But) not the dark | arch |
Nor the) black flowing | river |

---

[1] This and the following line are usually printed together, but the rhyme shews that they should be separated, just as much as the short lines preceding, 'But vainly thou warrest, For this is alone in,' etc.

So in the 3rd verse of *Pibroch of Donuil Dhu* the dactylic
rhythm of the other verses is changed into the anapaestic,

> Leave untend|ed the herd |
> The flock | without shel(ter
> Leave the corpse | uninterr'd |
> The bride | at the al(tar.

I presume without any deliberate intention on the part of the
poet.

To take now a general view of the licenses or irregularities
admitted, we find, in trochaic, addition of an unaccented syllable
at the beginning, dropping of an unaccented syllable at the end,
and substitution of iamb or dactyl in the first foot (rarely in
others), giving rise to lines of pure iambic form, as "but let
them rave," or of strong dactylic colouring, as "half invisible to
the view." On the other hand, in iambic, we find addition of
an unaccented syllable at the end, dropping of an unaccented
syllable at the beginning, with trochaic and anapaestic substitution, giving rise to lines of pure trochaic form, as "Up there
came a flower," or the anapaestic "In there came old Alice the
nurse." So in anapaestic we have dropping of unaccented
syllables at the beginning, and addition of an unaccented
syllable at the end, with iambic substitution; in dactylic,
dropping of unaccented syllables at the end, and addition of an
unaccented syllable at the beginning, with trochaic substitution.
The general principle may be thus laid down, that one or two
unaccented syllables preceding the initial accent or following
the final accent of the line are non-essential to the rhythm,
and may be added or omitted without necessarily changing the
metre.

So far we have considered cases in which one of the four
principal metres has assumed the appearance of another. We
will now proceed to examine cases in which the disguise
assumed is that of the amphibrach. Dr Abbott (*English Lessons*,
p. 212) reads Browning's line as an amphibrach,

> Dirck galloped | I galloped | we galloped | all three |

Prof. Bain (*Eng. Comp.* p. 239) does the same with

> There came to | the shore a | poor exile | of Erin |

and Mr Higginson (*Eng. Gramm.* p. 164) with

> Distracted | with care |
> For Phyllis | the fair |
> Since nothing | could move her |
> Poor Damon | her lover | .

Probably most readers would on a first reading pronounce the same of the following lines from *Christabel*,

> That in the | dim forest |
> Thou heardst a | low moaning |
> And foundst a | bright lady | surpassing|ly fair |

and from Southey's *Lodore*,

> Collecting | projecting |
> Receding | and speeding |
> Dividing | and gliding | and sliding |
> Retreating | and beating | and meeting | and sheeting | .

But a more careful examination will, I think, in each case shew that the normal metre is anapaestic. It would evidently be impossible to read other lines from Browning's *Good News from Ghent* as amphibrachs, e.g.

> Not a word | to each oth|er we kept | the great pace |
> Neck by neck | stride by stride | never chang|ing our place |

Hence the apparent amphibrach must be divided as follows

> Dirck gal|loped I gal|loped we gal|loped all three |

making *anap.* 4 instead of *amphib.* 4. The fact is, wherever there is a complete anapaestic line, with iambic substitution in the first foot, it will be possible to read it as an amphibrach truncated at the end. In the same way we should divide

> There came | to the shore | a poor ex|ile of E(rin.

The lines beginning 'Distracted with care' are shewn to be anapaestic by those which follow almost immediately.

> To a pre|cipice goes |
> Where a leap | from above |
> Would soon fin|ish his woes | .

The lines from *Christabel* are preceded by the manifestly anapaestic

> In the touch | of this bo|som there lur|keth a spell |
> Which is lord | of thy ut|terance, Chris|tabel | .

As to *Lodore*, the general rhythm is undoubtedly anapaestic; thus in the 1st stanza we have lines like

> With its rush | and its roar |
> As man|y a time |
> They had seen | it before | .

In the 2nd

> It runs | and it creeps |
> For a while | till it sleeps |
> In its own | little lake | .
> And thence | at depar(ting
> Awake|ning and star(ting
> It runs | through the reeds |
> And away | it proceeds |

where the two middle lines might also be read as amphibrachs. In the 3rd stanza we have

> Ri|sing and leap(ing
> Sink|ing and creep(ing
> * * *
> Around | and around |
> With end|less rebound |
> * * *
> Diz|zying and deaf|ening the ear | with its sound | .

And the last stanza ends

> And so | never end|ing but al|ways descend(ing
> Sounds and mo|tions for ev|er and ev|er are blend(ing,
> All at once | and all o'er | with a migh|ty uproar |
> And this | way the wa|ter comes down | at Lodore | .

I think therefore that it is natural to scan the ambiguous lines as anapaests with feminine ending, thus

> Collect|ing project(ing.   Anap. 2
> Divi|ding and gli|ding and sli(ding.   Anap. 3.

Perhaps the following lines from Shakespeare have as much right to be called amphibrachs as any we can find ;

> Most friendship is feigning, most loving mere folly ;
> Then, heigh ho ! the holly !
> This life is most jolly.

But looking at the preceding line, which I should divide

> Heigh ho ! | sing heigh ho ! | unto | the green hol(ly,

I think it is best to treat all as anapaestic.

There remains one other method of disguising metre, which I may call the scriptorial, when either verse is written as prose, of which Dickens supplies the most marked examples (see Abbott, *Lessons*, § 61), or prose as verse, of which plentiful examples may be found in Walt Whitman ; or again when, though verse is printed as verse, the lines are not divided in accordance with the actual metre employed. We have had an instance of such mis-division in Coleridge's *Christabel* (see above p. 90). Compare also what is said below (p. 154) on the line usually printed

> Singing to welcome the pilgrims of the night.

The signs + and − may be conveniently used to denote the addition or omission of unaccented syllables whether at the beginning or the end of the verse. Thus the feminine heroic

> Cromwell | I charge | thee fling | away | ambi(tion

which shews an extra syllable after the last bar, would be classed as *iamb.* 5 + . The truncated trochaic

> Come not | here ∧

may be marked with a *caret* after the last accent, and classed as *troch.* 2 − .

A hypermetrical syllable at the beginning of the verse may be marked with a curved line following, as in the line from *Lilian*

> She) looking | through and | through me |

which would be classed as *troch.* + 3 ; while that from the *Deserted House* would receive both marks,

> So) frequent | on its | hinge be|fore ∧

and be classed as *troch.* + 4 − . Conversely an iambic verse, which suffers truncation at the beginning and has a feminine ending, would be thus written

> ∧ Sub|tle-thought|ed myr|iad mind(ed

and described as *iamb.* − 4 + .

In the trisyllabic metres, where there is often a loss of two unaccented syllables, the mark may be doubled : thus the verses

> ∧ ∧ Few | and short | were the prayers | we said |
> And we spoke | not a word | of sor(row

might be described as *anap.* $= 4$ and $3 +$.

Dawn on our | darkness and | lend us thine | aid $\wedge$ $\wedge$

might be described as *dact.* $4 =$.

Verses with hypermetrical syllables may be conveniently divided into *prae-hypermetrical* and *post-hypermetrical*, according as the extra syllable comes at the beginning or end; but, as the latter are generally known as feminine lines, I shall use hypermetrical in a special sense, of a verse which has the extra syllable at the beginning.

CHAPTER VII.

EXAMINATION OF TWO RECENT METRICAL SYSTEMS[1].

Mr Robert Bridges in his book entitled *Milton's Prosody* (Oxf. 1893) has given a careful and instructive study of the peculiarities of Milton's blank verse and of the choruses in *Samson Agonistes*. He classifies the divergences from typical blank verse under four heads, as follows:

A. Supernumerary Syllables, which he subdivides into (1) Extra-metrical Syllables at the end[2], or in the middle of the line, and (2) Elided Syllables. Of medial extra syllables he gives examples from *Comus*, but says that it does not occur in *P. L.*, such lines as

> Departed from (thee); and thou resemblest now. iv. 839.
> Of high collateral glo(ry): Him thrones and powers. x. 86.

being better explained on the principle of Elision.

The analogy of the Greek would lead most persons to understand by this term the entire disappearance of the first vowel in a sequence of two vowel sounds, but Mr Bridges expressly says that it is not meant 'to imply that anything is cut off, or lost, or not pronounced' (p. 8), and again 'It has been taken by some that I meant that the elided syllable should be cut out of the pronunciation; but I chose the term, because I wished not to imply any theory of prosody as to how the supernumerary syllables were to be accounted for in rhythm.

[1] Read before the Philological Society.

[2] On p. 7 he gives examples from *P. L.* of two extra syllables at the end of the line; but in p. 41 says that, though such a thing is possible in the looser metre of *Samson*, 'it would be quite out of the question in *P. L.*, though a few lines might seem to support it.'

I did not think that there could be any doubt as to whether they should be pronounced.' 'Though Milton printed *th' Almighty* &c., it cannot be supposed that he wished it to be so pronounced' (p. 49). We are thus to understand the term 'elision' as covering three different explanations, which I have distinguished by the terms *elision* (in the strict sense), *slurring*, and *trisyllabic feet*: or rather 'since it is not intended to imply that anything is cut off or not pronounced,' we have simply to consider the two latter alternatives. And so we find Mr Bridges (in p. 48) allowing that 'the theory of trisyllabic feet best suits' the lines quoted above, as well as such lines as

> Innumerable. As when the potent rod   i. 338
> Of depth immeasurable. Anon they move   i. 549

though 'as a question of Miltonic prosody they are all examples of elision[1].' 'In cases where there is doubt, it is better to regard the syllable as extrametrical: the test is this, that if it is extrametrical, it does not signify to the ear whether it is long or short, whereas in a trisyllabic foot it must be short.'

I cannot but think that considerable confusion is caused by this attempt to treat the trisyllabic foot merely as a species of

---

[1] In p. 27 however he seems to hold to the strict theory of elision. Quoting *S. A.* 651

> The close of all my miseries and the balm

he says that "elsewhere Milton always insists on all the three syllables of the word 'misery,' which is the more expressive pronunciation of the word." But surely, however we scan the line, whether we end the 4th foot with 'miseries' making the 5th foot trisyllabic, or make the 4th foot trisyllabic closing it with 'and,' the pronunciation of 'miseries' is precisely the same as in every other line where it occurs. I am inclined to make the last foot trisyllabic, as giving a more pathetic rhythm, but Mr Bridges (p. 29) speaks of "a trisyllabic foot in the 5th place not resolvable by the fictions" as "without parallel in all the verse of *P. L.*, *P. R.*, and *S. A.*" Again in p. 34 there is a discussion as to the line

> Oft on a plat of rising ground

where it is said that it reads as if it began with a dactyl, though there is no "difference of opinion as to its metrical device" (meaning, I suppose, its scansion), "but if we substitute 'softly' for 'oft on,' it is clear that, according as we admit or refuse an elision of the open *y* before the *a*, we have a seven-syllable line with falling stress throughout, or an eight-syllable line of rising stress with the first foot inverted." It is hard to reconcile this with his previous explanation of the term 'elision.'

elision[1], especially as Mr Bridges confesses that 'true dactylic verse, or verse made of true trisyllabic units, was quite common in Milton's time' (p. 45), 'that in all the best blank verse the trisyllabic feet are made up almost exclusively of open vowels or vowels separated by liquids; and that after these the most frequent condition is that of short *i*....I think it impossible to doubt that in *P. L.* Milton purposely excluded all trisyllabic feet but those made by open vowels and the three liquids, and that he afterwards relaxed this rule to admit *m* and short *i*,' always rejecting such licences as

> Like to | a vag|abond flag | upon | the stream | *Ant. Cleop.* i. 4.
> 　　　　　　 0　 0　　　　 1
> To try | thy el|oquence, now | 'tis time | : dispatch | *ib.* iii. 10[2].
> 　　　　　　 0　 0　　　　　 2

I feel some doubt as to what would be Mr Bridges' explanation of a line such as the following

> That cruel ser|pent. On me | exercise most. *P. L.* x. 927.

I should be inclined to treat it myself as containing an extrametrical syllable, but he has laid down the rule that this is not allowed in *P. L.* (p. 7). Nor can the 3rd foot be trisyllabic, since that is only permitted under the above-stated limitations. It is impossible to elide the emphatic *me* before *exercise*; and thus the only remaining course is to scan the latter half of the line

> on | me ex|ercise most |
> 　 2　 1　 0　　 0　　 1

with a final anapaest, but this would be far harsher than the examples taken from Shakespeare's *Antony*, which we were told were un-Miltonic.

B. We go on now to the 2nd variety admitted by Milton, that connected with the number of stresses. Of these only two kinds are specified, (1) lines with four, (2) lines with three stresses; *excess*[3] in the number of stresses being altogether ignored, though it is just as common as *defect*, compare

---

[1] In p. 45 he even uses the word 'contraction' to explain the metre of

> But now | he's gone |, and my | *idol*|*atrous* fan(cy. *All's Well*, i. 1. 91.

[2] p. 31. The limitations mentioned in the use of the trisyllabic foot are just those which in p. 8 foll. are said to govern the use of elision.

[3] In p. 56 however he recognizes the occurrence of a spondee following two unstressed syllables.

Say Muse | their names | then known | who first | who last |.
 2   1   0   1   1   2   1   2   1

P. L. i. 376.

Rocks, caves, | lakes, fens, | bogs, dens, | and shades | of night |.
 2   2   2   2   2   2   0   1   0   1

ib. ii. 621.

C. The third variation arises from inversion of rhythm. Examples of inversion in every foot are given and also examples of double inversion in the 1st and 2nd, the 3rd and 4th, and 2nd and 4th foot. In the note on p. 22 we read that ' Milton came to scan his verses one way and read them in another.' I have insisted upon it as a general rule that scanning is not to fetter the reading, but I cannot think the examples here given are well chosen. I should prefer to read, as well as scan,

Of rain|bows and | starry eyes. | The wa|ters thus | *P. L.* vii. 446.

rather than to read with him the second foot as a trisyllabic and the 3rd foot as a regular iamb. My reason is that I think a pause should be made both before and after *and*, so as to emphasize *starry*, which would make it difficult to treat the 2nd foot as an anapaest.

His second example he reads thus

Shoots in|visible | virtue ₁ even to | the deep | *P. L.* iii. 568.

which would give a falling rhythm in four feet. I do not see why we might not follow the scansion given in p. 13 for the first three feet

Shoots in|visi|ble vir|tue even to | the deep |

but, instead of his 4th foot, which is simply a receptacle for syllables otherwise unaccounted for, I should read

vir|tue e'en | to the deep |.
 0   1   0   0   1

D. A fourth source of variation is in the position of the caesura or break in the verse, of which Mr Bridges gives examples after every syllable.

The next chapter deals with Milton's later metre as illustrated by the *P. R.* and *Samson*. The comparison of this with that of *P. L.* shews that he ' did not think it worth while to

7—2

keep strictly to his laws of elision, but that he approved of the great rhythmical experiments he had made, and extended these' (p. 26). As examples of 'elision'—what I should rather call trisyllabic feet—we find

> Thy pol|itic max|ims or | that cum|bersome | *P. R.* III. 400.
>   0 0   1
> She's gone | a man|ifest ser|pent by | her sting | *S. A.* 997.
>   0 0   2

And we may add

> Their own | destruc|tion, to come | speedy | upon (them   *S. A.* 1681.
>   0   0   1   2 0
> Tongue-dough|ty gi|ant, how | dost thou prove | me these |
>   0   0   1
>   *S. A.* 1181.
> Out, out, | hyae|na ! these | are thy wont|ed arts | *S. A.* 748.
>   0   0   1

[The three last might also be explained as examples of extrametrical syllables. Mr Bridges indeed says 'the system of prosody in *Samson* plainly forbids extrametrical syllables in the midst of the line, and there is certainly no other example,' but there seems no ground for such a statement. He is even driven by his theory to the impossible suggestion that, in the last line, 'hyaena' constitutes the 2nd foot with inverted stress and elision of the 1st syllable.]

I proceed to examine the chapter on the verse of *S. A.* Mr Bridges finds in it 19 lines in falling rhythm. Several of these should rather, I think, be treated as anapaests. Thus the chorus begins (l. 115) with the 4-foot iamb, where the 3rd foot has the accent inverted.

> This, this, is he; softly, awhile.

Mr Bridges makes line 116 a 4-foot trochaic.

> Let us | not break | in up|on him.

But, if regarded as anapaestic, the rhythm is far more vigorous

> Let us not | break in | upon (him

and corresponds better with the 3-foot iambs which follow

> As one | past hope | aban(doned
> And by | himself | given o(ver.

I also find two anapaestic lines in 169—175

iamb. 5.	For him | I rec|kon not | in high | estate.
iamb. 3.	Whom long | descent | of birth |
anap. 3+	Or the sphere | of for|tune rai(ses
	0 0 1
iamb. 5.	But thee | whose strength | while vir|tue was | her mate |
iamb. 3.	Might have | subdued | the earth |
anap. 4+	Univer|sally crowned | with high|est prai(ses.
	0 0 2 0 0 1

Also in 298

iamb. 5.	For of | such doc|trine ne|ver was | there school |
anap. 2.	But the heart | of the fool.
	0 0 1 0 0 1

And 329

iamb. 3.	Old Man|oah | advise |
anap. 3+	Forthwith | how thou ought'st | to receive (him.
	0 0 1 0 0 1

So in chorus beginning l. 606, where Mr Bridges treats 606, 607, 610, 614, 618 as trochaic, I should scan as follows:

anap. − 4[1].	∧ Oh | that tor|ment should not | be confined |
	0 0 1 0 1
anap. 2.	To the bod|y's wounds | and sores |
	0 0 2
iamb. 4+.	With mal|adies | innum|erab(le
iamb. 3.	In heart, | head, breast, | and veins |
anap. 3.	But must se|cret pas|sage find |
	0 0 1
anap. 2.	To the in|most mind |
	0 0 1
	* * *
anap. 3.	As on en|trails joints | and limbs |
	0 0 1
	* * *
anap. 3.	As a ling|ering | disease |
	0 0 1
l. 714. anap. 2.	Like a state|ly ship |
	0 0 1
l. 1269. anap. 4.	To the spir|its of just | men long | oppress'd |
	0 0 1 0 0 1
l. 1271. anap. − 3.	∧ Puts | invin|cible might |
	0 0 1
l. 1280. anap. 3.	And celest|ial vig|our armed |
	0 0 1

---

[1] By the caret (∧) and − prefixed to the number of feet is signified initial truncation of short syllable.

l. 1436. anap. 2.   In the camp | of Dan | .
 0 0 1

I have some doubt about 1668, which Mr Bridges reads as
5-foot trochaic

While their | hearts were | jocund | and sub|lime ∧

but the rhythm seems to be most inappropriate to the sense.
If there were any authority for giving the Latin and Italian
accent to *jocúnd*, I should take the line as composed of three
anapaests; otherwise I think we must scan

anap. 4.   While their hearts | were jó|cund and | sublíme |
 0 0 1

followed by anap. — 4

 ∧ Drunk | with idol|atry drunk | with wine |
 0 0 1 0 0 2
1686. anap. 3.   And with blind|ness inter|nal struck |
 0 0 1 0 1
1707. anap. 4.   A sec|ular bird | ∧ A|ges of lives |
 0 0 1 2 0 0 1

The following, which Mr Bridges treats as truncated trochaic, I think are better explained, on the principle referred to
by him in p. 35, as truncated iambic, i.e. iambic with the first
syllable omitted

1699. iamb. — 4.   ∧ Like | that self-|begot|ten bird |
1701. iamb. — 4.   ∧ That | no sec|ond knows | nor third |
1743 foll. iamb. — 4.   ∧ All | is best | though we | oft doubt |
 ∧ What | th' unsearch|able | dispose |
 iamb. 4.   Of high|est wis|dom brings | about |
1749. iamb. — 4.   ∧ Oft | he seems | to hide | his face |
So 1431. iamb. — 4.   ∧ Great | among | the heath|en round |

In p. 12 Mr Bridges proves that Milton usually pronounced
adjectives in -*able* with the stress on the penultimate, but he
allows an exception in *P. L.* v. 585

Innu|merable | before | the Almigh|ty throne |

so 'capital' and 'idolatry' are said to be exceptions to the rule
of 'elision' in pp. 27, 28.

Again he says that Milton always places the stress on the
penultimate of words ending in -*ary*, but allows an exception

in the case of 'luminary' in VII. 385. It would seem that an exception must also be made for 'sanctuary,' which, it is true, is followed by a vowel, and therefore may be considered to suffer 'elision,' in most of the passages where it occurs, but in Ps. 87. 3 we find the line

There seat|ed is | his sanc|tuary |

rhyming with

Among | the ho|ly moun|tains high | .

I think also that we should have to except 'extraordinary' in the only place where it is used by Milton (*S. A.* 1383) which Mr Bridges scans

To some|thing ex|traor|dinā|ry my thoughts |

though he shrinks very much from a trisyllabic fifth foot 'not resoluble by the fictions': and those who are indifferent to the 'fictions' will certainly condemn it as a very ugly line. Why may we not, in the absence of any evidence to the contrary, suppose that Milton pronounced it as he does 'luminăry' and 'sanctuăry' and 'contrăry' (in all but one place), as Shakespeare also does in

W. T. I. 2. Of head|piece ex|traor|dinary? Lo|wer mes(ses
0 0 1

(where the short *i* disappears altogether).

I proceed now to inquire what is meant by the 'fictions' referred to. They are first mentioned in p. 22, where it is said that 'Milton's system in *P. L.* was an attempt to keep blank verse decasyllabic by means of fictions.' Again in p. 68 we are told that Milton and Shakespeare threw off the syllabic trammels of their early style and came to determine their rhythm by stress. 'Immediately English verse is written free from a numeration of syllables, it falls back on the number óf stresses as its determining law.' 'If once the notion be got rid of that you must have so many syllables in a line to make a verse...then the stress will declare its supremacy; which...in Shakespeare and Milton it is burning to do.' 'The primary law of pure stressed verse is, that there shall never be a conventional or imaginary stress.' 'Coleridge proposed to write purely stressed verse in *Christabel*, counting the accents, not the syllables'; but he has not carried out his intention, and thus we find in him conventional stresses as in

> She ma|keth ans|wer tó | the clock |
> A fur|long fróm | the cas|tle gate |

(p. 71) 'If the number of stresses in each line be fixed [and such a fixation would be the metre], and if the stresses be determined only by the language and its sense, and *if the syllables which they have to carry do not over-burden them*[1], then every line may have a different rhythm.' 'This is very much what Milton was aiming at in the lyrical parts of *Samson*, but he still sought to accomplish it by fictitious units...He wrote... a rhythmical stressed line and scanned it by means of fictions. He need not have troubled himself about the scansion at all. If the stressed rhythm is the beauty of the verse, it is a sufficient account of it.'

I object here, first, to the use of the word 'fictions.' What is intended would be much better expressed by the word 'type.' The type or law of the metre is ascertained, like a botanical or anatomical type, by a comparison of a large number of recognized examples. It is the musical air or theme on which different variations are composed. It is Plato's one in the many, the permanent in the changeable, the persistent background in the mind of the poet and the reader. If however by 'fiction' is meant the minute conditions laid down for the use of trisyllabic feet by Mr Bridges, I am quite willing to throw these over at once. The unfettered trisyllabic foot used by Shelley or Tennyson is as satisfactory to my ear as the artificial foot allowed by Mr Bridges. The next point to which I should make objection is, that the metre is constituted simply by the number of stresses in the line, without regard to the number of syllables or to the position of the stress. Mr Bridges himself seems to be conscious that some limitation must be made on this wide definition, for in the words which I have italicized he slips in the condition that the stress must not be overburdened by the syllables it has to carry. What is this, but to re-

---

[1] The italics are mine.

introduce the syllabic principle? A few examples, prose and verse, will be sufficient to shew the absurd results which would follow from treating the number of syllables as unessential to metre. Take first these lines of six stresses

> Sir Ríchard spóke and he laúghed and we roáred a hurráh and só.
> With heád, hánds, wíngs, or feét pursués his wáy.
> Thát seéming to be móst which we indeéd leást áre.

five stresses

> Thén methoúght I heárd a méllow soúnd.
> A míxture of a lié doth éver ádd pleásure.
> Or thát stárr'd Éthiop queén that stróve.

four stresses

> The stág at éve had drúnk his fíll.
> Mílton a náme to resoúnd for áges.
> Revénge is a kínd of wíld jústice.

three stresses

> Nów the dáy is óver.
> The sójourners of Góshen who behéld.
> The slóthful man saith there is a líon in the wáy.

It is strange to find Mr Bridges, after he has said that metre is constituted by the number of stresses in each line and that it would have been better if Milton had not troubled himself about scansion in writing the *Samson* choruses,—it is strange, I say, to find him affirming that the laws of English stressed metre have still to be ascertained in regard to the questions 'What will a stress carry? What are the usual units of the verse?' and yet maintaining that, when these unknown laws are discovered, 'English poets will find open to them an infinite field of rhythm as yet untouched. There is nothing that may not be done in it.' How can he tell the effect of what is still *in nubibus*, or would he have us greet Walt Whitman as the harbinger of the new era? There may be some minds to which the fantastic visions of anarchy are more attractive than the waking realities of an ordered freedom, but Englishmen will be slow to believe that the poetry of the future is too big for the measures which sufficed the genius of Shakespeare and Milton and Shelley and Tennyson and

Browning, and the elasticity of which has been proved by a constant succession of new developments in metre and rhythm.

Happily Mr Bridges has not confined himself to theory, but has given practical illustration of what he means by the 'rhythmical stressed line' in his interesting dramas. In the Comedy entitled *The Feast of Bacchus* he adds the following note to explain his novel verse, which critics, he is told, will declare to be prose.

'The metre is a line of six stresses...Whatever a stress may carry, it should never be made to carry more than one long syllable with it,—the comic vein allowing some license as to what is reckoned as long;—but as there are no conventional, or merely metric stresses (except sometimes in the sixth place; and in the third, when the mid-verse break usual in English six-stressed verse is observed, or that place is occupied by a proper name), the accompanying long and short syllables may have very varied relation of position with regard to their carrying stress. Where more than four short unstressed syllables come together, a stress is distributed or lost; and in some conditions of rhythm this may occur when only four short syllables come together; and this distributed stress occurs very readily in the second, fourth, and fifth places. Such at least seem some of the rhythmic laws, any infringement of which must be regarded as a fault, or liberty of writing: and the best has not been made of the metre. A natural emphasizing of the sense gives all the rhythm that is intended.'

I don't know what may be the feeling of others, but to me the last sentence seems to be the expression of the author's despair of ever finding a satisfactory explanation of his metre. He puts forward tentatively, one after another, various rules, which can hardly be described as light-giving or convincing, and after telling us that 'such *at least seem to be some* of the rhythmic laws' which are essential to the verse, he ends by saying that after all it does not matter: the rhythm will be found all right if it is properly read.

I propose then to disregard the enigmatic rules, and consider whether Mr Bridges' verse admits of explanation according to the system which I have followed in my book, and what kinds of liberties are allowed. I think it will appear, as we proceed, that many of the lines are not in conformity with the author's own principles, and that, where they do conform, they are not rhythmical, unless they are subject to the recognized syllabic restrictions.

The 1st act begins with the lines

Good morn|ing Sir ! | good morn|ing ! He does | not hear | me—Sir ! |
Good morn|ing ! No | : he goes | on dig|ging away | for his life. |

which I should scan as shewn by the bars, calling them either 6-foot anapaestic with iambic substitution, or 6-foot iambic with anapaestic substitution. I·will give some examples where the scanning is more difficult.

p. 185, l. 37. Never do I go out, however early in the morning.

Written and read thus, I deny that this line is verse. If we read ' i' th' morning,' it will then be 6-foot iambic, ending with anapaest and extrametrical syllable.

l. 39. But here | I see | you dig|ging, hoeing, | or at all | events |

Here the word 'hoeing' is forced into a monosyllable or else the 4th foot is an amphibrach.

p. 186, l. 69. But af|ter the u|sual dic|tato|rial man|ner of fa(thers.

Here the 2nd, 3rd, 5th and 6th feet are anapaest and the line ends with an extrametrical syllable. The general effect is that of a hexameter with anacrusis.

l. 70. I ne|ver left | him in peace | don't think | my fine | fellow |

3rd foot anapaest, last foot trochee.

l. 79. You have not | enough | to do | . When I | was yo|ur age |

'your' has to be read as a disyllable to make the line rhythmical.

p. 187, l. 93. I returned | home to | my house | miser|able, | my mind

inverted stress in 2nd, 4th and 5th feet.

l. 100. So bus|ily are | engaged | all for | my com(fort
                      2   0   2   1

Here we have only five stresses, and the line must apparently be scanned as feminine 5-foot iambic with spondee in 5th foot and trochee in 4th.

p. 191, l. 270.　A hard|ship, was no|thing of the kind | : the so-|
called sever|ities |

The only way to make this rhythmical is to read the 3rd
foot as 'thing o' th' kind' (like 'o' th' morning' in p. 185, l. 37)
and apparently to treat 'called sevér' as an anapaest.

l. 277.　Of e|vil pas|sions, he is driven | of neces|sity from bad | to worse

It is absurd to call this verse.　To give any kind of scanning
one would be compelled to crush into a 3rd foot 'sions he's
driven,' into a 5th 's'ty from bad.'

l. 285.　Learn | this les|son : see | what shame | your friend | has brought

Here we find the 1st foot represented by a long syllable.

p. 194, l. 372.　Means well: | I would | not hurt | his feelings | but
　　　　　　　　　 1　　　1　　　 1　　　 2　　　　1
at an|y cost |
　2　　 1

If this is to be scanned, we have to allow an amphibrach in the
4th foot : there are 7 stresses.

p. 198, l. 512.　Have noth|ing to ans|wer.　No|body could | be in | a
worse plight |

2nd, 4th and 6th feet anapaests, the last having properly two
stresses.

p. 210, l. 921. With a mínd[1] most singularly sensible of grief, or else

Only 5 stresses.　I do not venture to scan it.　If read as a
5-foot iambic, the 3rd and 4th foot would each have four
syllables.

p. 216, l. 1146.　The stage is yóur hóme, the áctors your father
and moth(er

Here one would have said there were only five stresses, but
Mr Bridges accents the first 'your,' which I suppose he must
make a disyllable as in l. 79.　The 5th and 6th feet would then
be anapaests.

p. 220, ll. 1249, 1250.
A wom|an whose ve|ry pres|ence was an in|sult; and not | content |
With abu|sing my con|fidence | and kind|ness, my sheer | disgust | .

In the former line we must either assume an amphibrach in
the 3rd foot (see ll. 39, 372) or squeeze four syllables into the
4th, as in ll. 270, 277, 921.

[1] The accents are Mr Bridges'.

p. 221, l. 1292.

  To keep | your place | woman | . Wás there | ever | a thing |

Here we have three continuous trochees in the middle of the line.

l. 1197. Of the mat|ter in which | so con|fidently | you oppose | me. Fool! |

anapaests in 1st, 2nd, 4th, and 5th foot.

   p. 222, l. 1337.   That carries it: to hell with dumps! 'Twere poór
         mérriment

begins with 5 iambs. What it ends with I can't guess. It is certainly most unrhythmical.

   p. 1341.   You have made me, my dear Clinia the very happiest of
        fáthers

There seem to be only four stresses to 18 syllables. The rhythm reminds one of *Miserarum est neque amori dare ludum neque dulci* and is quite out of harmony with the general metre.

l. 1355.   What can | thát teach | ? Your tie | to me | your friend(ship

Here there are 6 stresses and 5 feet.

  p. 223, l. 1394.   That if | I can | be hap|py enough | to make | his
        peace | with his fath(er

Here we have 7 stresses and 7 feet.

p. 225, l. 1453.   Costly | to rear | costly | to keep | costly to | get rid (of

the 5th foot seems to be a dactyl.

  I turn now to the examination of Mr Bridges' 5-foot iambic, as exemplified in his tragedy of *Nero* Pt. 2. He has a note at the end which is not quite intelligible to me: ' pedantry refusing to conform to idiom will explain the occasion of many of the accents with which I have thought it necessary to disfigure my text ; for a good number of them will be found to be common enclitics. The rest are all put as guides to the dramatic rhythm, and many of them to ensure the usual pronunciation of words in verses the rhythm of which depends on it, but which I found some readers stumble at, so that they would rather mispronounce the word than accept the intended rhythm.' Not to dwell on this, I would call the attention of my readers to the following lines as illustrating his dramatic rhythm.

p. 233, l. 11.   Crackled | in flame | and smoke, | hath stilled | to a fire |
1st foot trochee, 5th foot anapaest.

l. 24.   Nay, while | she lives | I go | not from | the world |
contains 6 stresses and is therefore inadmissible in a line limited by theory to 5 stresses.

l. 35.   I had spo|ken of | to thee | openly, | but all
Here the 1st foot is an anapaest, the 4th a dactyl, and the line has only 4 stresses.

l. 57.   His cru|elty his | effem|inate blun|dering pas(sion
Four stresses, 2nd foot tribrach, 4th and 5th anapaest.

l. 116.   Wé res|tore the | repub|lic.   The | Repub(lic !
Here Mr Bridges accents 'we,' thus giving trochees in the 1st and 2nd foot: the 4th foot is a pyrrhic, and there are 4 stresses.

P. 235, ll. 220, 221.   Written as prose, but may be metrically divided as follows :

Sit and | drink gent|lemen. | Wine shall | be cheap |
To-day. | The life | in the earth | will crack | my jars. |
A few | more rumb|les like that | will drain | the cel(lars .

and so again at the end of the 2nd column

Your health, | sir ! If | you wish | to know | the cause |
*   *   *   *   *
I give | him his day | he cares | not for | the gods |

l. 503.   A sim|ple mind | a clear | head and | true heart |
six stresses.

l. 516.   Seal your | lips and | depart. | And thou | too neph(ew
begins like l. 116 with two trochees.

l. 620.   Sene|ca Cae|sar ? my hand | is trem|bling, my sense |
1st foot trochee, 3rd and 5th anapaests.

l. 629.   Stand firm ? with my | poor pal|sied limbs |
four feet with five stresses.

l. 773.   Scarce human.   'Tis soundest principle.
Here there are five stresses, but the line is unrhythmical

because it wants a syllable. It becomes rhythmical if 'the' is inserted after ''Tis.'

l. 842. Whose ar|my is | a creá|ture of dis|cipline |

only three stresses.

l. 888. Prece|dents for | my conduct. | The divine | Augus(tus

four stresses: the 3rd foot is amphibrach, unless it is meant to end with an extrametrical syllable before the stop.

l. 993. Snow from | the south | . Wóod must | búrn ; when | 'tis burnt |

trochee in the 1st, 3rd and 4th foot and spondee in 5th, six stresses.

l. 1048. Throw up | this all|men's joy? | Nay, here | the heart (rules
        1 2   2   1   2 2   2   1

eight stresses, strong extrametrical syllable.

l. 1715. For a stat|ue of Bru|tus and | outdo | the man |

four stresses, 1st and 2nd foot anapaests, 3rd pyrrhic.

l. 1803. Marriage | rúins | a wóm|an : and | how quick(ly

two trochees at the beginning of the line, 4th pyrrhic, 5th spondee.

l. 1875. Imme|diate ac|tion. That | madman | Scevi(nus

4th foot trochee.

l. 1943. Action | Rufus, | is now | your on|ly hope |

begins with two trochees like 1803, 516.

l. 2275. My rich | estates | cónfiscate, my innocent

The accent (which is given in the text) on the 1st syllable of 'confiscate,' destroys the rhythm. If it had been on the penultimate, the 4th foot might have been treated as an anapaest.

l. 2283. Our ill-|built ship | founders. | I am | your cap(tain

trochee in 3rd and 4th foot.

l. 2217. In a | conspir|acy | to mur|der ano(ther

only three stresses.

l. 2275. The lap-|dogs of | the pal|ace. Where | áre they? |

'are' is accented in the text, making up four stresses.

l. 2296.   My in|tima|cy with | the accused, | that oft |
three stresses.

l. 2396.   Defi|eth thee | as I, | curseth | thee as I |
4th foot trochee, 5th foot anapaest.

I think those who have followed me thus far will agree that
Mr Bridges' stressed line is of little value as a help to the
understanding of metre. A line is not necessarily rhythmical
when it accords with the system, nor unrhythmical when it
disagrees with it; and it is of no use for discriminating the
different kinds of verse.

In the *Transactions of the London Philological Society* for
1897—1898, pp. 484—503 there is a paper by Dr Skeat on
the Scansion of English Poetry. He considers that 'the usual
method of scansion of English poetry, which divides the line
into feet of equal length, is of small actual value. It is artificial, and conceals the facts which it ought rather to display.'
'It does not enable us to discriminate between the various
types of verse.' I am not quite sure what is the method of
scansion which Dr Skeat here condemns. If it is the same as
that which I have examined in my 3rd chapter, or, if we are
to take it as maintaining that the iamb is the only foot
admissible in English blank verse, I am not concerned to
defend it, though I think it nearer the truth than that which
Dr Skeat would substitute for it. For this system he claims,
that it will enable us 'to analyse any given poem in the five-
accent metre with a precision hitherto unattainable' (p. 487),
providing 'a most powerful and minute search-light, which, if
well directed, might easily enable us to distinguish the work of
one poet from another, and even the work of a poet in a
serious mood from that of the same poet when in a jocose or
pleasant one' (p. 495). He describes his system as 'the natural
method of grouping the syllables around the accented syllables
with which, in actual pronunciation, they are associated.' From
what follows it would at first seem that the grouped or associated
syllables are such as make up a single word, for he goes on to
say 'in pronouncing English words there are to be found four

forms of what I shall call an accent-group, i.e. a group in which only *one* accent occurs.   These groups are exemplified by the four words Tone, Ascent, Cadence, Extension...denoted by the symbols – ∪– –∪ ∪–∪, where the symbol – denotes a strongly accented, and ∪ an unaccented syllable.' It appears however that, in all words containing more than three syllables, and in some words of three syllables, we have to recognize a group of two accents, the strong and the weak, the latter of which may be denoted by a finer stroke, as in *indignātion, mērrimēnt.*

So far I think we should gather that the metrical groups of which the line is composed are simply the words themselves, and therefore that the words must not be broken up from any fancied considerations of rhythm.

It would appear however from the scanning on a later page that the 'accent-group' (which is the phrase he prefers to 'the misleading word *foot* with its absurd classical associations') is not limited to a single word.   We find not merely the article, pronoun, preposition, and conjunction attached to an accent-group, but we meet also such groups as *here - rests, save - where, how - bowed, some - heart, each - in, left - the.*   But how far from 'the natural method of grouping the syllables around the accented syllables with which, in actual pronunciation, they are associated,' is such a division as the following :

> [1] Each-in his-narrow•cell•for-ever laid
> Left-the warm-precincts•of•the-cheerful•day ?

It is plain that no good reader would separate the words *in, the, of,* from the following nouns, and that the natural grouping would be

> Each•in-his-narrow-cell,
> Left•the-warm-precincts of-the-cheerful-day.

Again, what are we to say of such lines as :

> Molest her-ancient soli•tary reign
> The-place of-fame and-ele•gy•supply

---

[1] The hyphens connect words belonging to the same group: a full stop is used to isolate the 'tones,' and also where the same word is divided into distinct groups.

If-chance by-lonely Contem•plation•led
Or-waked to-exta•sy•the-living•lyre,
Heaven-did a-recom•pense: as-largely•send.

where the 'accent-groups' *solitary, elegy, contemplation, extasy,*
recompense are each, according to the scansion, rudely broken
up into two distinct groups? In fact, if we choose to adopt
Dr Skeat's own vigorous language in p. 495, we might say
"nothing can be more hideous and artificial than such groups
of words as" Heaven-did a-recom•pense, Left-the warm-pre-
cincts•of· "and the like. A poet who really scanned his
lines according to such a system would hardly deserve a
hearing." My first charge then against Dr Skeat is that his
system, as applied by him, in no respect answers to his description of it, but separates naturally associated syllables, and joins
together alien syllables.

We should all of course agree in his general principle that,
in the reading whether of prose or verse, the first object of the
reader should be to bring out the natural relations of the
syllables of which the sentence is composed. The most elementary grouping is that in which syllables are combined into
words. Even this is not always made quite clear by an illiterate
reader. Nearly as intimate is the grouping which unites the
proclitic (article, preposition etc.) with the following word; and
we might go on tracing out the varying shades of intimacy, till
we come to distinct breaches of intimacy marked by commas,
colons, full stops and paragraphs. Dr Skeat limits his groups
to three syllables, but if we are thinking simply of how to read,
setting aside rules of scansion for the moment, we have to
reckon with single words containing six syllables or more, or
with longer compound groups of closely associated words, such
as 'from his heathery couch' following the word 'sprung'; so
that if, for convenience' sake, we choose to take no cognizance
of groups containing more than three syllables, we should at
least allow of the possibility of double or treble groups. But
confining ourselves to the groups recognized in his system, I
want to know, why the only trisyllabic group specified is the
amphibrach? If there are words like 'extension' there are
also words such as 'beauteous,' 'terrible,' 'counterfeit' with the

stress on the 1st syllable, and such as 'colonnade,' 'macaroon' with the stress on the last. The anapaestic group is no doubt rare, if we think only of single words, but it is extremely common as a compound group, such as 'the approach,' 'to return.' Again the disyllabic group, as exemplified in single words, may be generally divided into trochee or iamb, but if we consider compound groups, such as 'who first,' 'who last,' we are compelled to include the spondee. To illustrate this I will take the simplest of metres, the 4-foot iambic of the *Lady of the Lake* beginning with the normal

> The stag at eve had drunk his fill.

A little lower we come to a line which Dr Skeat would probably describe as made up of two extensions and two tones,

> Had-kindled•on•Benvoirlich's•head

but which seems to me more naturally divided, for the purpose of reading, into two groups, the former an extension, if we like to call it so, the other containing the remainder of the line.

But what are we to say of the following line

> The antlered monarch of the waste?

If we are to call the 1st group an extension, and the 2nd a cadence, we have surely just as good a right to call the 3rd an anapaest. And so, in

> Sprung from his heathery couch in haste

if we allow that 'sprung' may be called a 'tone,' we have equal right to say that it is followed by a double anapaest. So the following lines

> A moment | listened | to the cry
> That thickened | as the chase | drew nigh |

seem to me to fall naturally into three groups, as marked, the 1st consisting of extension, cadence, anapaest, the 2nd of extension, anapaest, ascent.

I go on to examine Dr Skeat's classification of the varieties of what is known as five-foot iambic. He begins by distinguishing four types, (A) commencing with two 'ascents' ($\smile -, \smile -$), (B) with 'ascent' and 'extension' ($\smile -, \smile - \smile$), ($C$) with 'extension'

and 'tone' (◡–◡, –), (*D*) with 'extension' and 'cadence' (◡–◡, –◡).
Of each of these there are four varieties determined by the
nature of the three following groups which make up the
end of the line, and which may be either ◡–, ◡–, ◡–, or ◡–,
◡–◡, –, or ◡–◡, –, ◡–, or ◡–◡, –◡, –.

This classification seems to me unsatisfactory (1) on the
ground that it is not exhaustive even for such strictly normal
metres as that of Gray's Elegy, which is taken as the type. Over
and above the sixteen varieties thus obtained, Dr Skeat has
afterwards to name one of far more importance in its effect on
the rhythm, i.e. the initial trochee, as in

Báck-to its-mansion•call•the-fleeting•breath.

He has also to open the door to many other varieties caused
by the varying position of the caesura and, still more, by the
greater or less number of accents and of syllables. (2) The
sixteen admitted varieties are purely arbitrary. No good
reader would separate between the 1st and 2nd group in the
line just quoted. 'Back' is certainly a monosyllabic 'tone,'
if we are to admit such things at all: 'to' belongs to the
following group, which, if we are to find names for all real
metrical groups, should be called a 'third Paeon' rather than
an 'extension' or amphibrach.

Look at some other instances of 'extension'

The-lowing•herd•winds-slowly•o'er•the-lea
The-cock's shrill-clarion•or•the-echoing•horn.

Extension, as we learn from p. 485, is a group of three syllables
in which only one accent occurs, that accent falling between
two unaccented syllables. Will any one say that *winds - slówly*
or *shrill - clárion* has only one accent, or that either *shrill -
clarion* or *echoing - horn* has only three syllables? To call
these by the name 'extension' is as purely arbitrary as to give
the name of 'tone,' defined as 'a strongly accented syllable,' to
the scarcely audible prepositions in the following lines :

The-rude forefathers•of•the-hamlet•sleep
No-more shall-rouse-them•from•their-lowly•bed
Some-hearts once-pregnant•with•celestial•fire
And-wastes its-sweetness•on•the-desert•air.

Surely if any scansion is to be called 'artificial,' to use Dr Skeat's own phrase, or 'fictitious' and 'conventional' in Mr Bridges' language, it is the scansion which puts the emphasis on the weakest word in the line. Properly read, the lines have only four accents and have therefore no claim to be reckoned specimens of the 5-accent verse. Thus in

> The rúde | forefá|thers of | the hám|let sléep |

I should describe the 3rd foot as a pyrrhic. Or, if we consider that we gain an additional accent in the first foot of such a line as

> Nó móre shall roúse them from their lówly béd,

this is at the expense of introducing a group unknown to Dr Skeat, in which two adjoining syllables have the same strong accent; the group which I should call a spondee. And that this is not exceptional, but a very effective and favorite variation is shewn by the following lines:

> And ăll that beăuty, ăll that weălth ĕ'er găve
> If mēmŏrў ŏ'er their tŏmb nŏ trŏphies răise
> Or flăttĕry sōōthe the dŭll cŏld ēar of dēath
> Sŏme hĕart ōnce prĕgnănt wĭth cĕlĕstĭăl fĭre
> Lĕft the wărm prĕcincts ŏf the chēērful dăy
> On sŏme fŏnd breăst the părting soŭl relīes
> Hărd by yŏn woŏd, nŏw smīling as in scōrn.

It will be observed that in most of these lines there are six accents, a number which is forbidden by the first law of Dr Skeat's system. In some there are pyrrhics, in some anapaests. Other examples of these are:

> They kept the noiseless tenoŭr ŏf their way
> Implores the passing tribŭte ŏf a sigh
> Now fades the glimmĕrĭng lăndscăpe ŏn the sight
> Some mute inglorĭoŭs Mĭlton here may rest
> To quench the blushĕs ŏf ingenŭoŭs shăme.

In one case the trisyllabic foot is better described as a dactyl,

> Mŭttĕrĭng his wayward fancies he would rove.

Dr Skeat would perhaps explain these away on the principle of elision, but at what a loss to the rhythm, if we are to pronounce 'glimm'ring,' 'ingenyous,' 'mutt'ring.'

(3) But if Dr Skeat's scansion breaks down in such a simple measure as the Elegy, how helpless and hopeless would it be in dealing with the bold experiments of Milton or Tennyson or Browning or with those of Mr Bridges which we have just been considering? What would he make of

> Rocks, caves, lakes, fens, bogs, dens, and shades of night,

or Tennyson's

> Galloping of horses over the grassy plain,

or

> The little innocent soul flitted away?

(4) Lastly, I contest the right to introduce such metrical groups as 'tones' and 'extensions' as being natural and ordinary substitutes for the normal ascents of the heroic metre. The cadence (i.e. the trochee) all will allow at any rate in certain parts of the line, but neither the tone nor the extension is found otherwise than as a rare exception. On the other hand the ascending and descending trisyllabic (i.e. the anapaest and dactyl) are closely allied with the iamb and trochee, often melting into them by means of slurring or glide. In conjunction with iamb and trochee they supply, as I have endeavoured to shew, all the feet required to explain any English metre, if we allow of occasional truncation or anacrusis. For the possible use of amphibrach in the iambic line cf. above, pp. 71, 74.

Dr Skeat (in p. 495) maintains 'that English verse admits neither dactyl nor anapaest,' and tries to explain all dactylic or anapaestic lines as consisting of amphibrachs. I have considered this question above, pp. 91—93. As an example of amphibrachic metre he takes Byron's lines, which I scan as alternate masculine and feminine anapaestic, with iambic substitution and occasional initial truncation, thus

> ∧ Knów | ye the lánd | where the cý|press and mýr(tle
> Are em|blems of deeds | that are done | in their clime |
> Where the rage | of the vul|ture, the love | of the tur(tle
> Now melt | into sad|ness now mad|den to crime |

Dr Skeat reads them thus

> Know-ye the-land-where the-cypress and-myrtle
> Are-emblems of-deeds-that are-done-in their-clime

Where•the-rage-of the-vulture the-love-of the-turtle
Now-melt-in•to-sadness now-madden to-crime.

I think no educated reader, who considers the matter without prejudice, would have any hesitation as to which scansion gives the better rhythm, which has the more natural division of the words, and which puts less strain on the metrical principles adopted.   Both systems admit of certain licenses, such as the omission of a short syllable before a long at the beginning of the line, or the omission of a short syllable after a long at the end of the line, what I have called initial or final truncation.   But Dr Skeat goes far beyond this in his 3rd line, where he prefixes a tone, i.e., according to definition, a long accented syllable, thus

Where•the-rage-of the-vulture the-love-of the-turtle.

But this gives us, not four accents, but five, which contradicts the essential principle of the metre.   Dr Skeat himself feels the difficulty, which he says ' must be disposed of before we can proceed in peace.'   He finds a means of escape by discarding the definition of the 'tone.'   Here, he says, it is used to denote an extremely slight accent (p. 496), for which he provides a new symbol, to remind us that the word is not to ' count as forming a true accent-group': it is merely in fact that ' insertion of additional syllables at the beginning of a line ' which ' is a strongly marked feature of this amphibrachic verse,' though ' it requires a good ear and careful handling, or the verse easily becomes lame and clogged ' (p. 497).   That is to say, his system breaks down when he has to apply it to a perfectly regular anapaestic line, just as it does in the lines cited on p. 499, as it would do in

Not a drum | was heard | not a fu|neral note |

How this magnificent anapaestic line would be murdered by the halting amphibrachic scansion

Not•a-drum-was heard-not a-funer•al-note !

Dr Skeat's paper concludes with an examination of Kingsley's hexameters, which of course turn out to be mere ' extensions.' I cannot say that I find his argument more convincing here than in the rest of his paper. I shall deal with the hexameter in a later chapter.

It may perhaps be worth while to give a specimen of dactylic metre, of which he denies the existence and which is certainly rarer than the anapaest. In p. 139 below I have cited Tennyson's

> Cannon in | front of them |
> Volleyed and | thundered | .

Hood's

> Take her up | tenderly |
> Lift her with | care ∧

Heber's

> Brightest and | best of the | sons of the | morning | .

We may add Scott's

> Come away | come away |
> Hark to the | summons |
> Come in your | war array |
> Gentles and | commons | .

Ruskin (*Elements of English Prosody*, p. 15) quotes Byron's line

> Bright is the | diadem | boundless the | sway ∧

as a perfect specimen of dactylic verse, and (p. 18)

> With the dew | on his brow | and the rust | on his mail |

as an equally faultless anapaestic. When, however, we compare the remainder of the poem from which the former line is taken, we find that it too is more properly described as anapaestic with initial truncation.

CHAPTER VIII.

NAMING AND CLASSIFICATION OF METRES.

Illustrated from Tennyson's Poems.

I propose in this chapter to test our metrical analysis upon a writer who furnishes examples of a great variety of rhythms, and as to whose readings and pronunciation there is no question, so that one may argue securely on the facts. Metrical writers are almost as much divided in regard to the general theory of metre and the scansion and naming of particular metres, as they are on the admissible varieties of the five-foot iambic; nor do I know of any one who has given an altogether consistent and satisfactory account of the matter. The best, I think, is that by Dr Abbott in *English Lessons*, but it is incomplete on the trisyllabic metres, and he errs, as we have seen, in the direction of a mechanical regularity.

Before classifying Tennyson's trochaic metres according to the number of feet employed, I must mention a variety which is common to them all, produced by the omission of the last unaccented syllable, thus giving rise to the truncated trochaic, the converse of the feminine iambic. We find examples of the two-foot trochaic, both complete and truncated, in combination with longer metres; of complete in *The Poet*—

In the | middle | leaps a | fountain |	(4)
Like sheet | lightning ¦	(2)
Ever | brightening |	(2)
With a | low me|lodious | thunder |	(4)

and of the truncated in *The Miller's Daughter*—

Love the | gift is | love the | debt ∧	(4 –)
Even ¦ so ∧	(2 –)

Deserted House—

Life and | thought have | gone a|way ʌ   (4 –)

Side by | side ʌ   (2 –)

Poet—

Hollow | smile and | frozen | sneer ʌ   (4 –)

Come not | here ʌ   (2 –)

I do not think Tennyson has any example of the complete three-foot trochaic, such as we find in Baring Gould's hymn for children—

Now the | day is | over | (3)

Night is | drawing | nigh ʌ   (3 –)

Shadows | of the | evening | (3)

Steal a|cross the | sky ʌ   (3 –)

But the truncated form is common in combination with longer metres, as in *Lilian*—

When my | passion | seeks ʌ

Pleasance | in love | sighs ʌ

Then a|way she | flies ʌ

Fairy | Lili|an ʌ

and the *Deserted House*—

Careless | tenants | they ʌ

Here no | longer | dwell. ʌ

In *Maud* xvii. we find twenty-eight consecutive lines in this metre, beginning " Go not | happy | day." In *Lilian* we have specimens of a variation of the complete three-foot trochaic formed by the prefixing of a hypermetrical syllable or anacrusis, analogous to the feminine rhythm in the iambic metre—

She) looking | through and | through me |

If) prayers | will not | hush thee |

The four-foot trochaic is by far the commonest, as in *Lilian*—

When I | ask her | if she | love me |

Claps her | tiny | hands a|bove me |

The Poet's Mind—

Clear and | bright it | should be | ever |

Flowing | like a | crystal | river |

Lady of Shalott—

Willows | whiten | aspens | quiver |

Little | breezes | dusk and | shiver |

Usually, however, it alternates with the truncated form, as in *Lord of Burleigh*—

> Deeply | mourned the | lord of | Burleigh |
> Burleigh | house by | Stamford | town ∧

This is the common 8s 7s of the hymn-books, like—

> Through the | day thy | love has | spared us |
> Now we | lay us | down to | rest ∧

Written as one line we know it as truncated eight-foot, the metre of *Locksley Hall*—

> Comrades | leave me | here a | little | while as | yet 'tis | early | dawn.

The truncated four-foot is the metre of the song in the *Vision of Sin*—

> Wrinkled | ostler | grim and | thin ∧

It is the 7s of hymn-books, the metre of

> Hark the | herald | angels | sing ∧

Deserted House is in the same metre with anacrusis in three of the lines—

> So) frequent | on its | hinge be|fore ∧
> Or) through the | windows | we shall | see ∧
> The) naked|ness | and vacan|cy ∧

The complete four-foot is rarely used alone in hymns, as in one of the translations of the *Dies Irae*—

> Day of | wrath, O | day of | mourning |
> See once | more the | cross re|turning |
> Heaven and | earth in | ashes | burning |

Five-foot trochaic is rare in either the complete or truncated form.   We find examples of the former in the *Vision of Sin*—

> Narrowing | into | where they | sat as|sembled |
> Low vo|luptuous | music | winding | trembled |

and in *Wellington*—

> He shall | find the | stubborn | thistle | bursting |
> Into | glossy | purples | which out|redden |

The rhythm has rather a tendency to run into Canning's *Needy Knife Grinder*, which indeed only differs from it by the

insertion of a short syllable, changing the initial trochee into
a dactyl—

> Story, God | bless you, | I have | none to | tell, Sir |

In both the poems just mentioned the truncated form is mixed
with the complete, as in the *Vision of Sin*—

> Then me|thought I | heard a | mellow | sound ∧
> Gathering | up from | all the | lower | ground ∧

and in *Wellington*—

> Once the | weight and | fate of | Europe | hung ∧
> He that | ever | following | her com|mands ∧
> On with | toil of | heart and | knees and | hands ∧

Six-foot is also rare. We find in the *Vision of Sin* the
complete form—

> Purple | gauzes | golden | hazes | liquid | mazes |

and in *Wellington* the truncated

> Who is | he that | cometh | like an | honoured | guest ∧

also in *Cauteretz*—

> All a|long the | valley | stream that | flashest | white ∧

I am not aware that Tennyson has any example of the complete seven-foot trochaic, though it has to my ear an easier and
more natural rhythm than the five and six-foot trochaics, e.g.

> In the | glowing | autumn | sunset | in the | golden | autumn |

but we find the truncated form in the *Lotos Eaters*—

> We have | had e|nough of | action | and of | motion | we ∧

and

> Like a | tale of | little | meaning | though the | words be | strong ∧

Locksley Hall supplies examples of the eight-foot trochaic,
both in the complete form, as

> Slowly | comes a | hungry | people | as a | lion | creeping | nigher |

and in the truncated form—

> Smote the | chord of | self that | trembling | past in | music | out of |
>   sight ∧

So the *Lotos Eaters*

Rolled to | starboard | rolled to | larboard | when the | surge was | seething | free ∧

In this metre the line is usually divided into two sections after the fourth foot, which I have marked with the double bar, e.g.

Comrades | leave me | here a | little || while as | yet 'tis | early | dawn ∧

In 194 lines of *Locksley Hall* we find this rule observed in all but forty-two, and in fifteen of these the fourth foot ends with 'and,' which softens the effect, as in

Saw the | vision | of the | world and || all the | wonder | which should | be
Love took | up the | glass of | time and || turned it | in his | glowing | hands

Otherwise it has a heavy dragging sound, as in

Many a | night from | yonder | ivied || casement | ere I | sunk to | rest
What is | fine with|in thee | growing || coarse to | sympa|thize with | clay
Glares at | one that | nods and | winks be||hind a | slowly | dying | fire

In one line we find both sections truncated—

As I have | seen the | rosy | red || flushing | in the | northern | night

Some have maintained that the basis of the metre is a double trochee with a weaker stress on the first syllable and stronger on the third.   There seems no ground for this.   If we have

In the | spríng a | fuller | crimson | comes up|on the | robin's | breast

we have also

Mány a | night from | yonder | ivied | casement | ere I | sank to | rest

The rationale of the two sections is of course that the line arose from the juxtaposition of a complete and truncated four-foot trochaic, as

Pilgrims | here on | earth and | strangers || Dwelling | in the | midst of | foes

In rhythmical effect it resembles the Greek trochaic tetrameter catalectic.

Having thus classified the various trochaic lines to be found in Tennyson, it remains for us to observe how they are combined into poems, and with what irregularities, either accentual or syllabic, they are used. One of these irregularities I have already referred to, the anacrusis. It may be well here to give reasons in support of such an explanation of an unaccented syllable at the beginning of the line. Why should not a line beginning thus be regarded as an iambic line? We will take *Lilian.* This is a poem of thirty lines, all but four of which are manifestly trochaic. Why should we wish to assign a distinct rhythm to these four, because they have an iambic beginning, more than we do to iambic lines which have a trochaic (i.e. a feminine) ending? Similarly in *A Dirge* we have forty-nine lines, all but four plainly trochaic, and one of these is formed simply by prefixing 'but' to the refrain, "let them rave." In the *Lotos Eaters,* after a number of long trochaic lines, we come to

Than) labour | in the | deep mid | ocean | wind and | wave and | oar ∧
Oh) rest ye | brother | mari|ners we | will not | wander | more ∧

I should certainly prefer to call these trochaic. The *Valley of Cauteretz* and the *Ode on the Duke of Wellington* present several examples of the same kind. No doubt there is a remarkable mixture of the iambic and trochaic rhythms in the latter; but taking the last eleven lines beginning

He is | gone who | seemed so | great ∧

it seems to me better to treat the exceptional lines

Than) any | wreath that | man can | weave him |
But) speak no | more of | his re|nown ∧
And) in the | vast cath|edral | leave him |

as examples of anacrusis rather than as iambics. So in the longer lines of stanza vi.—

Who is | he that | cometh || like an | honoured | guest ∧
With) banner | and with | music || with) soldier | and with | priest ∧

I should treat the second as a truncated six-foot trochaic, with anacrusis at the beginning of both sections. The line that follows

With a | nation | weeping || and) breaking | on my | rest ∧

has anacrusis at the beginning of the second section only. *Cauteretz* is six-foot truncated—

All a|long the | valley || stream that | flashest | white ∧

but anacrusis is freely used at the beginning of either or both
sections, as, in the first—

> For) all a|long the | valley || down thy | rocky | bed ∧

in the second—

> Deepen|ing thy | voice with || the) deepening | of the | night ∧

in both—

> The) two and | thirty | years were || a) mist that | rolls a|way ∧

and even with two short syllables prefixed to the second
section in

> Thy) living | voice to | me was || as the) vöice | of the | dead ∧

This last might of course be treated as a case of iambic intrusion; in either case the second " voice " is disyllabic.   D r
Abbott gives the historical explanation of anacrusis in *English
Lessons*, p. 189 : " In early English poets syllables which precede
the accented syllable are not necessary to the scansion."   He
gives to such syllables the name of the " catch."

The next irregularity which I will speak of is the substitution of the dactyl in the place of the trochee.   Dr Abbott confines this licence to the first foot, and it is, no doubt, most
frequent in that position, as in

> Thoroughly | to un|do me |
> Wearieth | me May | Lili|an ∧
> Shadowy | dreaming | Ade|line ∧
> But in a | city | glori|ous ∧
> Many a | chance the | years be|get ∧

but it is also found in other places, especially in long lines, as
in the *Lotos Eaters*—

Where the | *wallowing* | monster | spouted | his foam | fountains | in the |
> sea ∧

Wellington—

> He that | ever | *following* | her com|mand ∧

and the *Vision of Sin*—

> Moved with | *violence* | changed in | hue ∧
> Caught each | *other with* | wild gri|maces |
> Half in|*visible* | to the | view ∧
> Wheeling | with pre|*cipitate* | paces |
> To the | *melody* | till they | flew ∧

This is, however, a very irregular poem, and we should perhaps class the passage among those in which there is an intentional mixture of rhythms, the trochaic and dactylic.

The inversion of the accent is less common than in the iambic metre, but is occasionally found in the first foot, e.g.

> The góld-|eyed | kingcups | fine ʌ
> The fráil | blue bell | peereth | over |
> From déep | thought him|self he | rouses |

To speak now of the combination of trochaic lines. We find poems made up of the truncated three-foot, as the seventeenth stanza of *Maud*, but this is, I think, a solitary instance. The truncated four-foot is common, e.g. *The Owl, Adeline* (though in this we find anacrusis freely employed, giving an iambic colouring), the song in the *Miller's Daughter*; also the alternation of the complete and truncated four-foot, as in *Lord of Burleigh*. The truncated four-foot is often varied by the intermixture of longer and shorter lines, as in *Lilian* we find it associated with complete four-foot and truncated or hypermetrical three-foot; in *Deserted House* with truncated three and truncated two; in *The Dirge* with hypermetrical four, truncated two and complete four; in *Locksley Hall* we have truncated eight-foot varied by the occasional insertion of a complete line. I reserve the more difficult combinations till we have got the analysis of the trisyllabic metres.

Of the ascending disyllabic, or iambic, metre we find the following varieties in Tennyson: two-foot, as in *The Poet*—

> The love | of love |

three-foot—

> The la|dy of | Shalott |

three-foot with feminine ending—

> In days | of old | Amphi(on

four-foot—

> O had | I lived | when song | was great |

four-foot feminine-

> She on|ly said | my life | is · wea(ry

five-foot—

> The mel|low re|flex of | a win|ter moon |

five-foot feminine—

> The vex|ed ed|dies of | its way|ward bro(ther

six-foot—

> Give us | long rest | or death | dark death | or dream|ful ease |
> It is | the last | new year | that I | shall ev|er see |

seven-foot (usually divided into four-foot and three-foot)—

> I thought | to pass | away | before || but yet | alive | I am |

These are combined into poems as follows : we find three-foot masculine and feminine indiscriminately with anapaestic variations in *Claribel*—

> Where Cla|ribel | low li(eth
> The bree|zes pause | and die |
> *But the sol*|emn oak | tree sigh(eth

Four-foot alternating with three-foot is very common, as in *The Talking Oak*—

> Once more | the gate | behind | me falls |
> Once more | before | my face |

It is known in the hymn-books as ' common metre.' Sometimes we have stanzas of 4-4-4-3, as

> Of old | sat free|dom on | the heights |
> The thun|ders break|ing at | her feet |
> Above | her shook | the star|ry lights |
> She heard | the tor|rents meet |

And there are other combinations, as in *Sir Galahad,* etc. In *Amphion* and the *Brook* we have four-foot masculine alternating with three-foot feminine. It has usually a light playful touch—

> My fa|ther left | a park | to me |
> But it | is wild | and bar(ren
> A gar|den too | with scarce | a tree |
> And was|ter than | a war(ren

> And out | again | I curve | and flow |
> To join | the brim|ming ri(ver
> For men | may come | and men | may go |
> But I | go on | for ev(er

Will Waterproof is in eight-line stanzas, the first half of the stanza consisting of alternate masculine four-foot and three-foot; the latter half of four-foot masculine and three-foot feminine. The four or eight-line stanza of four-feet (the 'long metre' of hymn-books) is the commonest of all. It is used in *Lady Clara Vere de Vere, Day Dream, Love thou thy Land,* which last, as well as the whole of *In Memoriam,* takes a peculiar character from the rhyming of the first and fourth and second and third lines. The five-foot line is found in combination with others, as in *Dream of Fair Women,* where we have a four-line stanza of 5-5-5-3—

> I read | before | my eye|lids dropt | their shade |
> The leg|end of | good wom|en long | ago |
> Sung by | the morn|ing star | of song | who made |
> His mus|ic heard | below |

In the beautiful *Requiescat* we find it in combination with four and three—

> Fair is | her cot|tage in | its place |
> Where yon | broad wa|ter sweet|ly slow|ly glides |
> It sees | itself | from thatch | to base |
> Dream in | the sli|ding tides. |

The *May Queen* is composed of six and seven-foot lines.

The first irregularity I shall mention is the use of the monosyllabic first foot (as in Chaucer), what I have distinguished as initial truncation, in opposition to the final truncation of the trochaic line. Usually it is found in poems where anapaestic substitution is common; as in the lines quoted in a former chapter from the *Arabian Nights* and *Lady Clara Vere de Vere.* Compare also
Ode to Memory—

> ∧ Streng|then me | enligh|ten me |
> ∧ Sub|tle-though|ted, my|riad-mind(ed

Lady Clare—

> I trow | they did | not part | in scorn |
> ∧ Lov|ers long | betrothed | were they |
> ∧ False|ly false|ly have | ye done |
> O mo|ther she said | if this | be true |
> ∧ Dropt | her head | in the mai|den's hand |

The *Sailor Boy*—

> ∧ Fool | he ans|wered death | is sure |
> To those | that stay | and those | that roam |

The poem in which truncation occurs most frequently is the *Flower*, which is so irregular that it should perhaps be reckoned among the examples of anapaestic rhythm—

> ∧ Up | there came | a flower |
> The peo|ple said | a weed |
> But thieves | from o'er | the wall |
> ∧ Stole | the seed | by night |

The second irregularity is that of feminine rhythm, of which I need say nothing. The third, substitution of anapaest for iambic, as in the *Sailor Boy*—

> *They are all* | to blame | *they are all* | to blame |

A Dedication—

> Dearer | and near|er as | the rap|*id of life* |

The fourth, substitution of trochee (and even dactyl in the first foot) for iamb. Example of dactyl in *Arabian Nights*—

> Serene | with ar|gent-lid|ded eyes |
> *Amorous* | and lash|es like | to rays |

So Wordsworth's exquisite line—

> *Murmuring* | from Gla|rama|ra's in|most caves |

The trochee is sometimes found in the middle of the line—

> Of all | the glad | new year | *Mother* | the mad|dest mer|riest day |

Pyrrhic and spondaic substitution, though not so common in the shorter iambic verse, as in the heroic, are still far from unfrequent: compare

> Come then | pure hands | and bear | the head |
>   2   1   1   1
> Thou comest | much wept | for : such | a breeze |
>   1   1
> Compelled | thy can|vas, and | my prayer |
>   0   0
> Was as | the whis|per of | an air |
> 1   0   0   0

Trisyllabic metre is either ascending like the iambic, which we know as anapaestic, or descending like the trochee, which we know as dactylic. We find examples of anapaestic lines, consisting of one foot, in the *Song* beginning "A spirit haunts"—

> At his work | you may hear | him sob | and sigh | 4
> In the walks | 1
> At the moist | rich smell | of the rot|ting leaves | 4
> And the breath | 1

In the same poem we have the two-foot anapaest—

> Of the moul|dering flowers |

We find the three-foot line in *Maud*—

> In the mead|ow un|der the hall |
> To the death | for their na|tive land |

The four-foot in the *Song*—

> For at e|ventide lis|tening ear|nestly |

and in the *Poet's Mind*—

> In the heart | of the gar|den the mer|ry bird chants |

The five-foot in *Maud*—

> Till I well | could weep | for a time | so sor|did and mean |

And also the six-foot—

> Did he fling | himself down | who knows | for a vast | specula|tion had failed |

which is the metre of the *Northern Farmer*—

> "The Amoigh|ty's a taa|kin of you | to 'issen | my friend " | a said |

The seven-foot in *Sea Fairies*—

> ∧ ∧ Whith|er away | from the high | green field | and the hap|py bloss|oming shore |

The eight-foot in the same—

> ∧ ∧ Whith|er away | lis|ten and stay | mar|iner mar|iner fly | no more |

In this the first, third, and fifth feet are monosyllabic, a license of which I shall speak directly.

The variations are (1) the iamb, of which all the longer lines quoted afford instances, even in the last foot, where Dr Abbott denies its use (*Lessons*, p. 211). Sometimes a line is made up of these without a single anapaest, as in the *Song*—

> The air | is damp | and hushed | and close |

The iamb may, of course, be represented by a spondee, as—

And the year's | lāst rōse |

But (2) at the beginning of the line the anapaest may be represented by a monosyllable, the two unaccented syllables disappearing without altering the character of the verse. Thus the line

I would kiss | them of|ten un|der the sea |

is repeated in the form

And kiss | them again | till they | kissed me |

Leave out 'and' and the rhythm is unaltered. This law of the anapaestic metre is not, I think, noticed by Dr Abbott, yet examples of such initial truncation are innumerable. The truncated two-foot is found in the *Merman*—

∧ ∧ Who | would be |
∧ A mer|man bold |
∧ ∧ Sit|ting alone |
∧ ∧ Sing|ing alone |
∧ ∧ Un|der the sea |
With a crown | of gold |
∧ ∧ On | a throne |

truncated three-foot in *Maud*—

Maud | with her ex|quisite face |

truncated four-foot in the same—

Sing|ing alone | in the morn|ing of life |

truncated five-foot—

Knew | that the death|white cur|tain meant | but sleep |

truncated six-foot—

Why | do they prate | of the bless|ings of peace | who have made | them
a curse |
Glo|ry of war|rior glo|ry of or|ator glo|ry of song |

It may be asked what reason is there for calling these lines 'metamorphous anapaestic,' rather than 'metamorphous dactylic'? The answer has been already given in a former chapter; it is that the rhythm of the lines must be interpreted by the general rhythm of the piece, and all the lines quoted come from passages, which are either distinctly anapaestic, or which at any rate contain lines which can only be explained as anapaestic, while they have no lines which must necessarily be taken as dactylic. Thus the last line, taken alone, would naturally be classed as truncated dactylic; but in the same poem (*Wages*) we find the indisputable anapaest

The wa|ges of sin | is death | if the wa|ges of vir|tue be dust |
She desires | no isles | of the blest | no qui|et seats | of the just | .

So in Byron we have

Bright	be the place	of thy soul		(=3)
No love	lier spir	it than thine		(−3)
E'er burst	from its mor	tal control		(−3)
In the orbs	of the bless	ed to shine		(3)

Verses like these were long a puzzle to me. Their melody was indubitable, but I could not see what was the scientific account of the rhythm till I was struck by the analogy with the old monosyllabic initial foot in the iambic line.

Besides these main variations, we find the use of feminine rhythm; as in *Maud*—

Ah what | shall I be | at fif(ty
If I find | the world | so bit(ter.

And she knows | it not | oh if | she knew (it
To know | her beau|ty might half | undo (it.

The anapaestic rhythm is a great favourite with Tennyson, especially in his later poems. It is used with much freedom as regards the number of feet employed. One of the most uniform in this respect is the *Welcome to Alexandra*, written in the four-foot anapaest. Initial truncation is very common: in fact there is only one line which commences with the pure anapaest—

We are each | all Dane | in our wel|come of thee |

In one line we have initial and sectional truncation—

Roll | and rejoice | ju|bilant voice |
Roll | as a ground|swell dashed | on the strand |

The two-foot trochaic 'Alexandra' forms a refrain.

The six-foot anapaest is used in many important poems, as the two *Northern Farmers*, the *Grandmother*, the *Higher Pan-*

theism, Wages, a good deal of *Maud, Rizpah, First Quarrel, Northern Cobbler, Entail, Children's Hospital, Maeldune,* and the very irregular *Revenge.* I will notice here a few peculiarities in the use of the metre. In the *Grandmother* we have two lines which would naturally be read as instances of the seven-foot anapaest—

> Sev|enty years | ago | my dar|ling sev|enty years | ago |

but this may be reduced to six by reading the first 'seventy' as a disyllable. In the other, a seven-foot line could only be avoided by the heroic remedy of giving four syllables to the first foot—

And whit whit whit | in the bush | beside | me chir|rupt the night| ingale |

The first four sections of *Maud* are in six-foot anapaest. There is a considerable variety in the use of the metre. In section iii. almost every line suffers initial truncation, which is rare in section i. In section iv. we find the usual break at the end of the third foot disregarded, e.g.

> Half lost | in the li|quid a|zure bloom | of a cres|cent of sea |
> The si|lent sap|phire-spang|led mar|riage ring | of the law |

The normal line of the *Revenge* is also six-foot anapaest, as

He had on|ly a hun|dred sea|men to work | the ship | and to fight |
Sir Rich|ard spoke | and he laughed | and we roared | a hurrah | and so |

This is occasionally divided into two sections, sometimes rhyming, as

> And the half | my men | are sick ||. I must fly | but fol|low quick |

and admitting a superfluous syllable after either section, or both, as

Then sware | Lord Thom|as How(ard ||: 'Fore God | I am | no cow(ard
By their moun|tain-like | San Phil(ip || that of fif|teen hun|dred guns |

We sometimes find initial truncation giving rise to a trochaic rhythm in the first half of the line, as

∧ Thou|sands of | their sol(diers || looked down | from their decks | and laughed |

It admits also lines varying in length from two to seven feet, as

> *Anap.* 2. And a day | less or more |
> At sea | or ashore |

sometimes truncated

            ∧ Long | and loud |
Anap. 3.   So they watched | what the end | would be |
Anap. 4.   But Sir Rich|ard cried | in his Eng|lish pride |

In two instances a pyrrhic takes the place of an anapaest, unless we give four syllables to one foot,

        But he rose | ŭpŏn | their decks | and he cried |
        And he fell | upon | their decks | and he died |

Anap. 5.   And a wave | like the wave | that is raised | by an earth|-quake grew |

7.   And the sun | went down | and the stars | came out | far o|ver the sum|mer sea |

Truncated in

∧ God | of bat|tles, was ev|er a bat|tle like this | in the world | before |

The three-foot anapaest is usually combined with others; thus in *Maud* (sections v. and vi.) it is joined with four-foot and occasional five-foot lines. In vii. we have the three-foot preserved throughout, sometimes with feminine rhythm, except for two four-foot lines; viii. is a mixture of three-foot and four-foot; ix. joins two, three, and four-foot. In x. the first three stanzas are of four feet, the fourth and fifth mixed of three and four; xi. is three-foot throughout; xii. is mainly three-foot, but has occasional four-foot lines, and is disguised by prevalent truncation and feminine rhythm; xiii. is almost entirely four-foot, with only three lines of three feet; xiv. is mainly three-foot, but rises into four and even five-foot; xv. is four-foot, with one line of two-foot; xvi. mainly four varied with three and two. In xvii. and xviii. the feeling changes to a tone of more assured happiness, and we have a corresponding change in the rhythm, xvii. consisting of truncated three-foot trochaic, and xviii. (perhaps the most perfect example of the flowing richness of Tennyson's rhythm) consisting of iambic with anapaestic variation, in lines varying from two to six feet. The four which follow are three and four-foot anapaests. The more passionate movement of xxiii. (Part II 1 in new arrangement) shews itself in three, four, and five-foot anapaestic lines, with occasional iambic variation; xxiv. (Pt. II 2) is three and four-foot anapaest, with marked initial truncation; xxv. (Pt. II 3) and xxvi. (Pt. II 4) three and four-foot anapaest, with iambic variation, the latter also with feminine ending; xxvii. (Pt. II 5), as suits its subject, is the most violent in rhythm of any, consisting of anapaestic lines, varying from two to five feet in length, and shewing examples not only of initial truncation, as in

Dead | long dead |

but of monosyllabic feet in other parts of the verse, e.g.

Long | dead |
And the hoofs | of the hor|ses beat | beat |

The last section of *Maud* is regular five-foot anapaest.

In "Break, break, break," we have three-foot anapaest arranged in verses of four lines. In three verses the third line contains four feet, and in two the first line is represented by the three monosyllables "Break, break, break." The *Poet's Song* is mainly four-foot, but is varied by several three-foot lines. In the *Song* "A spirit haunts," the metre is variously four, two, and one-foot. The song in *Sea Fairies* varies from three to eight-foot, and truncation, as I mentioned above, is very freely used: thus we have

Whi|ther away || whi|ther away || whi|ther away || fly | no more ||

the line being divided into four sections, admits of four mono-syllabic feet. In the *Islet* the four-foot anapaest prevails—

Whi|ther O whi|ther love | shall we go |

varied with three-foot—

That it makes | one wea|ry to hear |

truncated two-foot—

No | love no |

and complete five-foot running into pure iambic—

With ma|ny a riv|ulet high | against | the sun |
The fa|cets of | the glor|ious moun|tain flash |

The *Flower* has been treated above as a specimen of iambic, but it might be viewed as a three-foot anapaest, broken by one four-foot, and with prevailing disyllabic substitution—

Once | in a gold|en hour |
I cast | to earth | a seed |

The *Victim* is mainly four-foot, with disyllabic substitution—

> A plague | upon | the peo|ple fell |
> The priest ǀ in hor|ror about | his alt(ar
> To Thor | and O|din lift|ed a hand |
> The mo|ther said | they have ta|ken the child |
> Sud|denly from | him breaks | his wife |

But some of the verses are followed by lines of two feet, forming groups equivalent to eight-foot lines in rhythm, *e.g.*

Help | us from fa|mine And plague | and strife || What | would you have | of us ? Hu|man life |

But, it may be said, is it not easier to take these as dactylic, dividing as follows

> Help us from | famine And | plague and | strife ∧ ∧
> What would you | have of us ? | Human | life ∧ ∧

the two last dactyls being represented by trochee and long syllable ? The answer is that in either case the metre will be metamorphous or disguised, and that we shall best preserve the unity of the poem by interpreting the disguise so as to agree with the undisguised corresponding lines in other stanzas, e.g.

> They have ta|ken our son | They will have | his life |
> Is he | your dear|est Or I | the wife | ?

The same question arises about the metre of *Lucknow,* which may be generally represented by the following scheme

_ ◡ ◡ _ ◡ ◡ _ ◡ ◡ _ ◡ ◡ _

Is this to be treated as anapaestic or dactylic ? That is, at which end of the line must the inevitable truncation be placed? Are we to regard the first syllable as representing an anapaest, or the last as representing a dactyl ? The pauses sometimes seem to suit the one, sometimes the other. If the question had to be settled for each line taken separately, we should, I think, naturally scan the first of the two which follow as a dactyl, and the second as an anapaest, as marked by the bars ;

Bullets would | sing by our | foreheads and | bullets would | rain at our | feet ∧ ∧

∧ ∧ Mine ? | yes a mine | Countermine | . Down, down | and creep | through the hole |

There is no difficulty however in scanning the first as anapaestic, while it is almost impossible to scan the second as dactylic; and the refrain

And ev|er upon | the top|most roof | our ban|ner of Eng|land blew |

thus schematized ($\smile - \smile \smile - \smile - \smile - \smile \smile - \smile -$) divides into seven iambs or anapaests more naturally than into seven dactyls with anacrusis and final truncation.

The dactylic metre is much more rarely used than the anapaest. There is, I think, only one example of the pure dactyl, viz. the *Light Brigade*. The essential point of course is that the stress is not on the last syllable—

Cannon to | right of them |
Cannon to | left of them |
Cannon in | front of them |
Volleyed and | thundered |

The metre is two-foot, with frequent substitution of the trochee for the second foot. Sometimes the rhythmical stress is opposed to the verbal accent, as in

While horse and | hero fell |

We do not find in Tennyson the monosyllable for the dactyl, as in Hood's

Take her up | tenderly |
Lift her with | care $\wedge$ $\wedge$

In Heber's hymn—

Brightest and | best of the | sons of the | morning $\wedge$
Dawn on our | darkness and | lend us thine | aid $\wedge$ $\wedge$

we have the last foot represented alternately by a monosyllable and a trochee.

The last line of the alcaic stanza might be described as a four-foot dactyl with trochaic substitution in the last two feet—

Milton a | name to re|sound for | ages |

Since the different metres are thus capable of interchange and transmutation, it is easy to understand how a poem commencing in one metre will run into another. Thus *Madeline* begins with two iambic lines (4 + and 4), the third line is truncated four-foot trochaic; the fourth again is four-foot iambic;

fifth trochaic truncated; sixth and seventh iambic; and so, throughout, the two rhythms alternate. The *Deserted House* is one in which trochaic rhythm passes into iambic. In *Oriana* the second and third verses have a predominant trochaic rhythm, while the others are iambic with the trochaic refrain. The *Lady of Shalott* begins with iambic, but there are many pure trochaic stanzas. *Eleanore* is mainly iambic, with ana-paestic variation—

> With the hum | of swar|ming bees |
> Into dream|ful slumb|er lulled |

but in stanza iv. changes to trochaic, e.g.

> How may | full-sailed | verse ex|press ∧
> How may | measured | words ad|ore ∧

The Choric Song in *Lotos-Eaters* begins with iambic, of length varying from three to six feet. In the third stanza we find occasional trochaic substitution, e.g.

> Nightly | dew-fed | and tur|ning yel|low

and initial truncation,

> Falls | and floats | adown | the air |

which prepares us for the trochaic commencement of iv.,

> Hateful | is the | dark-blue | sky
> Vaulted | o'er the | dark-blue | sea

and for the series of long trochaics (seven and eight-foot) which close the eighth stanza. In the *Vision of Sin* the rhythms are appropriated to separate sections of the poem, and express different tones of thought. In the *Ode on Wellington* we have anapaestic rhythm in the first and fifth stanzas, iambic in third, fourth, and seventh, trochaic mixed in sixth, eighth, and ninth.

Iambic is found mixed with anapaest, sometimes irregularly, sometimes according to a fixed law. Thus *Mariana in the South* is regular four-foot iambic, but the last two lines have invariably the trisyllabic rhythm—

> And ah | she sang | to be all | alone |
> To live | forgot|ten and die | forlorn |

Similarly, *The Sisters*, which is in regular four-foot iambic, is broken by the trisyllabic refrain

> The wind | is how|ling in tur|ret and tree |

In *The Daisy* the stanza consists of four four-foot iambic lines, the third with feminine rhythm, and the fourth with anapaestic substitution in third place—

> I stood | among | the sil|ent stat|ues
> And stat|ued pin|nacles mute | as they |

In the *Verses to Maurice* the first three lines are the same as in *The Daisy*, but the fourth has anapaestic substitution in the second place as well as the third, and the first foot is a monosyllable: with which the superfluous syllable of the preceding line naturally connects itself—

> And fur|ther on | the hoar|y chan(nel
> Tumb|les a break|er on chalk | and sand |

Of course it is possible to treat the fourth line as dactylic, with the substitution of a trochee for the third and a monosyllable for the fourth dactyl. In that case the last two lines of the verse would be a slight modification of the alcaic

> God-gifted organ voice of England
> Milton a name to resound for ages

this latter having two trochees at the end of the fourth line.

Of irregular mixture we have many examples. The *Dying Swan* begins with four-foot varied by three-foot iambic: the third line suffers initial truncation: anapaestic substitution is frequent—

> With an in|ner voice | the riv|er ran |
> Adown | it float|ed a dy|ing swan |

In the second stanza the anapaestic character becomes more marked, and in the third it becomes pure anapaestic. The *May Queen* commences with seven-foot iambic, with free anapaestic substitution, as in

And the wild | marsh mar|igold shines | like fire | in swamps | and
    hol|lows gray |
And the riv|ulet in | the flow|ery dale | will mer|rily dance | and play |

Occasionally we have six-foot iambics, e.g.

> If you do | not call | me loud | when the day | begins | to break |
> As I | came up | the val|ley || whom think | ye should | I see |

We have one example of initial truncation, accompanied by feminine caesura,

All | the val|ley mo(ther || will be fresh | and green | and still |

One line appears to have eight feet, unless we compress four syllables into the first, or make 'so' extra-metrical—

So you | must wake | and call | me ear|ly call | me ear|ly mo|ther dear |

There is some difficulty in the rhyming of the following—

> For I would see the sun rise upon the glad new year.
> To-night I saw the sun set : he set and left behind[1].

Regarding this as a six-foot line, we find a superfluous syllable at the end of the third foot, which is hardly possible to connect with what follows as the first syllable of an anapaest, because the word itself requires some stress, and in the second line is followed by a decided pause. I am inclined to think we must treat *rise* and *set* as monosyllabic feet, thus making a seven-foot line.

Death of the Old Year is mainly three or four-foot iambic, but we find it diversified with anapaests, as marked as

> He gave | me a friend | and a true | true love |
> And the new | year will take | 'em away |

Some lines shew initial truncation, e.g.

> ʌ Toll | ye the church-|bell sad | and slow |
> ʌ And | tread soft|ly and | speak low |
> ʌ Ev|ery one | for his own |

Lady Clare is in four-line stanzas of four-foot iambics, diversified with three-foot. Some verses are regular, but in most there is a strong anapaestic colouring, e.g.

> Are ye out | of your mind | my nurse | my nurse |
> Said La|dy Clare | that ye speak | so wild |

There are several examples of initial truncation, as

> Dropt | her head | in the maid|en's hand |

The *Flower* has been already mentioned. The *Ringlet* is about

---

[1] Mr Roby compares the 73rd line of the *Atys*

> *jam jam dolet quod egi, jam jamque pœnitet*

and refers to his *School Lat. Gr.* § 934.

equally divided between iambic and anapaestic. Beginning with the feminine anapaest—

> Your ring|lets your ring(lets

it proceeds with five regular iambics, and then bursts into the strong anapaests—

> And then | shall I know | it is all | true gold |
> To flame | and spark|le and stream | as of old |

falling back into the quiet iambic—

> And all | her stars | decay |

It contains three examples of initial truncation—

> ∧ I | that took | you for | true gold |
> ∧ She | that gave | you's bought | and sold |
> ∧ Burn | you glos|sy her|etic burn |

and the refrain consists in two instances of monosyllabic feet—

> Sold, sold,
> Burn, burn.

as may be seen by comparing the intermediate refrain—

> You gol|den lie |

The *Victim* begins with regular four-foot iambic, breaking into anapaestic towards the end of each eight-line stanza, as

> The priest | in hor|ror about | his al(tar
> To Thor | and O|din lif|ted a hand |
> He caught | her away | with a sud|den cry |

Maud contains several instances of mixed iambic and anapaestic, cf. xi., xviii., xxiii.

I proceed now to mixed trochaic metres. The mixture of trochaic and iambic has been already treated of. Trochaic, varied by the intermixture of dactyls according to a fixed law, is found in *Boadicea*, which is mainly eight-foot trochaic, sometimes complete, but usually truncated, with one or more dactyls in the last three feet—

While a|bout the | shore of | Mona || those Ne|ronian | legiona|ries ∧
Girt by | half the | tribes of | Britain || near the | colony | Camulo|dune ∧

In the following we have four consecutive dactyls—

There the | hive of | Roman | liars || worship a | gluttonous | emperor | idiot |

I think the rhythm would have been improved by omitting *emperor*, thus making a truncated eight-foot: but the final dactyl, giving eight complete feet, is also found in

Hear it | gods the | gods have | heard it || O I|cenian | O Cori|tanian |
Tho' the | Roman | eagle | shadow thee || though the | gathering | enemy |
    narrow thee |
Up my | Britons | on my | chariot || on my | chargers | trample them |
    under us |

In one line we find three dactyls in the first half—

Bloodily | bloodily | fall the | battle-axe || unex|hausted in|exora|ble

There is only one line in which the dactylic substitution is not found in the last three feet—

There they | dwelt and | there they | rioted || thère | there they | dwell no |
    more

The metre is in length, and in trisyllabic final rhythm an imitation of the *Atys* of Catullus, of which the type is

    Phrygium nemus citato || cupide | pede te|tigit |

The *Poet's Mind* begins with four and three-foot trochaic, but passes by a rather unusual combination into anapaestic—

    Holy | water | will I | pour |
    Into | every | spicy | flower |
    Of the lau|rel shrubs | that hedge | it around |
    In your eye | there is death |
    There is frost | in your breath |

The hendecasyllabic is a five-foot trochaic, in which the second foot is a dactyl—

    Look I | come to the | test a | tiny | poem |
    All com|posed in a | metre | of Ca|tullus |

I think I have now noticed all the metres which occur in Tennyson, except his alcaics. These being, like the hendecasyllabics, pure imitation from a foreign source, might be omitted in an examination of English metres; but they admit of simple analysis in the terms which I have employed. The first two lines are made up of five iambs, the fourth of which suffers anapaestic substitution[1],

> O might|y mouthed | inven|tor of har|monies |

The final iambic is usually pyrrhic, so as to give the impression of a double dactyl at the end, and we might if we pleased describe the line as consisting of two sections, the first a two-foot iambic with feminine ending, the second two dactyls. The third line is four-foot feminine—

> God-gift|ed or|gan voice | of Eng(land

The fourth, two dactyls followed by two trochees—

> Milton a | name to re|sound for | ages |

It has been observed that Tennyson's classical metres are conformed to the law of quantitative, as well as of accentual rhythm.

---

[1] On the alcaic metre see Roby's *School Gr.* § 936 and p. 366 B.

CHAPTER IX.

NAMING AND CLASSIFICATION OF METRES.

ILLUSTRATED FROM THE HYMN-BOOK.

I PROCEED now to test our metrical analysis on the hymns contained in the ordinary collections, such as *Hymnal Companion* and *Hymns Ancient and Modern*. In old-fashioned hymn-books each hymn is marked with certain mystic signs, which serve as guide-posts to the corresponding tunes. Sometimes these marks are references to psalms of the same metre in the old version by Sternhold and Hopkins; thus 'ps. 104' denotes an eight-line stanza of anap. 2

Oh wór|ship the Kíng || All-gló|rious abóve |

'ps. 148' denotes an eight-line stanza, four lines consisting of 3 iambs, and four of 2 iambs, as

Ye bound|less realms | of joy || Exalt | your Ma|ker's name |
His praise | your song | employ || Above | the star|ry frame |
Your voi|ces raise | Ye cher|ubim |
And ser|aphim | To sing | his praise |

Sometimes they denote the number of syllables in each line; thus 8s 7s stands for a stanza of alternate troch. 4 and troch. 3, as in

Through the | day thy | love has | spared us |
Now we | lay us | down to | rest ʌ

7s 6s stands for alternate iamb 3 + and iamb 3, as

From Green|land's i|cy moun(tains
From In|dia's cor|al strand |

It is evident that the same figures might have been used for the converse rhythms, thus 8s 7s might have stood for an iambic stanza of 4 and 3 + feet alternately, such as

> The Lord | of might | on Si|nai's brow |
> Gave forth | his voice | of thun(der

But the great majority are marked LM, SM, CM, PM, denoting respectively Long, Short, Common, and Peculiar Measures. The first three are four-line iambic stanzas; in LM all the lines contain 4 iambs; in SM the third line has 4, the rest 3 iambs; in CM the first and third have 4, the alternate lines 3 iambs. Peculiar Measure is the general receptacle for all hymns that do not come under any of the other heads.

We will begin by classifying all under their genera, Iambic, Trochaic, Dactylic, Anapaestic, and Mixed; subdividing them into species according to the number of feet, and mentioning any particular varieties which are found in each species.

IAMBIC. *Stanzas of not more than four lines*[1].

3.2.3.3   The sun is sinking fast, The daylight dies.
3.3.3.3   We love the place O Lord, Wherein thine honour dwells.
3+.3.3+.3 Brief life is here our portion, Brief sorrow, short-lived care.
var.   There's a friend for little children Above the bright blue sky.

[Here an anapaest is substituted for the first iamb in every stanza.]

3.3.4.2   The God of Abraham praise, Who reigns enthroned above. Ancient of everlasting days, And God of love.
3.3.4.3 (SM)   My soul repeat his praise.
3+.3.4.3   I want to be like Jesus, So lowly and so meek; For no one marked an angry word, That ever heard him speak.
4.3.4.2   Our bless'd Redeemer ere He breathed.
4.3.4.3 (CM)   God moves in a mysterious way.
4.3+.4.3+   The King of love my Shepherd is, Whose goodness faileth never.

---

[1] I include under this all stanzas, though they may contain more than four lines, which merely repeat the metre. It will be noticed that many of the subjoined examples suffer trochaic substitution in the first foot.

4.4.4.−2   Fierce raged the tempest o'er the deep,
            Watch did thine anxious servants keep,
            But thou | wast wrapped | in dream|less sleep |
                        ∧ Calm | and still |

4.4.4.2   My God, my Father, while I stray.

4.4.4.3   Just as I am without one plea.

4.4.4.4 (LM)   Before Jehovah's awful throne.

var.   Come Holy Ghost our souls inspire.
            *   *   *   *

            That through the ages all along
            ∧ This may be our endless song ;
            ∧ Praise to thy eternal merit.

[In the last line we have feminine ending, and both in it and in the preceding there is initial truncation.]

4+.4.4+.4   Bread of | the world | in mer|cy bro(ken
            Wine of | the soul | in mer|cy shed |

5.5.5.5   Abide with me, fast falls the eventide.

var. (couplet) Come take by faith the body of your Lord.

   (triplet)   For all the saints who from their labours rest.

5+.3.5+.3   A voice | is heard | on earth | of kins|folk weep(ing
            The loss of one they love.

5+.5+.5+.2+   Lord of | our life | and God | of our | salva(tion,
            *   *   *   *

            Lord God | Almigh(ty

5+.5.5+.5   O for | the peace | which flow|eth as | a riv(er
            Making earth's desert places bloom and smile.

IAMBIC. *Stanzas of more than four lines.*

3.3.3.3.2.2.2.2   (148th ps.)   Ye boundless realms of joy.

[Not unfrequently the last four lines are thrown into two, as in

            Hills of the North rejoice,
              River and mountain spring,
            Hark to the Advent voice,
              Valley and lowland sing:
            Though absent long, your Lord is nigh ;
            He judgment brings and victory.

A peculiar effect is given in this specimen by the initial trochaic substitution in most of the short lines.]

3.3.2.3.3.3.2   (God save the Queen) Thou, whose Almighty word.

3.2.3.2.3.3.2   Nearer my God to thee.

3.2.3.2.3.3.3.2   There is a happy land.

[There is a dactylic ring about these verses, and the sixth line in each stanza is irregular.   In the second and third stanzas it seems to begin with an anapaest ('when from sin,' 'be a crown'): in the first with a dactyl ('worthy is').   I think however that the line 'And bright | above | the sun |' is too decisively iambic to allow of the hymn being assigned to any other genus.]

3.3+.3.3+.3.3.3.3   Now thank | we all | our God |
                                    With heart | and hands | and voi(ces.
3+.3+.2.2.3+ (twice)   Head of | the church | trium(phant,
                                    We joy|fully | adore (thee;
                                    Till thou | appear, |
                                    Thy mem|bers here |
                                    Shall sing | like those | in glo(ry.
3+.3.3+.3.4.4   The day is past and over, All thanks O Lord to thee.
4.3.4.3.3.3.3.3   O Paradise, O Paradise,
                                    Who doth not crave for rest.
3.3.4.3.4.4   Change is our portion here.
4.3.4.3.4.4   Lord of my life whose tender care.
4.3.4.4.3   Eight days amid this world of woe
                                    The holy Babe had been.
4.3.4.3.4.3 var.   Father I know that all my life.
4.4.3.4.4.3   O Lord how happy should we be
                                    If we could cast our care on thee
                                    If we from self could rest.
4.4.3+.4.4.4.3+   For ever to behold him shine
                                    For evermore to call him mine
                                    And see | him still | before (me.

[Frequent anapaestic substitution in the first foot.]

4.4.4.4.2.2.4   Lord of the harvest, thee we hail.
4.3+.4.3+.4.3+.4.3+.4.4   O Rock of Ages, since on thee
                                    By grace | my feet | are plan(ted.
4.2.4.2.4.2   My God I thank thee, who hast made
                                    The earth so bright.
4.3+.4.3+.4.4.3+ (Luther's Hymn)
                                    Great God what do I see and hear.
3+.3 (four times repeated) var.   The sands | of time | are sink(ing.

[The eighth line of each stanza seems to be iamb − 3, thus

         ∧ In | Emman|uel's land |]

4.3.4.3.4.3.3+.3   var.   ∧ Broth|er thou | art gone | before (us.

[In this very irregular hymn of Milman's, the normal verse is shown to be iambic by such lines as

> The toil|some way | thou'st trav|elled o'er |
> And borne | the heav|y load; |

but there is frequent anapaestic substitution in the first foot; the first line of the first stanza and of the refrain have a feminine ending; and several lines suffer initial truncation, as

> ∧ Earth | to earth | and dust | to dust |
> ∧ Sin | can ne|ver taint | thee now]

2.5.5.5.2   Come labour on,
            Who dares stand idle on the harvest plain.
5.2.5.2.5.2 O Lord my God, do thou thy holy will.
            I will lie still.
5.2.5.2.5.5
Lead kindly Light amid the incircling gloom, Lead thou me on.
5+.5.5+.5.5.5 Thou know|est, Lord, | the wea|riness | and sor(row
            Of the | sad heart | that comes | to thee | for rest. |

TROCHAIC. *Stanzas of not more than four lines.*

3.3−.3.3−   Now the | day is | over |
            Night is | drawing | nigh ∧
3.3.3.3   Jesus meek and lowly.
4.3−.4.2−   Art thou weary, art thou languid,
            Art thou sore distrest?
4−.4−.4−.2− Christian seek not yet repose.
4−.4−.4−.3− Three in One and One in Three.
4−.4−.4−.4− ('7s') Hark the herald angels sing.
            (triplet) Lord in this thy mercy's day.
4−.4.4−.4   Jesus lives; no longer now
            Can thy terrors, death, appal us.
4.4−.4.4−   Jesus calls us o'er the tumult
            Of our life's wild restless sea.
4.4.4 (triplet) Day of wrath, O day of mourning.

TROCHAIC. *Stanzas of more than four lines.*

3−.3−.4.4.3−.3− Jesus still lead on
                Till our rest be won.
4−.2−.4−.4−.2−   O, they've reached the sunny shore
                Over there.
4.4−.4.4−.2.4−   Lo! He comes with clouds descending.
4.4−.4.4−.2.2.4− Lead us, heavenly Father, lead us.
4.4−.4.4−.4−.4−   Who are these like stars appearing.

4.4−.4.4−.4.4   Once in royal David's city.

4.4−.4.4.4−   O the bitter shame and sorrow.

4−.4−.4−.4−.4.4   Now the labourer's task is o'er.

4−.4.4−.4.4−.4−   Gentle shepherd thou hast stilled.

4.4−.4.4.4−.4−.4−.4−   Thou art coming O my Saviour.

DACTYLIC.

2−.2=.2−.2=   Rest of the | weary ∧

                Joy of the | sad ∧ ∧

2.2−.2.2−(twice)   Breast the wave | Christian |

                When it is | strongest ∧

[The sixth line begins with anacrusis and ends with a trochee (dact. + 2 −)

                The) rest that re|maineth ∧]

2.2= (four times)   Fierce was the | wild billow |

                Dark was the | night ∧ ∧

2.2=.2.2=.2.2.2.2=   No not des|pairingly |

                Come I to | thee ∧ ∧

2.2.2=.2.2.2.2=   Father of | heaven above |

                Dwelling in | light and love |

                Ancient of | days ∧ ∧

4−.4=.4−.4=   Brightest and | best of the | sons of the | morning ∧

                Dawn on our | darkness and | lend us thine | aid ∧ ∧

4=.4=.4=.4=   Raise the tris|agion | ever and | aye ∧ ∧

ANAPAESTIC.

2.2.2.2 (twice)   ∧ O, wor|ship the King |

                ∧ All glor|ious above |

[The two lines are often printed as one; usually, the first foot is an iamb.]

3.3.3.3   ∧ We speak | of the realms | of the blest |

[Iambic substitution common in first foot.]

      var.   ∧ One sweet|ly sol|emn thought |

          ∧ ∧ Comes | to me o'er | and o'er |

          I am near|er my home | today |

          Than I ev|er have been | before | .

[Iambic substitution common in all the feet. First foot often represented by monosyllable.]

4.3.4.3　　ʌ I think | when I read | that sweet sto|ry of old |
　　　　　　　ʌ When Je|sus was here | among men |

var.　　ʌ ʌ Christ | is gone up | with a joy|ful sound |
　　　　　　He is gone ı to his bright | abode |

[Monosyllabic substitution common in first foot, iambic in first and last.]

4.4.4.4　　O Thou | that dwell'st | in the heav|ens high |
　　　　　　Above | yon stars | and within | yon sky |

[Iambic substitution common in all the feet.]

4.3.4.3.4.4　There were nine|ty and nine | that safe|ly lay |
　　　　　　In the shel;ter of | the fold |

[Iambic substitution common in all the feet, and monosyllabic in first foot.]

4+.4.4+.4

Thou art gone | to the grave | but we will | not deplore (thee
　　Though sor|rows and dark|ness encom pass the tomb |

[Iambic substitution in first foot.]

MIXED.　*Iambic and trochaic.*

Alternate iamb. 3, troch. 3 − (thrice).

We close | the wea|ry eye |
Saviour | ever | near ʌ
We lift | our souls | on high |
Through the | darkness | drear ʌ

Alt. troch. 4 −, iamb. 3 (four times, except iamb. 4 in sixth line).　Printing two lines in one, we may describe this as troch. 7 −. 7 −. 8 −. 7 −.

God of | my sal|vation | hear ʌ
And help | me to | believe |
Simply | do I | now draw | near ʌ
Thy bles|sing to | receive |
Dust and | ashes | is my | name ʌ
My all | is sin | and mis|ery |
Friend of | sinners | spotless | Lamb ʌ
Thy blood | was shed | for me |

[This hymn is by C. Wesley, who has another in the same metre beginning

Lamb of | God whose | bleeding | love ʌ]

Troch. 6. 7 —. 6, iamb. 5.

Holy | holy | holy | all the | saints a|dore thee |
Casting | down their | golden | crowns a|round the | glassy | sea ∧
Cheru|bim and | seraphim | falling | down be|fore thee |
Which wert | and art | and ev|ermore | shalt be |

[In the third line ' seraphim ' is a dactyl for trochee.   In the
lines which follow we must disyllabize ' Lord ' and ' our ' to preserve the metre, unless we think that the solemnity of the
subject justifies a monosyllabic foot in the former case.

troch. 6   Holy | holy | holy | Lörd | God Al|mighty |
troch. 7 –   Early | in the | morning | oür | song shall | rise to | thee ∧]

Troch. 4, iamb. 2, troch. 4, iamb. 2, troch. 4 . 4 . 4, iamb. 2.

God that | madest | earth and | heaven |
Darkness | and light |
Who the | day for | toil hast | given |
For rest | the night |
May thine | angel | guards de|fend us |
Slumber | sweet thy | mercy | send us |
Holy | dreams and | hopes at|tend us |
This live|long night |

Iambic SM with trochaic refrain 2 . 4 —.

From E|gypt's bon|dage come |
Where death | and dark|ness reign |
We seek | our new | our bet|ter home |
Where we | our rest | shall gain |
Halle|lujah |
We are | on our | way to | God ∧

Troch. 4 —. 4 —, iamb. 3, trochaic refrain 3 . 3 . 3 . 4 —.

Here we | suffer | grief and | pain ∧
Here we | meet to | part a gain ∧
In heaven | we part | no more |
O that | will be | joyful |
Joyful | joyful | joyful |
O that | will be | joyful |
When we | meet to | part no | more ∧

[The ranting tune makes the refrain dactylic, turning *O,
that will be*, and *joyful* into trisyllables.]

The long irregular hymn beginning "The strain upraise," consists of iambic lines varying from $3.3+.4.5.5+$ to 7 feet, and closes with troch. $4-$.   A few lines are given as specimens.

iamb. $5+$ Here let | the moun|tains thun|der forth | sono(rous
iamb. 7   This is | the strain | the eter|nal strain | the Lord | of all |
              things loves |
troch. $4-$ Now from | all men | be out|poured ∧

Iambic with dactylic refrain.

Iamb. $5+.5.5+.5$, dact. $2-.2=.2-$, iamb. 3.

Hark, hark | my soul | angel|ic songs | are swel(ling
O'er earth's | green fields | and o|cean's wave|beat shore |
          *   *   *   *
              Angels of | Jesus ∧
              Angels of | light ∧ ∧
              Singing to | welcome ∧
              The pil|grims of | the night |

I cannot help thinking that the metre of the last line must have been intended to be dactylic, and that 'the' before 'night' either crept in by mistake, or that we should read *o' th' night.* Its metrical index would then be dact. $+2=$.

Iambic with anapaestic refrain.

Iamb. $3+.3$ (four times).

              When his | salva|tion bring(ing
              To Zi|on Je|sus came |

refrain, anap. 3.

              ∧ Hosan|na to Je|sus they sang |

Trochaic and dactylic.

Dact. $2.2.3-.2-.2-$, troch. $4-$.

              O most | merciful |
              O most | bountiful |
              God the | Father Al|mighty ∧
              By the Re|deemer's ∧
              Sweet inter|cession ∧
              Hear us | help us | when we | cry ∧

Trochaic and anapaestic.

Troch. 4.4 − .4.4 − .4, anap. 3 + .3 + .3.

    Shall we | gather | at the | river |
    Where bright | angel | feet have | trod ʌ
       *   *   *   *
       *   *   *   *

    Yes we'll | gather | at the | river |
    ʌ The beau|tiful beau'tiful riv(er
    Gather with | the saints | at the riv(er
    ʌ That flows | by the throne | of God |

A Riddle.

It seems at first sight impossible to reduce to rule Oakley's translation of *Adeste Fideles*. What common scheme will suit the two following stanzas?

        O cóme, all ye faíthful,
        Jóyful and triúmphant,
    O cóme ye, O cóme ye to Béthlehém ;
        Cóme and behóld him
        Bórn the Kíng of ángels :

        Gód of Gód,
        Líght of Líght,
    Ló he abhórs not the Vírgin's wómb ;
        Véry Gód,
        Begótten nót creáted.

It looks as though there were no more regularity of rhythm in them than in the words of a chanted psalm, where the number and accent of the syllables bear no fixed relation to the musical notes; and certainly the translator in his desire to reproduce the literal sense, has been much more erratic in his metre than the original. In the Latin, the first line of the second verse, *Deum de Deo*, is only one syllable short of *Adeste fideles*, the first line of the first verse, and, in singing, the first syllable of *Deum* occupies the same time as the two first of *adeste*, while the English is three syllables short. We may observe that even in the English, the accents correspond, and I think by comparing the different verses and picking out the more regular lines we may make out a common scheme, and explain the variations, thus

dact. 2 –   Síng choirs of | ángels ʌ
troch. 3   Síng in | éxul|tátion |
dact. 2 –, iamb. 2   Ló he ab|hórs not | the Vír|gin's wómb |
dact. 2 –   Wórd of the | Fáther ʌ
troch. 3   Nów in | flésh ap|peáring |

refrain, iamb. 3+. 3+. 5

　　　　　　O come | let us | adore (him
　　　　　　O come | let us | adore (him
　　　　O come | let us | adore | him, Christ | the Lord |

If this is the correct scheme, the first verse departs from it
by anacrusis in the 1st and 3rd lines, and the second verse represents the two dactyls of the 1st and 4th lines by a trochee
and monosyllable, and has anacrusis in the 5th line. Its 2nd
line departs furthest both from the normal line and from the
Latin *lumen de lumine*, as it has only two trochees (troch. 2 –)
where there ought to be three. The third verse also varies in
its 3rd, 4th, and 5th lines.

dact. 2, iamb. 2   Sing all ye | citizens | of heaven | above |
dact. 2 =   Glory to | God ʌ ʌ
troch. 2   In the | highest |

CHAPTER X.

Blank Verse of Surrey and Marlowe.

The earliest specimen of English blank verse, that is, of the unrhyming five-foot iambic, is found in the translation of the second and fourth books of the Aeneid by the Earl of Surrey, beheaded Jan. 1547, in the 30th year of his age. In the edition by Mr Bell it is said (p. 141), that 'the dexterity with which he manages his metre prevents it from falling with monotony on the ear,' 'he mixes the iambic and trochaic feet so skilfully, that his constancy to the measure escapes observation in the pleasure derived from the music with which he fills it'; yet 'crudenesses of sundry kinds are by no means infrequent'; 'the ear is sometimes wounded by such lines as these

By the divine science of Minerva.'

Mr Symonds on the other hand, as we have seen above (p. 53), joins him with Sackville, Greene and Peele as being very averse 'to any departure from iambic regularity.' We will endeavour to give a more exact account of the matter. The initial trochee is as common in Surrey as in Milton. It is often found in combination with a trochee in the third foot, as

p. 152. He with | his hands | strave to | unloose | the knots |
       2   0   0   1   2   0   0   1   0   1

  156. Then the | Greeks' faith, | then their | deceit | appeared |
       2   0   2   2   2   2   0   0 1   0   1

  158. Finding | himself | chanced | amid | his foes |
       2   0   0   1   2   0   0   1   0   2

Trochee in the second foot is not uncommon, and is sometimes preceded or followed by another trochee, as

p. 148. Yea, and | either | Atride | would buy | it dear |
          2   1   2   0   1   0   1   0 1

    156. Wherewith | Panthus | scaped from | the Greek|ish darts |
           0   1   2   0   2   0   0   1   0   1

    158. Holding | alway | the chief | street of | the town |
           1   0   1   0   1   0   1   0   0   1

    160. Of the | virgin | from them | so res|cued |
          1   0   2   0   0   1   1   2   0 1

    161. The gilt | spars and | the beams | then threw | they down |
          0   1   2   0   2   1   2   0   1

    165. Which re|pulsed from | the brass | where it | gave dint |
          1   0   2   0   0   1   1   0   1   2

    173. Till we | came to | the hill | whereas | there stood |
          1   0   2   0   0   1   0   1   0   1

         The old | temple | dedi|cate to | Ceres |
          0   1   2   0   2   0   1   0   2   0

    174. Holding | backward | the steps | where we | had come |
          1   0   2   0   0   1   1   1   0   1

    175. Long to | furrow | large space | of stor|my seas |
          2   0   2   0   1   1   0   2   0   1

    186. And the | hope of | Iu|lus' seed | thine heir |
          1   0   2   0   01 0   1   0   1

    193. Blowing | now from | this quar|ter now | from that |
          2   0   2   0   2   1   0   2   0   2

    197. Shall I | wait? or | böard | them with | my power |
          0   1   2   1   1 0   0   1   0   1

[The rhythm is harsher if we take *board* as one syllable forming the first part of a trochee. The fifth foot would then be the trochee *power*.]

         Without | taste of | such cares ? | is there | no faith |
          0   1   2   0   0   1   1   0   2   1

    199. From the | bounds of | his king|dom far | exiled |
          1   0   2   0   0   1   0   1   0   1

For examples of trochee in the fourth place compare

p. 144. And where|of no | small part | fell to | my share |
           0   1   0   1   2   1   1   0   2   1

    145. In the | dark bulk | they closed | bodies | of men |
          1   0   2   2   0   1   2   0   0   1

    147. What news | he brought | what hope | made him | to yield |
          1   1   0   1   1   1   1   0   0   1

         Into | his band | young and | near of | his blood |
          1 0   0   1   2   0   2   0   0   1

    148. This horse | was made, | the storms | roared in | the air |
          0   1   0   1   0   2   2   0   0   1

    149. With blood | likewise | ye must | seek your | return |
          0   1   2   1   0   0   1   1   0   1

         And that | that erst | each one | dread to | himself |
          0   1   0   1   1   0   2   0   0   1

156. Toward | the tower | our hearts | brent with | desire |
     0   1   0   1   0   1   2   0   0 1

158. Each pal|lace and | sacred | porch of | the gods |
    0   1 0   0   1 0   2   0   0   1

And plen|ty of | grisly | pictures | of death |
   0   1   0 0   2 0   2   0   0   1

[Here perhaps the 2nd foot should be taken as an anapaest, *grisly* being pronounced with three syllables, as seemingly in p. 196,

Erebus | the gri|sly | and Cha|os huge |]
1 0 0   0   2 0 1   0   1 0   1

p. 159. We went | and gave | many | onsets | that night |
        0   1   0   1   1 0   1 0   1   1

To hope | on aught | against | will of | the gods |
  0   1   0   1   0   1   2 0   0   1

162. From that | high seat | which we | razed and | threw down |
     0   1   1   1   0   1   2   0   1   2

183. Whom our | mother | the earth, | tempted | by wrath |
     1   0   1 0   0   1   2   0   0   1

196. Bent for | to die | calls the | gods to | record |
     2   0   0   1   2   0   2   0   0 1

And if | there were | any | god that | had care |
  0   1   0   1   2 0   2   0   0   1

202. And her | dying | she clepes | thus by | her name |
     0   1   1 0   0   1   2   0   0   1

The black | swart gore | wiping | dry with | her clothes |
  0   1   1   1   2 0   2   0   0   1

For trochee in fifth place compare

p. 160. The fell | Ajax | and ei|ther A|trides |
       0   1   2 0   0 1 0   0 1 0

163. I saw | Pyrrhus | and | ei|ther A|trides |
     0 1   2 0   0   1 0   0 1 0

165. Esca|ped from | the slaugh|ter of | Pyrrhus |
     0 1 0   0   0   1   0 0   1 0

Without | sound hung | vainly | in the | shield's boss |
  0   1   1   1   1   2 0   0   2   2

168. Nor bla|med Pa|ris yet | but the | gods' wrath |
     0   1   0   1 0   1   1 0   2   1

171. With sud|den noise | thundered | on the | left hand |
     0   1   0   1   2   0   0   0   2   1

172. Worship | was done | to Ce|res the | goddess |
     1 0   0   1   0 1 0   0   1 0

173. The old | temple | dedi|cate to | Ceres |
     0 1   2 0   2 0 1   0   2 0

175. Unto | the son | of Ve|nus the | goddess |
     1 0   0   1   0 1   0 0   1 0

181. Before | her go | with glad|some I|ulus |
     0   1   0   1   0   1 0   0 1 0

184. That now | in Car|thage loi|tereth | reckless |
     0   1   0   1   0   1 0 1   2 0

187. And that | the feast|ful night | of Ci|theron |
     1   0   0   1 0   1   0   1 0

Doth call | her forth | with no|ise of | dancing |
  0   1   0   1   0   1 0   0   1 0

192. Nor cin|ders of | his fa|ther An|chises |
        0   1   0   0   0   1   0   1   0

       I with | the Greeks | within | the port | Aulide |
       1   0   0   1   0   1   0   1   1 0

       So hard | to ov|ertreat ? | Whither | whirls he ? |
       0   1   0   1   0   1   2   0   2   0

196. Stood near | the al|tar, bare | of the | one foot |
        0   1   0   1 0   1   0   0   2   1

199. What said | I ? but | where am | I ? what | phrensy |
        1   1   0   1   1   2   0   1   2   0

201. With wai|ling great | and wo|men's shrill | yelling |
        0   1   0   1   0   1   0   1   2   0

145. By the | divine | science | of Min|erva |
        0   0   0   1   2   0   0   0   1   0

The rhythm in some of these lines is so harsh, that we might be disposed to think Surrey's pronunciation must have differed from ours, but in almost every case it might be shown that he has elsewhere used the same word with the common accent. It would almost seem as if he were satisfied with the metre, so long as he got ten syllables into the line. I do not think he has any example of truncation, like Chaucer before him or Marlowe afterwards. He admits however trisyllabic feet, as

p. 146. Or this | an en|gine is | *to annoy* | our walls |
    150. The al|*tar and sword* | quoth he | that I | have scaped |
    153. O na|tive land | *Ilion* | and of | the gods |
           Four times | it stopt | *in the en*|try of | our gates |
    157. As fu|ry gui|*ded me and* | whereas | *I had heard* |
    162. Like to | the ad|*der with ven*|*omous her*|bes fed |
    163. There He|cuba | I saw | *with a hun*|dred mo |
    167. *To revenge* | my town | unto | such ru|in wrought |
    168. *Doth Creü*|sa live | and As|*canius* | thy son |
    174. *In the void* | porches | Phœnix | Ulys|ses eke |
    184. A wo|*man that wan*|dering in | our coasts | hath bought |
    199. Infer|nal fu|ries eke | , ye wreak|*ers of wrong* |

Surrey pays as little regard to Dr Guest's rules in regard to the pauses, as in regard to the accent and number of syllables. As often as not, he has no middle pause. Sometimes the end of the line separates closely connected words, as

p. 174. The rich|es here | were set | , reft from | the brent |
           Temples | of Troy | .

He puts a stop after the ninth syllable, as

p. 151.   His tale | with us | did pur|chase cred|it ; some |
          Trapt by | deceit | ; some, for|ced by | his tears |

While his most common pause is after the fourth syllable, we sometimes find a pause after the first and second syllables, even though the latter is unaccented, and also after the third, occasionally with very harsh effect, as in

p. 160.   And, by | sound, our | discord|ing voice | they knew |
   161.   The gilt | spars, and | the beams | then throw | they down |
   165.   Without | sound, hung | vainly | in the | shield's boss |
   168.   Anchi|ses, thy | father | fordone | with age |
   196.   The fields | whist, beasts | and fowls | of di|vers hue |
   197.   Shall I | wait ? or | board them | with my | power |
   198.   Follow | thee, and | all blithe | obey | thy call |

One of the least pleasant pauses is that in the middle of the third foot, when it is a trochee or spondee, as

p. 203.   Command|ed I | reave ; and | thy spir|it unloose |
               0   1   0   1   2   0   0   1   0   0   1
   164.   An old | laurel | tree, bow|ing there|unto | [1]

Surrey sometimes uses the feminine ending, as in

p. 196.   Him she | requires | of jus|tice to | remem(ber
   196.   And three | faces | of Di|ana | the vir(gin

He generally imitates Virgil's broken lines   The only other unfinished line I have observed is the third below,

p. 184.   His fair | mother | behight | him not | to us |
          Such one | to be | , we there|fore twice | him saved |
          From Greek|ish arms | , but such | a one |
          As might, &c.

where probably we should insert *to be* before *such*.

    Occasionally we meet with Alexandrines, as

p. 196.   Her cares | redou|ble ; love | doth rise | and rage | again |
   200.   But fall | before | his time | ungraved | , amid | the sands |

Not to confine myself to specimens of eccentricity, I add the following passage as a favourable example of his ordinary metre.

---

[1] Compare, for examples of similar harshness, the lines from Marlowe at the end of this chapter, and those from Tennyson and Browning in the chapter on Modern Blank Verse (pp. 206 foll.).

p. 201. Sweet spoils | , whiles God | and des|tinies | it would, |
 Receive | this sprite | , and rid | me of | these cares : |
 I lived | and ran | the course | fortune | did grant ; |
 And un|der earth | my great | ghost now | shall wend : |
 A good|ly town | I built | and saw | my walls ; |
 Happy | , alas | , too hap|py, if | these coasts |
 The Troy|an ships | had nev|er touch|ed aye. |

Before going on to Marlowe, it may be worth while to give Gascoigne's rule of metre contained in his *Instruction concerning the making of verse in English*, which was first published in 1575. There he tells us (p. 36, Arber) that 'there are certain pauses or rests in a verse, which may be called Caesures, whereof I should be loth to stand long, since it is at the discretion of the writer, and they have been first devised, as should seem, by the musicians; but yet thus much I will adventure to write that, in mine opinion, in a verse of eight syllables the pause will stand best in the midst, in a verse of ten it will be best placed at the end of the first four syllables....In Rhithm Royall (which he afterwards explains to be a seven-line rhyming stanza, each line containing ten syllables) it is at the writer's discretion, and forceth not where the pause be until the end of the line.' He further says (p. 33) that 'nowadays in English rimes we use none other order but a foot of two syllables, whereof the first is depressed or made short, and the second elevate or made long,' whereas in former poets, such as Chaucer, there was much greater liberty in regard to the number of syllables. In observing the rule of alternating accented and unaccented syllables, we are to remember to keep 'the natural and usual sound of the word.'

The rhythm of Marlowe (d. 1593) is very different from that of Surrey. It is much more regular in accentuation, but, if the text is correct, it occasionally admits of initial truncation, leaving only nine syllables in the line. I have noted the following instances : the pages are Dyce's ed. 1850.

Vol. I. p. 48. Bar|barous | and blood|y Tam|burlaine |
 Treach|erous | and false | Therid|amas |
 49. Blood|y and | insa|tiate Tam|burlaine |
 51. Long | live Tam|burlaine | and reign | in A|sia
 145. Arm | dread sov|ereign and | my no|ble lords |

164. Now | my boys | what think | you of | a wound |
146. Trai|tors vil|lains dam|ned Chris|tians |

and almost in the same words in pp. 178, 203,

Vil.lain trai|tor dam|ned fu gitive |
Vil.lains cow|ards trai tors to | our state |
189. Con|quer sack | and ut|terly | consume |
198. Save | your ho|nours, 'twere | but time | indeed |
199. Let | us not | be id|le then | my lord |
63. Kings | of Fez | Moroc|co and | Argier |
83. Cap|oline | hast thou | surveyed | our powers |
98. What | is beau|ty? saith | my suf|ferings then |
18. Duke | of Af|rica and | Alba|nia |

I am doubtful about the last, because Marlowe is so capricious in his pronunciation of proper names. If Africa was pronounced Afrīca or Affarica, the line would be regular. I find in three several passages Euphrătes, viz.[1]:

p. 110. As vast | a deep | as Euph.rates | or Nile |
157. That touch | the end | of fam|ous Euph|rates |
212. Of Euph|rates | and Tig|ris swift|ly run |

So in pp. 139, 71, we find Gibrălter—

We kept | the nar|row strait | of Gib|ralter |
And thence | unto | the straits | of Gib|ralter |

In the latter passage some editions spell it Jubaltar. In 85 we have Bajāzeth long—

And now | Baja|zeth hast | thou an|y stom|ach

There are three other passages in which Affarica would set the rhythm right—

p. 209. A 'cit|adel | that all | Affa|rica |
14. Create | him pro|rex of | Affa|rica |
20. To safe | conduct | us through | Affa|rica |

It should be mentioned, however, that in the last two lines the 8vo. of 1592 has a different reading, inserting in one *all*, in the other changing *through* into *thorough*.

[1] So in Greene's *Friar Bacon*, p. 214 (Dyce)—
Circled | with Gi|hon and | first Eu|phrătes |
Shakespeare's *Antony and Cleopatra*, i. 2. 105—
Extend|ed A|sia | from Eu|phrătes |

The monosyllabic foot is more frequent in *Tamburlaine* than in Marlowe's other plays, but I think examples may be found in all. The following are taken from *Edward II.*—

Vol. II. p. 177.   No | but we'll | lift Gav|eston | from hence |

(This would be regular if we read 'we will.')

        p. 219.   Lan|caster | why talk'st | thou to | the slave |
          252.   Mor|timer | who talks | of Mor|timer |

(Here it would be easy to prefix an 'of.')

        p. 273.   Where|fore stay | we? On | sirs to | the coast |
          277.   Mor|timer | I did | he is | our king |

(Here 'aye' might naturally precede.)

In *Faustus* we find

    p. 8.   Jer|ome's bi|ble, Faus|tus ; view | it well |
     19.   Now | Faustus | what wouldst | thou have | me do |
     36.   Faus|tus thou | art damn'd | ; then swords | and knives |

It is doubtful, however, how far we can trust our text of Marlowe, as the metre frequently halts in other feet besides the first, e.g. in *Edward II.*—

    p. 174.   'Tis true, the bishop is in the Tower.
     180.   Lay hands on that traitor Mortimer.

(where probably we should read *upon*).

    p. 188.   Plead for him that will, I am resolved.

(where we should probably insert *he* before *that*).

    p. 193.   Diablo, what passions call you these?

(where perhaps we should read *diavolo*).

    p. 207.   'Twas in your wars; you should ransom him.

(perhaps *and* should be inserted before *you*).

    p. 211.   Pardon me sweet; I forgot myself.

(perhaps *I had forgot* or *did forget*).

    p. 227.   And Spenser spare them not, lay it on.

(we might insert *but* before *lay*).

    p. 255.   Well that shall be, shall be: part we must.

(probably *that* should be doubled).

    p. 257.   Should drink his blood, mounts up to the air.

(perhaps we should read *into* for *to*).

p. 269. Sister, Edward is my charge ; redeem him.

(which would make better sense if we read thus,

> Sister, Edward's my charge ; let me redeem him.)

p. 281. To murder you, my most gracious Lord.

(where perhaps *nay* should be inserted before *my*).

Sometimes a missing syllable may be accounted for by the presence of the letter *r* as in

p. 172. Eȧrl | of Corn|wall king | and lord | of Man |
231. Eȧrl | of Gloces|ter and | Lord Cham|berlain |
287. Because | I think | scórn | to be | accused |

(though it would be easy to insert *so* before *accused*).

p. 168. Were swȯ|r̈n to | your un cle at | his death |

Here the *r* precedes a consonant, but the same effect is produced where it follows a long vowel, as in *fire, sure, assure,* or a consonant, as in *hundred, entrails, nostril, monstrous,* e.g.

As mons|tr̈ous | as Gor|gon prince | of hell |

So we find in *Edward II*. Mowbr̈ay, Pembr̈oke, gentr̈y, frustr̈ate, secr̈et, thr̈ust. The letter *l* sometimes has the same effect, as

I. 47. Resolve | I hope | we are | resem|bled | II. 173, chaṗlain,
251, deeṗly.

We also have prïest, heär, despäir, and even Edüard twice, pp. **234, 269**.

Feminine rhythm is more frequent in Marlowe than in Surrey. We even find two superfluous syllables at the end of the line, unless we are to reckon as Alexandrines verses like the following from vol. II. (Dyce, ed. 1850).

p. 13. Faustus | these books | thy wit | and our | expe(rience
12. Yet not | your words | only | but mine | own fan(tasy
21. What, is | great Meph|istoph|ilis | so pas(sionate
28. And Faus|tus hath | bequeathed | his soul | to Lu(cifer

Anapaests are common in any part of the line, e.g.

p. 7. *Bid econ*|omy | farewell | and Ga|len come |
9. Are but | obeyed | *in their sev*|*eral prov*|inces |
28. Alread|y Faus|*tus hath haz*|*arded that* | for me |
32. Speak Faus|tus, do | *you deliv*|er this | *as your deed* |
75. Sweet Hel|en make | *me immor*|tal with | a kiss |
289. And with | the rest | accom|*pany him* | to his grave |

And we occasionally meet with dactyls, as

> p. 9. Shall be | at my | command | *emperors* | and kings |
> 13. *Shadowing* | more beau|ty in | their air|y brows |
> 233. Edward | with fire | and sword | *follows at* | thy heels |

Trochees are common in the first foot, and in the third and fourth after a stop.

> p. 245. Gallop | apace | bright Phoe|bus through | the sky |
>   2   0
> 231. Let them | not un|reveng'd | murder | your friends |
>   1   0   2   0

Examples such as the following are much rarer in Marlowe than in Surrey :.

> p. 199. I am | none of | these com|mon ped|ants, I |
>   1 0   1   0
> 269. Brother | Edmund | strive not, | we are | his friends |
>   1   0   1   0   1   1   1   0
> 255. And hags | howl for | my death | at Cha|ron's shore |
>   2   0
> 270. My lord | be not | pensive, | we are | your friends |
>   1   0   2   0
> 193. Repealed | : the news | is too | sweet to | be true |
>   1   0
> 36. Why should | I die | then or | basely | despair |
>   2   0
> 269. Hence will | I haste | to Kil|lingworth | castle |
>   1 0
> 51. Caro|lus the | fifth at | whose pal|ace now |
>   1 0   0   0   1   0   0   1   0   1

(The last line is not worse than several in Surrey, but I think it is impossible in Marlowe. I suspect that an epithet such as *high* has been lost before *palace,* making the 1st foot a dactyl.)

As to the pauses, most lines have only the final pause. An internal pause is most commonly found after the fourth or sixth syllable, but it is also found after the second, as

> p. 261. Take it. What, are you mov'd ? pity you me ?

and the third, as

> p. 261. Receive it ? no, these innocent hands of mine
> 239.   Noble minds contemn
>   Despa|ir. Will | your grace | with me | to Hain(ault ?
> 270. Therefore, come ; dalliance dangereth our lives
> 278. Art thou king ? must I die at thy command ?

The last two verses are rendered harsher by the accent falling on the first syllable of the second foot.   We also find the same effect in the third foot, as

p. 198.   A vel|vet-caped | cloak, faced | before | with serge |
            Or mak|ing low | legs to | a nob|leman |
   199.   And being | like pins' | heads, blame | me for | the bus(iness

But, making all allowance for occasional harshness, there can be no question of the great superiority of Marlowe to Surrey in point of rhythm.   Such a passage as the following fully justifies Ben Jonson's praise of 'Marlowe's mighty line,'

p. 257.   The griefs of private men are soon allay'd ;
            But not of kings.   The forest deer, being struck,
            Runs to an herb that closeth up the wounds :
            But when the imperial lion's flesh is gor'd,
            He rends and tears it with his wrathful paw,
            And, highly scorning that the lowly earth
            Should drink his blood, mounts up *into* the air.

CHAPTER XI.

SHAKESPEARE'S BLANK VERSE.

MACBETH.

I PROCEED now to the examination of Shakespeare's rhythm as seen in the play of *Macbeth*[1], limiting myself to the two kinds of variation before mentioned, viz. that through the number of syllables and that through the number or position of accents. Variation in the number of syllables may be either by way of defect (*A*.), or of excess (*B*.).

A.—A line which is defective may be plainly fragmentary, wanting either the beginning or the end (*I*.), or it may be a skeleton line wanting some of its internal syllables (*II*.). The latter I shall call specially 'defective,' the former 'fragmentary.'

I. 1.—Of fragmentary lines, which are still rhythmical, the majority are brief sentences occurring in rapid dialogue. These frequently combine to make up regular lines, as

Len. Good-morrow, noble sir.   *Mac.* Good-morrow both

But they are also irregularly combined, the metre being obscured by the division of parts, and in this way they give rise to Alexandrines which are otherwise rare in Shakespeare (*a*), and to what Dr Abbott has called 'amphibious sections'— a more business-like name might be 'common sections'—where an intermediate sentence does double work, supplying the close

---

[1] It was in lecturing on this play that my attention was first drawn to what appeared to me to be defects in the existing treatises on English metre. I have used it here to illustrate the different ways in which Shakespeare gives variety to the regular iambic line, not with any view of tracing the historical development of his own metre.

of a preceding fragmentary line, and also the commencement of
a following fragmentary line (*b*), e.g.

IV. 3. 219. *Macd.* At one | fell swoop | . *Malc.* Dispute | it like | a man |.
 [Dispute | it like | a man | .] *Macd.* I shall | do so | .

There are many examples in *Macbeth* both of the common
section and of Alexandrines formed by the union of two fragmentary lines. Examples of the latter will be given further on.

I. 2.—Fragmentary lines are also found at the beginning,
middle, and end of longer speeches.

(*a*) Those at the beginning are frequently short introductory phrases, as V. 5. 30, "Gracious my lord"; III. 2. 26, "Come on";
II. 3. 86. "What's the business" (which becomes rhythmical if we
either read 'what is' for 'what's' or pronounce 'business' as a
trisyllable, of which Walker gives examples). Most commonly
such a broken line is the second half of a preceding broken
line; as Lady Macbeth's "What beast was't then" follows on
Macbeth's "Who dares do more is none." So III. 4. 99, "What
man dare I dare," seems to take up the fragmentary line
which ends Macbeth's previous speech "which thou dost
glare with," no notice being taken of Lady Macbeth's intermediate address to the guests. Sometimes it becomes metrical
by treating a portion of a preceding regular line as a common
section, e.g.

II. 4. 33. *Macd.* To be | invest|ed. *Ross.* Where | is Dun|can's bo(dy ?
[Where's Dun|can's bo|dy ?] *Macd.* Car|ried to Colme(kill.
III. 2. 12. *L. Mac.* Should be | without | regard | ; what's done | is done |.
[What's done | is done.] *Macd.* We've scotched | the snake | not killed (it.
V. 8. 23. And break | it to | our hope | ! I'll not | fight with (thee
[I will | not fight | with thee.] *Macd.* Then yield | thee, cow(ard.
V. 3. 34. *Macb.* Give me | my ar|mour. *Sey.* 'Tis | not need|ed yet |.
[It is | not need|ed yet.] *Macb.* I'll put | it on | .

It will be noticed that in three of these examples the common
section is of greater rhythmical importance in one of the two
lines, owing either to feminine rhythm or to contraction, *I'll* for
I will, *'tis* for *it is*. Some may perhaps doubt the applicability
of the principle in these cases, or even deny its use altogether ;
but whoever will go through any play, noting every fragmentary
line, as I have done in *Macbeth*, will, I think, be surprised to

find the very small residuum of lines which remain unmetrical if treated on this method. Whether Shakespeare consciously intended it is another matter. I believe he simply wanted harmonious lines, and the common section contributed to this result without his thinking about it.

(*b*) Speeches are often closed by a fragmentary line. This is sometimes a short final phrase, as I. 5. 74, " Leave all the rest to me "; I. 6. 31, " By your leave, hostess "; IV. 1. 156, " Come, bring me where they are "; III. 3. 56, " So, prithee, go with me." It seems to be especially used in the absence of the rhyming couplet as the natural close of the scene or of an important speech, e.g. I. 4. 52, " It is a peerless kinsman "; V. 4. 21, " Towards which advance the war "; III. 4. 144, " We are yet but young in deed "; II. 3. 95, " And say it is not so "; III. 2. 26, " Can touch him further "; V. 2. 31, " Make we our march towards Birnam "; V. 7. 23, " And more I beg not." Sometimes there is a special impressiveness in the words thus isolated, e.g. I. 4. 14, " An absolute trust "; V. 5. 28, " Signifying nothing "; II. 2. 63, " Making the green one red." Where the broken final line does not conclude the scene, it is usually taken up and completed by a broken initial line, e.g.

I. 5. 55.   To cry | hold, hold ! || Great Gla|mis, wor|thy Caw|dor.

or by a portion of a complete initial line used as a common section, as III. 4. 68,

Lady Mac. You look | but on | a stool | . *Macb.* [Prithee | see there |]
          Prithee | see there | Behold | look, lo | I pray (you.

(*c*) Far less common are fragmentary lines in the middle of speeches, and those which occur may often be resolved into cases of either (*a*) or (*b*); what is printed as a single speech consisting really of several speeches uttered continuously by the same person, e.g. I. 5. 62, Lady Macbeth ends one topic with the broken line " Shall sun that morrow see," and goes on, possibly after a pause, to appeal more directly to her husband, " Your face, my thane," which, it is to be observed, itself forms a common section. So I. 2. 41, " I cannot tell " ends the sergeant's description of the battle, and in the following line he asks for help for his own wounds. III. 4. 4, " And play the humble host " may be the end of an address to one guest, Macbeth turning to another in the next line. III. 4. 99, "What man dare I dare," is addressed to Lady Macbeth, and followed by "Approach thou like," etc. addressed to the Ghost. II. 1. 41, "As this which now I draw" is followed by a pause for drawing the sword, and watching the imaginary dagger. III. 2. 51, "Makes wing to the rooky wood" may suggest a pause for watching the coming on of night, while the following lines give the general reflection, "Good things of day," etc.

Short phrases or titles are sometimes given in broken lines in the middle of speeches, e.g. III. 1. 40, "Farewell," and a few lines below we should read with Abbott

> Sirrah,
> A word with you : attend those men our pleasure ?

So in III. 2. 15, it seems better to print

> But let
> The frame of things disjoint, both the worlds suffer,

expressive of a pause before the imprecation, rather than as an Alexandrine. Similarly, in I. 2. 37, we should read (with the Cambridge edition, not the Clarendon) "so they" as fragmentary, and not join it to either line. The pause gives more force to the following line "doubly redoubled strokes upon the foe." Some of the broken lines in *Macbeth* may be the result of corruption of the text, e.g. III. 2. 32, "Unsafe the while that we," which is also suspicious from the harsh construction ; and I. 2. 20, "Till he faced the slave." In other places wrong printing has given the appearance of broken lines, e.g. II. 3. 120 (reading 'let us away' for 'let's away')

> Let us | away | our tears | are not | yet brewed |

and IV. 3. 28, which should be read

> Without | leave tak|ing ? I | pray you | let not |
> My jea|lousies | be your | disho|nours, but |
> Mine own | safeties | . You may | be right|ly just | .

(For the double trochee in the last line see pp. 38 and 76.)

II.—We go on to the consideration of lines which are not fragmentary, mere heads or tails, but defective in their internal structure. Such defectiveness is sometimes only apparent, arising from difference of pronunciation (1), or it may be real, but supplied by a pause (2), or by a compensative lengthening of some long syllable (3).

(1).—The most common case of what we pronounce as a monosyllable being treated as a disyllable, is where the letter *r* occurs either following a long *vowel* (*a*), as in I. 2. 45,

> Who comes | hére | ? The wor|thy thane | of Ross |

unless (which I should prefer) we adopt Pope's reading and prefix a 'but' to the beginning of the line. 'But' is wanted, and *who* and *here* would then get their right emphasis. Moreover, the phrase 'but who comes here' is common in Shakespeare. Abbott quotes four examples of it in p. 414.

I. 6. 6.   Smells woo|ingly | hére | : no jut|ty frieze | .
II. 3. 128.   What should | be spo|ken he|re, where | our fate | .
I. 6. 30.   And shall | conti nue ó|úr gra|ces towards | him.
II. 1. 20.   I dreamt | last night | of the | three we|ird sis(ters.
IV. 3. 111.   Died ev|ery day | she lived | Fáre | thee well | .

[so better than by dividing ' liv|ed '].

Also where *r* follows a *consonant* (*b*), as *ent*(*e*)*rance* I. 5. 40, *rememb*(*e*)*rance* III. 2. 30, *monst*(*e*)*rous* III. 6. 8, *child*(*e*)*ren* IV. 3. 172; and even where it precedes a consonant, as in III. 1. 102,

> Not in | the wor|(e)st rank | of man|hood, say (it.

Examples will be found in Walker's *Versification*, p. 32, and in Abbott. So Burns (quoted by Guest, vol. I. p. 57) has—

> Ye'll try | the wá|rld soon | my lad | .
> On ev|ry blade | the peá|rls hung | .

Other examples of words pronounced with more syllables than we should now give to them are *sergèant* I. 1. 3, *cap*(*i*)*tains* I. 1. 34, *prayers* III. 6. 49. Mr Wagner, in his edition, goes too far when he tells us, on I. 2. 5,

> 'Gainst my | captiv|ity. | Hail | brave friend |

" *brave* zu sprechen wie *bra-ave*." And Dr Abbott is almost as daring in making 'hail' a disyllable (*S. G.* § 484).

(2) and (3).—It will be best to consider together all the cases of really defective lines, as they are usually capable of

being explained either on the principle of the pause or of the lengthened syllable. The former explanation is the one which commends itself the most to myself. In many cases indeed I should treat the defective line as consisting of a final and initial fragmentary line. Thus in I. 2. 5, "'gainst my captivity" is the end of the speech to the king; "hail, brave friend" is the commencement of the speech to the sergeant; and the pause between the two takes the place of the omitted syllable. In I. 4. 14, "an absolute trust" ends Duncan's address to Malcolm; "O worthiest cousin" begins the address to Macbeth, the pause, occasioned by the entrance of the latter, occupying the place of two syllables. In I. 5. 41, "under my battlements" closes Lady Macbeth's reflections on the hoarse messenger, and then, after a pause, begins the invocation of the powers of evil, "come, you spirits." In II. 3. 83, "the great doom's image. Malcolm! Banquo!" we have a final fragmentary line followed by a pause and an extra-metrical exclamation. The pause will also sufficiently explain I. 4. 35, "In drops of sorrow. Sons, kinsmen, thanes"; II. 1. 19, "which else should free have wrought. *Banq.* All's well" (this line, which consists properly of two fragments, is reduced to regularity by Dr Abbott, who reads 'all is,' and disyllabizes 'wrought'); II. 4. 29, "Thine own life's means! Then 'tis most like" (here too Dr Abbott obtains a regular line by reading 'it is' and disyllabizing 'means'); I. 2. 7, "As thou didst leave it. Doubtful it stood" (but I should prefer here to read 'doubtfully'); IV. 3. 218, "did you say all? O hell-kite! all?" (though, if it were desired, the cry expressed by the conventional symbol *O* might fill the space of three syllables), and v. 7. 22, "seems bruited. Let me find him fortune," though I confess I should prefer to read with Steevens, 'let me but find him fortune,' not only as more rhythmical, but as more expressive. In the famous line—

    I. 7. 28. And falls | on the o|ther. | How now | what news | ?

the loss of a syllable is quite accounted for by the pause, but I should prefer to insert 'side.' It seems to me more probable that we have here a piece of carelessness on the part of the printer, of which there is such abundant evidence throughout, rather than that Shakespeare was guilty of what I should be disposed to call the affectation of expressing surprise by the cutting short of one little word.   Other passages in which the pause is perhaps a less satisfactory expedient are the following : II. 1. 51, "The curtained sleep : witchcraft celebrates," where the pause after 'sleep' is scarcely sufficient to justify the omission of a syllable.   Dr Abbott would make 'sleep' a disyllable, supporting this by *Richard III.*, v. 3. 130, which he divides thus—

    Doth com|fort thee in | thy sle|ep : live | and flou|rish.

[The true scanning has been given in a former chapter.] In the line before us I should prefer to read 'sleeper' as more suited to the definite article.   In IV. 1. 122, "Horrible sight ! Now I see 'tis true," there is a decided pause, but the rhythm is so harsh that I am inclined to think that an exclamation must have dropped out of the text. . Such a cry would be very natural on catching sight of Banquo's ghost.   Dr Abbott disyllabizes 'sight.'   In IV. 3. 44, "Of goodly thousands : but, for all this," there is a pause both before and after 'but'; not enough, how- ever, to account for the rhythm.   Dr Abbott disyllabizes 'but.' I should be rather disposed, if the line is correct, to give a disyllabic weight to 'all' with its long vowel and final liquid.

B.—Where there is excess in the number of syllables, the extra syllables may be either outside the feet, producing what is called the feminine ending (*I.*), or they may be included in the feet (*II.*).

I.—The first kind of superfluous syllable is frequently found at the end of the line, and its presence or absence has been used as a test for determining the genuineness or the age of the Shakespearian Plays, the prevalent taste in the end of Elizabeth's reign inclining more and more to a broken rhythm, just as we find in Euripides a growing tendency to the use of trisyllabic feet.   Sometimes we find two such unaccented syllables, which generally admit of being slurred, as in 'conference.'   Examples will be given further on under the head of apparent Alexandrines. As I am not now treating of specialities of rhythm, but merely illustrating the general manner of its variation, I shall say nothing more of this (a), but go on to the rarer use of the superfluous syllable at the close of the second or third foot (b). This is acknowledged by Dr Guest and Dr Abbott, but Mr Ellis would treat all such cases under the head of trisyllabic feet. I observe in the passage from M. Gaston Paris, printed in the Appendix, that two of the four types of the old French deca-syllabic metre are what he calls feminine at the hemistich. I make twenty-five lines in *Macbeth* with the superfluous syllable after the second foot, and thirty-two with it after the third foot. In almost all there is a full stop after the superfluous syllable, which makes it more difficult to join it with what follows, so as to form a trisyllabic foot. In several instances, however, it would be possible to get rid of the superfluous syllable on the principle of slurring, of which I shall shortly speak. Thus several end in r and s, which have a tendency to obscure the sound of a preceding vowel, e.g.

I. 7. 26. Of his | own chamb'r | and used | their ve|ry dag(gers.
II. 3. 138. Of trea|s'nous mal'ce | . And so | do I | . So all | .

Superfluous after second foot:

I. 3. 72. But how | of Caw|dor | ? The thane | of Caw| dor lives |
I. 3. 150. With things | forgot|ten | . Kind gen|tlemen | your pains |
I. 4. 42. On all | deserv|ers | . From hence | to In|verness |
II. 2. 53. Give me | the dag|gers | : the sleep|ing and | the dead |
II. 3. 147. The near|er blood|y | . This mur|d'rous shaft | that's shot | .
III. 1. 35. Craving | us joint|ly | . Hie you | to horse | , adieu | .
III. 1. 84. Say thus | did Ban|quo | . You made | it known | to us | .
III. 1. 128. Your spirits | shine through | you | . Within | this hour |
            at most | .
III. 2. 19. That shake | us night|ly | . Better | be with | the dead | .
III. 2. 22. In rest|less ecs|t'sy | . Duncan | is in | his grave | .
III. 4. 36. 'Tis given | with wel|come | . To feed | were best | at home | .
III. 4. 87. To those | that know | me | . Come love | and health | to
            all | .
III. 4. 103. Shall ne|ver trem|ble | : or be | alive | again | .
v. 6. 4. Lead our | first bat|tle | . Worthy | Macduff | and we | .

Sometimes we find the double feminine ending, both after the second and after the last foot, e.g.

I. 3. 43. That man | may ques|tion | You seem | to un|derstand (me.
I. 7. 10. To plague | the inven|tor | This ev|en-hand|ed just(ice.
II. 2. 66. At the | south | en|try | : retire | we to | our cham(ber.

[Though here we might divide | at the south | entry |, and there is a further explanation in the repeated *re*.]

II. 3. 109.   Upon | their pil|lows | : they stared | and were | distrac(ted.

III. 1. 26.   'Twixt this | and sup|per |.   Go not | my horse | the bet(ter.

III. 1. 80.   In our | last con|ference |, passed in | proba|tion with (you?

IV. 2. 17.   The fits | of the sea|son |, I dare | not speak | much fur(ther.

IV. 2. 35.   Why should | I, mo|ther |.   Poor birds | they are | not set (for.

IV. 3. 220.   Convert | to an|ger |.   Blunt not | the heart | enrage (it.

Superfluous after third foot:

v. 3. 7.   Shall e'er | have power | upon | thee |.   Then fly | false thanes |.

v. 3. 4.   Was he | not born | of wom|an |?   The sprites | that know |.

v. 4. 3.   What wood | is this | before | us |?   The wood | of Bir(nam.

v. 2. 11.   Protest | their first | of man|hood |.   What does | the ty(rant?

v. 1. 65.   Do breed | unnat|ural troub|les |.   Infect|ed minds |.

IV. 3. 223.   That were | most pre|cious to | me |.   Did heaven | look on | ?

IV. 3. 156.   The heal|ing ben|edict|ion |.   With this | strange vir(tue.

IV. 3. 177.   Each mi|nute teems | a new | one |.   How does | my wife | ?

IV. 3. 117.   To thy | good truth | and hon|our |.   Devilish | Macbeth |.

IV. 3. 33.   For good|ness dare | not check | thee |.   Wear thou | thy wrongs |.

IV. 2. 77.   Account|ed dang|'rous fol|ly | :   why then | alas |.

IV. 2. 14.   So runs | against | all rea|son |.   My dear|est coz |.

III. 6. 43.   That clogs | me with | this ans|wer |.   And that | well might |.

III. 6. 44.   Advise | him to | a cau|tion |, to hold | what dis(tance.

III. 4. 110.   With most | admired | disor|der |.   Can such | things be |.

III. 4. 112.   Without | our spe|cial won|der | ?   You make | me strange |.

III. 4. 84.   Your no|ble friends | do lack | you |.   I do | forget |.

III. 4. 60.   That might | appal | the de|vil |.   O pro|per stuff |.

III. 1. 126.   For sun|dry weight|y rea|sons |.   We shall | my lord |.

III. 1. 107.   Which in | his death | were per|fect |.   I'm one | my liege |.

III. 1. 57.   Mark An|tony was | by Cae|sar |.   He chid | the sis(ters.

I. 3. 113.   With hid|den help | and van|tage |, or that | with both |.

I. 4. 56.   It is | a ban|quet to | me |.   Let's af|ter him |.

I. 6. 3.   Unto | our gen|tle sens|es |.   This guest | of sum(mer.

II. 1. 26.   It shall | make hon|our for | you |.   So I | lose none |.

II. 2. 52.   Look on't | again | I dare | not |.   Infirm | of pur(pose.

II. 2. 54.   That fears | a pain|ted dev|il |.   If he | do bleed |.

II. 2. 74.   Wake Dun|can with | thy knock|ing |.   I would | thou couldst |.

III. 6. 2.   Which can | inter|pret fur|ther |.   Only | I say |.

II. 2. 23. That they | did wake | each o|ther | . I stood | and heard
(them.

v. 8. 6. With blood | of thine | alrea|dy | . I have | no words | .

v. 8. 27. Here may | you see | the ty|rant | . I will | not yield | .

II.—Extra syllables within the feet may either disappear
through elision (*a*) or slurring (*b*), or they may be distinctly
perceptible and form trisyllabic feet (*c*), or finally they may
form an extra foot, giving rise to an Alexandrine (*d*).

(*a*) As regards the mark of elision, there seems to have
been no principle in the First Folio, and not much in later
editions. I have by me a complete collation of the elisions
in the Folio and in the Clarendon edition, and in several
cases syllables essential to the metre are cut out, e.g. 'let's
away' in

II. 3. 129. Let us | away | our tears | are not | yet brewed | .

In others, syllables are unelided, the absence of which would
certainly improve the rhythm, e.g. I should prefer *'gan* and
'would, to *began* and *I would* in the following

I. 2. 53. The thane | of Caw|dor 'gan | a dis|mal con(flict.

II. 2. 73. Wake Dun|can with | thy knock|ing. 'Would | thou couldst | .

So I should prefer *thou'rt* and *I'm* to *thou art* and *I am* in

I. 4. 16. Was heav|y on | me. Thou'rt | so far | before | .

III. 1. 168. Which in | his death | were per|fect | . I'm one | my liege | .

Perhaps the sign of elision should only be used where there
is a complete disappearance of the syllable. There are three
degrees of evanescence, (1) where the syllable is distinctly pronounced, but is metrically superfluous (as in a trisyllabic foot),
(2) where it is slurred, blending more or less with a preceding
or succeeding sound, (3) where it is entirely inaudible. It will
depend very much on the taste of the individual reader what
view he will take of any particular syllable, and I doubt whether
it is possible to arrive at any certainty with regard to the usage
in Shakespeare's time. Perhaps as *the* is constantly printed as
th in the Elizabethan writers, even in prose and before consonants, we may assume that, in colloquial use, the *e* was
entirely lost before vowels, where we should make a glide or
slur it.

M. M. 12

The commonest elisions in the First Folio are *'d* for *ed* in the preterite and past participle, even where the present ends with *e*, as 'fac'd,' 'carv'd' : *th'* for *the*, as 'to th' chops,' 'o' th' milk,' 'th' utterance.' Not unfrequently this elision is wrongly given where the syllable is required for the metre : e.g. III. 4. 101,

> The armed | rhino|ceros or | the Hyr|can ti(ger.

is better than 'th' Hyrcan' of the Folio. And there can be no doubt that 'th' expedition' and 'th' Tiger' are wrong in

II. 3. 92.   The ex|pedi|tion of | my vi|olent love | .
I. 3. 7.   Her hus|band's to | Alep|po gone | master o' | the Ti(ger.

Equally common with these is the elision of *'s* for *is*. 'When the battle's lost and won.'

's also stands for *us*, 'betray's' in I. 8. 125 (unnecessarily, though the Clarendon adopts it).

> Win us | with hon|est trifl|es to | betray (us.

So in 'let's' (several times), 'upon's' (unnecessarily, though adopted by Clarendon) in

III. 1. 36.   Ay, my | good lord | : our time | does call | upon (us.

And V. 6. 5.

's for *his*. II. 2. 22, 'in's sleep.' II. 3. 99, 'make's love known.'

Another very common elision is *st* for *est*, e.g. cam'st, anticipat'st, got'st, kind'st, stern'st, near'st, secret'st, dear'st.

'll for *will*. *I'll* (always *ile* in the Folio), *we'll*, *you'll*.

'ld for *would* ; *thou'ldst*, *we'ld*, *I'ld*, *you'ld*.

'lt for *wilt*, *thou'lt*.

'dst for *hadst*, 'thou'dst rather hear it.'

'rt for *art*, 'thou'rt mad.'

't for *it*, prefixed, *'twas*, *'twere*, *'tis*, *'twould*.

> suffixed, *is't*, *was't*, *were't*, *may't*, *please't*, *done't*, *be't*, *bear't*, *goes't*, *take't*, *pull't*, *deny't*, *on't*, *in't*, *for't*, *to't*, *before't*, *under't*, *if't*, *an't*.   This is adopted by Clarendon.

t' for *to*, *t'hold* III. 6. 44, *t'appease* IV. 3. 18.   Not adopted by Clarendon.

o'er for *over, o'erleap, o'erbear, o'erfraught.*

ne'er, for *never.*

o' for *of, o' th', o' that,* adopted by Clarendon.

i' for *in, i' faith* once, *i' th'* many times, adopted by Clarendon.

'em for *them* several times, adopted by Clarendon.

Surd vowel omitted in *murth'ring* I. 5. 47, *temp'rate* II. 3. 90, *mock'ry* III. 4. 106, *vap'rous* III. 5. 24, *med'cine* IV. 3. 210, and v. 2, *whisp'rings* v. 1, not adopted by Clarendon ; of course, if employed at all, it ought to be used in very many more instances.

Loss of initial short syllable : *'gainst* for *against, 'bove* for *above, 'twixt* for *betwixt, 'gin* for *begin,* adopted by Clarendon, which also reads *'scape, 'cause,* for *escape, because,* where the Folio gave the abbreviation without mark of elision.

The Clarendon edition also gives the apostrophe after *highness',* used for the genitive, where there is none in the Folio.

Two special words, *god'ild, sev'night,* complete the list of elisions contained in the Folio.

It has already been seen that some of these are incorrect. The other errors which I have noticed are as follows : I. 3. 18, " I'll drain him dry as hay," corrected in C.

II. 3. 102 Fol. and C.

> What is | amiss | ? You are | and do | not know 't | .

the elision of *it* is quite unnecessary.

> III. 1. 102. Not in | the wor|st rank | of man|hood say (it.

F. and C. read *i', say't,* and F. gives *th'.*

> III. 4. 89. I drink | to the gen|eral joy | of the | whole ta(ble.

F. gives *th'* for *the* and *o'* for *of;* C. only the latter.

> IV. 3. 180. Be not | a nig|gard of | your speech | : how goes (it?

F. and C. unnecessarily elide *it.*

I will lastly give a list of passages in which a necessary elision is unmarked.

It is singular that with the exception of *thou'dst* for *thou hadst,* F. never contracts *have.* Otherwise *I've, we've, they've,*

I'd, he's, would be naturally written in the following lines, among others, where F. and C. both give the words at full length :

I. 4. 20.   Might have | been mine | : only | I've left | to say | .
I. 4. 18.   To o|vertake | thee : would | thou'dst less | deserved | .
v. 2. 73.   We've wil|ling dames | enough | , there can|not be | .
II. 1. 21.   To you | they've showed | some truth | .   I think | not of (them.
II. 2. 6.   Do mock | their charge | with snores | .   I've drugged | their pos(sets
III. 4. 20.   Then comes | my fit | again | I'd else | been per(fect.

So in the following lines we should read, instead of *I am, thou art, we would,* etc.

III. 1. 108.   Which in | his death | were per|fect | .   I'm one | my liege | .
I. 3. 133.   Commenc|ing in | a truth | .   I'm thane | of Caw(dor.
I. 4. 16.   Was hea|vy on | me, thou'rt | so far | before | .
II. 1. 23.   We'ld spend | it in | some words | upon | that bus(iness.
II. 4. 17.   Contend|ing 'gainst | obe|dience as | they'ld make | .
I. 5. 21.   The ill|ness should | attend | it, what | thou'ldst high(ly.

So ' *to his home,*' ' *what is,*' ' *Macduff is,*' are better contracted in

I. 6. 24.   To's home | before | us.   Fair | and no|ble hos(tess.
II. 3. 77.   Is left | this vault | to brag | of.   What's | amiss | .
III. 6. 29.   Takes from | his high | respect | .   Thither Mac|duff's gone | .

(*b*)   Dr Abbott makes great use of the principle of slurring, and is proportionately chary of admitting trisyllabic feet. As a rule I prefer the latter explanation, while allowing the possibility of the former explanation in the cases which follow. The commonest case is where the roll of an *r* obscures a neighbouring vowel. Thus we may slur the following vowel in

III. 4. 107.   The ba|by of | a. girl | hence hor|r'ble shad(ow.
v. 3. 44.   Cleanse the | stuffed bo|som of | that per'|lous stuff |

and so with *ceremony, warranted, nourisher, tyranny, verity.*

Similarly we may slur the *preceding* vowel in

v. 1. 78.   Foul whisp|'rings are | abroad | unnat|'ral deeds.

and in *corp'ral, discov'ry, temp'rance, persev'rance, gen'ral, moment'ry, conf'rence, ev'ry, murd'rous,* and perhaps *power, chamber, supper, disorder, Caesar, wonder, answer.* The spell-ings *sprite* for *spirit*, and *parlous* for *perilous* seem to shew that in certain cases at any rate the vowel was lost.

We also find the short vowel slurred with other liquids, as in *devil, devilish, heaven*, perhaps *villain* in

v. 3. 13. There is | ten thou|sand—geese | , vill'n—sol|diers Sir | .

and with *s*, as *min'ster, maj'sty, ecst'sy*. Compare III. 4. 2:

And last | the hear|ty wel|come. Thanks | to your maj('sty.

[Also I. 6. 18, II. 3. 75, III. 4. 121.]

III. 2. 22. In rest|less ecst|'sy | . Duncan | is in | his grave | .
I. 5. 49. And take | my milk | for gall | you murd|'ring min('sters.

In v. 3. 5,

All mor|tal cons|equences have | pronounced | me thus |

there seems a double slurring due to the sibilant. In this and other cases the alternative lies not between slurring and trisyllabic feet, but between slurring and the Alexandrine, which to my ear would have a weak dragging effect in such a passage. Dr Abbott gives several examples (§ 471) of the dropping of the final *s* in the plural of words ending with a sibilant.

Possibly we ought to admit slurring of vowels after other consonants, as *surf'ted, fantast'cal*. One vowel preceding another is sometimes slurred, as *furiõus, unusũal*. Sometimes more than one letter seems to be omitted in pronunciation, as *instruments* is disyllabic according to Abbott, § 468. See examples in note[1].

---

[1] Perhaps it will be best to give the complete list of such doubtful lines for the reader to form his own judgment upon them.

I. 7. 80. Each corporal agent to this terrible feat.
III. 2. 19. In the affliction of these terrible dreams.
III. 4. 78. Too terrible for the ear: the time has been.
III. 4. 36. From thence, the sauce to meat is ceremony.
IV. 3. 138. Be like our warranted quarrel. Why're you silent?
II. 2. 40. Chief nourisher in life's feast. What do you mean?
V. 4. 6. The numbers of our host, and make discovery.
IV. 3. 67. In nature is a tyranny: it hath been.
IV. 3. 92. As justice, verity, temperance, stableness,
Bounty, persev'rance.

(c) It is difficult to find examples of undoubted trisyllabic feet; what would at first sight be taken for such being so often capable of other explanation, either on the principle of

III. 4. 89. I drink to the general joy o' the whole table.
III. 4. 55. The fit is momentary; upon a thought.
III. 1. 79. In our last conference; passed in probation with you.
IV. 3. 59. Sudden, voluptuous, smacking of every sin.
II. 3. 123. The near|er blood|y | . This mur|derous shaft | that's shot | .
I. 7. 76. Of his own chamber, and used their very daggers.
III. 1. 87. Your patience so predominant in your nature.
III. 1. 105. Whose execution takes your enemy off.
III. 2. 31. Present him eminence both with eye and tongue.
III. 6. 40. He did, and with an absolute 'Sir, not I.'
[cf. I. 4. 14. An ab|solute trust | . . | O worth|iest cou|sin.]
III. 1. 117. To thy | good truth | and hon|our | . Devilish | Macbeth | .
V. 7. 8. The devil himself could not pronounce a title.
[cf. III. 4. 60, II. 2. 54.]
IV. 3. 182. Which I have heavily borne, there ran a rumour.
IV. 3. 57. In evils to top Macbeth. I grant him bloody.
V. 3. 40. Canst thou not minister to a mind diseased.
[cf. V. 3. 46, I. 5. 49.]
III. 4. 86. I have a strange infirmity which is nothing.
III. 2. 45. Be innocent of the knowledge, dearest chuck.
[cf. I. 5. 63, II. 2. 36.]
IV. 3. 64. All continent impediments would o'erbear.
V. 4. 19. Thoughts speculative their unsure hopes relate.
IV. 2. 17. The fits | o' the sea|son | . I dare | not speak | much fur(ther.
IV. 1. 152. His wife, his babes, and all unfortunate souls.
III. 4. 36. 'Tis given | with wel|come | : to feed | were best | at home | .
III. 1. 68. Given to the common enemy of man.
[here *given* may be a trochee, making the next foot an anapaest.]
IV. 3. 223. That were | most pre|cious to | me | . Did heaven | look on | .
II. 2. 62. The multitudinous seas incarnadine.
III. 1. 57. Mark An|tony's was | by Cae|sar | . He chid | the sis(ters.
V. 4. 8. We learn no other but the confident tyrant.
V. 2. 5. Excite the mortified man. Near Birnam wood.
III. 2. 47. Scarf up the tender eye of pitiful day.
II. 2. 5. The doors are open and the surfeited grooms.
I. 3. 140. My thought | whose mur|der yet | is but | fantas(tical.
II. 4. 14. And Duncan's horses, a thing most strange and certain.
[*horses* probably one syllable, as Abbott, § 471.]
III. 2. 48. And with thy bloody and invisible hand.
V. 8. 41. The which no sooner had his prowess confirmed.
II. 3. 114. Who can | be wise | , amazed | , temperate | , and fur(ious.
II. 1. 12. He hath | been in | unu|sual plea|sure and | .

feminine rhythm or of slurring. The following seem to me the most probable :

 ɪ. 7. 22. Striding | the blast | or heav|en's che|rubim[1] horsed | .
 ɪɪ. 3. 121. Unman|nerly breeched | with gore, | who could | refrain | .
 ɪ. 5. 17. What thou | art pro|mised. Yet | do I fear | thy na|ture.
 ɪ. 2. 45. What a haste | looks through | his eyes | ! So should | he look | .

(d) Alexandrines are most commonly found in lines divided between different speakers after the 3rd foot, e.g.

 ɪɪɪ. 1. 139. I'll come | to you | anon | —We are | resolved | my lord | .
 ɪ. 2. 58. The vict|ory fell | on us | —Great hap|piness | —That now | .
 ɪɪ. 1. 3. And she | goes down | at twelve | —I tak't, | 'tis la|ter Sir | .
 ɪɪɪ. 3. 11. Alread|y are in | the court | —His hor|ses go | about | .
 ɪᴠ. 2. 30. I take | my leave | at once | —Sirrah | your fa|ther's dead | .
 ɪɪɪ. 4. 121. Attend | his maj|esty | —A kind | good-night | to all | .

[though this may be read as an ordinary line by disyllabizing ' majesty.']

The following have the feminine rhythm at the end.

 ɪ. 6. 10. The air | is del|icate | —See, see | our hon|oured hos(tess.
 ɪɪ. 3. 79. The sleep|ers of | the house | —Speak, speak | —O gen|tle la(dy.
 ᴠ. 5. 17. The queen | my lord | is dead | —She should | have died | hereaf(ter.

  ɪɪ. 1. 17. In mea|sureless | content | . Being un|prepared | .
  ɪɪ. 3. 62. And pro|phesying | with ac|cents ter|rible | .
  ᴠ. 5. 28. Signi|fying no|thing | . Thou comest | to use | thy tongue | .
  ɪɪ. 3. 121. Unmannerly breeched with gore ; who could refrain.
  ɪ. 4. 45. I'll be myself the harbinger and make joyful.

[Abbott (§ 468) considers *messenger* and *passenger* to be disyllabic, and so perhaps *harbinger* here.]

  ɪ. 3. 129. Of the imperial theme. I thank you, gentlemen.

[See Abbott (§ 461) for the pronunciation of *gentlemen*.]

  ɪᴠ. 3. 239. Put on their instruments, Receive what cheer you may.

  ɪɪɪ. 1. 81. How you were borne in hand, how crossed, the instruments.

[We escape an Alexandrine by making *instruments* disyllabic. See Abbott, § 468.]

  ɪ. 3. 111. Which he deserves to lose. Whether he was combined.

  ᴠ. 7. 18. Are hired to bear their staves: either thou Macbeth.

  ɪɪɪ. 6. 29. Takes from his high respect: thither Macduff's gone.

[On the shortening of *whether, either, thither,* in pronunciation, see Abbott, § 466.]

---

[1] That *u* of ' cherubim ' is always short in Shakespeare.

IV. 1. 89. And top | of sov'|reignty | —Listen | but speak | not to (it.

III. 6. 49. Under | a hand | accursed | —I'll send | my pray|ers with (him.

[As the emphasis is on *with* rather than *him*, it seems best to divide it thus.]

III. 4. 73. Shall be | the maws | of kites | —What quite | unmanned | in fol|ly.

In the following instances the division is after the 1st, 2nd or 4th foot, or in the middle of the 4th.

III. 2. 4. For a | few words | —Madam | I will | —Nought's had | all's spent | .

III. 3. 15. Stand to't | —It will | be rain | to-night | —Let it | come down | .

III. 6. 39. Prepare | for some | attempt | of war | —Sent he | to Mac(duff.

V. 3. 37. How does | your pa|tient, doc|tor?—Not | so sick | my lord |.

III. 4. 38. Meeting | were bare | without | it—Sweet | remem|brancer | .

IV. 2. 72. I dare | abide | no lon|ger—Whi|ther should | I fly.

V. 7. 11. I'll prove | the lie | thou speak|est—Thou | wast born | of wom(an.

[If we read *speak'st* as in the Clarendon, we should have to compress *thou'st*, making a regular line.]

III. 4. 2. And last | the hear|ty wel|come—Thanks | to your ma|jesty |.

[Or the line may be divided into five feet if we slur the last part of *majesty*; it will then have a double feminine ending.]

The following Alexandrines have an extra syllable at the hemistich :

II. 2. 30. When they | did say | God bless | us | —Consid|er it not | so deep(ly.

II. 3. 58. For 'tis | my lim|ited ser|vice | —Goes the | king hence | to-day | .

V. 3. 8. Like syl|lable | of dol|our | —What I | believe | I'll wail | .

I. 3. 85. That takes | the reas|on pris|oner | —Your chil|dren shall | be kings | .

Where the lines are not thus divided between two speakers, it is often possible to explain away apparent Alexandrines, either as containing trisyllabic feet, or by hypermetric syllables at the end or before the caesura, or, if we follow Dr Abbott, on the principle of slurring, as—

III. 1. 80. In our | last con|f'rence | ; passed in | probat|ion with (you.

I. 3. 140. My thought | whose mur|der yet | is but | fantast(ical.

I. 3. 129. Of the | imper|ial theme | , I thank | you gen(tlemen.

III. 1. 81. How you | were borne | in hand |, how crossed, | the inst(ruments.

IV. 3. 239. Put on | their inst'|ments |. Receive | what cheer | you may |.

III. 2. 22. In rest|less ec|st'sy. | Duncan | is in | his grave |.

I. 3. 111. Which he | deserves | to lose | whether he | was combined | .

IV. 3. 97. Acting | it ma|ny ways | . Nay 'd | I power | I should | .

Sometimes the Alexandrine is due to wrong arrangement of lines. I have already mentioned that it seems better to treat the first two words of the following as a broken line ;

III. 2. 15. But let | the frame | of things | disjoint | both the | worlds trem(ble.

The only remaining Alexandrines in *Macbeth* are, I believe, the following, some of which seem to me corrupt :

I. 4. 26. Which do | but what | they should | by do|ing ev|erything | .

This line which is followed by the obscure 'safe toward your love and honour,' is so feeble in rhythm that it can hardly be genuine. Is it possible to contract 'every' into a monosyllable ?

IV. 3. 20. In an | imper|ial charge | . But I | shall crave | your par(don.

Here there is a decided pause, and I should take the line as made up of two fragments, and therefore to be classed with what Dr Abbott calls the trimeter couplet, of which we spoke before.

III. 2. 11. With them | they think | on ? Things | without | all rem|edy |.
Should be without regard, what's done is done.

In the former line, I think *all* is an interpolation ; it injures the antithesis 'without remedy '—'without regard,' and gives a feeble dragging rhythm. In the same way, in I. 2. 66,

Our bo|som inte|rest. Go | pronounce | his pre|sent death | ,
And with | his for|mer ti|tle greet | Macbeth |

'present' seems to me interpolated, like 'all,' with the view of giving more force.

IV. 1. 153. That trace | him in | his line | . No boast|ing like | a fool.
This deed | I'll do | before | this pur|pose cool.

Here too I should wish to reduce the former line to the same length as that with which it rhymes, by omitting ' him in.'

I. 3. 102.   Only | to her|ald thee | into | his sight | , not pay (thee.

Here I should prefer to read ' to ' for ' into.'

It remains for me now to say a word or two on the variation produced by means of accentuation. This may arise either from defect of accent (the pyrrhic), from excess of accent (the spondee), or from inversion of accent (the trochee). They are all extremely common, and it will not be worth while to do more than give an example of each,

II. 2. 1.   What hath | quenched them | hath given | me fire |
                     1 1 1 1

hark ! peace | .
1 1

Spondee in second, fourth, and fifth.

Thy let|ters have | transpor|ted me | beyond | .
            0 0 0 0

Pyrrhic in second and fourth.

With regard to trochees, I have only looked for such as would be excluded by Dr Abbott's rule, that the trochee is inadmissible except in the first foot or after a stop. Of these I have found about twenty-five.

Trochee in second place :

I. 4. 52.   The eye | wink at | the hand | yet let | that be | .
                        2 0

Trochee in third place :

II. 4. 7.   And yet | dark night | strangles | the trav|elling lamp | .
                        1 1 2 0

Trochee in fourth place :

III. 6. 41.   The clou|dy mes|senger | turns me | his back | .
                                                2 0

It is rare to find a trochee in the last place. I have only two examples.

IV. 2. 4.   Our fears | do make | us trai|tors. You | know not.
                                                        2 1

and

V. 5. 3$_{2.}$ But know | not how | to do | it. Well | say, Sir | .
                                                        1 0

Mr Ellis kindly allows me to reprint from the *Proceedings of the Philological Society* his remarks on the preceding analysis of Shakespeare's metre as exhibited in *Macbeth.*

"Lines which cannot be naturally divided into measures readily acknowledged by the ear when read, need not be noticed. No poet, I believe, ever writes such lines. When we find them in Shakspeare, we are bound to assume that we have not the whole or the correct version of the poet's words before us. Such lines may be exercises for ingenuity in correction; but they are at any rate *not* suited to become a basis for a metrical theory. This observation at once disposes of some of Dr Abbott's certainly original, but as I cannot help thinking, impossible scansions.

"If we were determining Shakspeare's own rhythmical habit as opposed to that of other writers,—a research now carefully pursued by many members of the New Shakspeare Society,— then we should have at once to reject from consideration all lines about which critics are yet doubtful as to whether they are Shakspeare's or not. It is evident that no theory should be founded except on undoubted instances. But we are not dealing with this investigation. Any line not rejected as defective or erroneous, or doubtful, or as simply a modern or possible emendation, is sufficient for our present purpose, whether Shakspeare wrote it or not.

" In considering the rhythm of any single line, we should also, as I have already said, remember that it is part of a passage, and that the poet rhythmises whole passages, not single lines— except at a very early stage of his art. This is more particularly the case in dramatic poetry, where the author will even change the metre, by reducing or extending the number of his measures, to produce an emotional effect. And this leads to the difficult question how far the dramatic poet intended his actors to give oral effect to his rhythms, how far he intended them to distinguish his verse from measured prose, and how far he himself felt the transition from verse to prose. It would take too much time to consider this, and I therefore content myself with indicating the point. In the mean time I shall assume, as the basis of a rhythmical inquiry, that a poet always means to be rhythmical, whether he writes prose or verse ; but, as Dionysius and Cicero well put it, verse is *in rhythm*, and prose is merely *rhythmical*, that is, verse follows a conscious and mainly enunciable law in the juxtaposition of syllables of different kinds (long and short in Sanscrit, Greek, Latin, Arabic, Persian ; strong and weak in Modern Greek, Italian, Spanish, German, English), and prose follows a subjective and mainly non-enunciable feeling.

" Now I will endeavour to notice the principal points in Professor Mayor's notes on *Macbeth* in his own order.

" *A. I.*—Lines in defect, that is, having fewer than the normal five measures, are *not* necessarily defective.   These may be called ' short lines,' and are common enough in conclusions and in parts of dialogue, but they also occur in the body of a speech, as in the following examples, where I mark the odd and even measures as I previously proposed.

I. 2. 20.	Till he faced	the slave].
I. 2. 51.	And fan	our peo]ple cold	.
I. 5. 60.	Shall sun	that mor]row see	.
II. 1. 41.	As this	which now] I draw ¦ .
III. 2. 32.| Unsafe	the while] that we	.
III. 2. 51.	Makes wing	to the rook]y wood ¦ .
IV. 3. 217.	Did you	say all ?] O hell/kite ! all ?].

" So many speeches end and begin with such short-measured lines, that when there is an ' amphibious section,' as Dr Abbott strangely calls it, the break of the sense must determine to which one of the two short lines, that it is able to complete into a full line, the poet meant it to be joined.   To assume that it was intended to be part of both, seems almost ludicrous. Using this test I should divide

IV. 3. 219.	At one	fell swoop].	[short]
	Dispute ¦ it like] a man. ¦—I shall] do so	.	
V. 3. 18.	The En/glish force] so please	you.	[short]
	Take thy	face hence] Seyton ! ¦ I'm sick] at heart	.	
II. 4. 33.	To be	invest/ed.	[short]
	Where is Dun/can's bod]y ? Car/ried to] Colmekill	.	
III. 2. 12.	Should be	without] regard,	what's done] is done	.	
	We've scotched	the snake] not kill'd	it.	[short]
V. 3. 34.	Give me	my ar]mour. 'Tis	not need]ed yet	.	
	I'll put	it on.]	[short]

v. 8. 23. And break | it to] our hope | .   [short]
          I will | not fight] with thee ! |—Then yield] thee cow(ard.

"Observe that in 'I will not fight with thee,' the utter
tonelessness of the speech takes it almost beyond the bounds
of rhythm. There is scarcely a strong syllable in the phrase,
as I read it; the strongest is *not*, and the *I will* would be
naturally contracted to *I'll*. Still it is possible to read:

I will | not fight] with thee | .

"There seems no reason anxiously to avoid these short
lines. Thus, why not read ?

III. 1. 44. Sirrah | a word] with you | .
          Attend | these men] our pleas(ure.

"No thought of an Alexandrine need occur. Yet, as the
omission of 'Sirrah' or 'with you,' would produce a regular
line, no certainty is possible—or of consequence.
"In III. 2. 15, 'but let the frame of things disjoint, both the
worlds suffer,' there is no such reason as in I. 2. 37 ('So they ')
to make one line of one measure, and another of five measures.
Such a division is, I think, really unusual. Considered as one
line, although there are six measures, there is no Alexandrine
rhythm. The conclusion, 'both the worlds suffer,' is that of a
regular five-measure line, with a pause at 'disjoint,' where the
Folios divide the line. There is possibly some error. The
initial 'but' is not required, and is rather prosy. By omitting
it, and making an initial trisyllabic measure, regularity is
restored :

Let the frame | of things] disjoint: | both the] worlds suf(fer.

It is therefore a line from which we can conclude nothing.
"I also cannot accept the scansion of IV. 3. 28, given by
Professor Mayor on p. 171. It seems to me entirely unlike the
rhythm of the rest of *Macbeth*, especially in ending a line with
'but' after a comma, that is, the 'weak ending,' and in the
two initial measures of the strong-weak form. I would rather
divide

Without | leave ta]king.   [short, pause]
I pray | you,   [short, initial]

Let not | my jeal]ousies | be your] dishon(ours,
But mine | own safe]ties. *You* | may be right]ly just,
Whatev|er *I*] shall think | .—Bleed, bleed,] poor coun(try.

" But I strongly suspect the genuineness of the text throughout this scene ; and here the words, 'I pray you,' which are quite unnecessary, may be a mere insertion, or part of a player's 'cut.'

" *A. II.*—'Lines defective in their internal structure,' for reasons already explained, may be omitted. Each requires a separate critical examination, either on the ground of pronunciation or alteration, which takes it out of the present investigation.

" *B. I.*—A superfluous syllable at the end of a line, or even two such, when both are very weak, must be admitted as common in heroic rhythm, especially when dramatic. The greater or less liking for it by particular poets is altogether another inquiry. But as to the existence of such syllables at the end of the second or third measure, after a pause, or closing a speech, Professor Mayor is right in supposing that I should treat them in almost every case as cases of trisyllabic measures. And for this reason : the continuation may or may not begin with a weak syllable ; when it does not, the final syllable of the preceding section is evidently effective, that is, *not* superfluous. Why should it not be so in other cases, when it merely introduces a regular variety, namely a trisyllabic measure. Thus in

       I. 4 . 11.   As 'twere | a care]less tri|fle.—There's] no art |

the last syllable of 'trifle' acts in the usual way. But read ' there *is*] no art |,' with an emphasis (which the passage allows), and we have a trisyllabic fourth measure. There is, therefore, no reason for considering '-fle' a superfluous syllable in this case rather than the other.

      I. 4. 27.   Safe toward | your love] and hon|our.—Wel]come hith(er.

Here '-our' is effective. Had the reading been ' Thou'rt wel]come hith|er,' would '-our' have ceased to be effective ? I find no need for such a supposition.

      I. 5. 36.   Than would | make up] his mes|sage.—Give] him tend(ing.

Here ' -sage ' is effective, why then not ' -stant ' in

      I. 5. 57.   The fu|ture in] the in|stant.—My dear|est love ?

Might we not omit ' my,' without the slightest influence on the rhythm of the first section ? But then '-stant' must be effective, not superfluous. Without considering every line, I will mark the measures in a few, where this ' superfluous' syllable is *not* part of the trisyllabic measure which it introduces. Generally it will be seen that when this weak syllable is followed by a strong one, we have a regular weak-strong measure. But the final weak syllable of the first section may be followed by another weak one, making a weak-weak measure; though it is then more commonly part of a trisyllabic measure of the weak-weak-strong class, and even a weak-weak-weak measure is possible.

III. 1. 25. 'Twixt this | and sup]per : go | not my horse] the bet(ter.
III. 1. 34. Craving | us joint]ly. Hie | you to horse :] adieu | .
III. 1. 79. In our | last con]ference, passed | in proba]tion with (you.
III. 2. 19. That shake | us night]ly. Bet|ter be with] the dead.
IV. 3. 229. Convert | to an]ger. Blunt | not the heart,] enrage (it.
V. 6. 4. Lead our | first bat]tle. Worth|y Macduff] and we |
IV. 3. 117. To thy | good truth] and hon|our. Dev']lish Macbeth | .

[Read 'dev'lish' in two syllables, it is not once necessarily of three syllables in Shakspeare, even at the end of a line, as in *Rich. III.*, I. 4. 265,

> Not to | relent] is beast:ly sav]age dev'(lish.]

IV. 3. 33. For good|ness dare] not check | thee. Wear] thou thy wrongs | .

[Perhaps ' thou' is erroneous, as it is quite superfluous.]

III. 6. 2. Which can | inter]pret fur|ther. On]ly, I say, |
V. 8. 27. Here may | you see] the ty|rant. I'll | not yield | .

[Read *I'll* and emphasise *not*, saving the rhythm by the weight of *yield.*]

III. 4. 86. I have | a strange] infir|mity, which] is noth(ing
To those | that know] me.   [short line, decided pause]
Come, love | and health] to all ; | then I'll] sit down | .
Give me | some wine !] fill full ! | [short, order]
I drink | to the gen]eral joy | o' the] whole ta(ble.

[This might be divided thus, if the text is correct—Pope omits ' come' in v. 88, but it seems better left in.]

" *B. II.*—Much of the so-called ' slurring,' and almost all the ' elision,' when not usual in common conversation, I find unnecessary, that is, I see no reason for not reading the words fully, with a natural pronunciation. As to Alexandrines divided among two speakers, there is always a doubt, because only two short lines may have been intended. These lines, therefore, lie out of my present province. When a five-measure line ends with two light superfluous syllables, it does not become an Alexandrine to the feeling of the reader, and there is no occasion to suppose one of these light syllables to be elided. The words ' fantastical, gentlemen, instruments,' give rise to such terminations. In the middle of lines they simply produce trisyllabic feet, as

III. 2. 22.   In rest|less ec]stasy.   Dun|can is in] his grave | .

IV. 3. 239 may be divided thus

> Put on | their in]struments.   [short, pause]
> Receive | what cheer | you may,   [short, initial]
> The night | is long] that nev|er finds] the day.

I suspect, however, some error in ' receive.' A monosyllable, such as ' have,' would suit the rhythm, and occurs with ' cheer ' in other passages, *Rich. III.*, v. 3. 74 : ' I have not that alacrity of spirit, Nor cheer of mind,' and *All's Well*, III. 2. 67 : ' I prithee, lady, have a better cheer.' Whereas ' receive cheer ' is not used elsewhere. Certainly an Alexandrine would be very much out of place as the first line of a final rhyming couplet, and even the break, with short lines, is not what we should expect. But this enters into the region of conjecture and criticism which I wish to avoid. I pass over all the other lines where Professor Mayor suspects errors. And the rest of his remarks referring to the measures strong-strong and strong-weak, (which he calls spondees and trochees), in place of the theoretical weak-strong, merely bear out my own observations.

" In reading through *Macbeth* afresh for this purpose, the general impression made on me is that the character of five-measure lines is well preserved. The fifth measure of each verse ends strongly, with often one, and occasionally two additional very weak syllables. I have not observed any so-called ' weak-endings.' Sometimes, not often, the fifth measure has two weak syllables. But two weak syllables[1] are also allowed to form a measure elsewhere, as the second in

> III. 1. 96. Distin|guishes] the swift | the slow] the sub(tle.
> III. 1. 97. Accor|ding to] the gift | which bount]eous na(ture.

"Trisyllabic measures are common enough, perhaps more common than our present utterance shews. The lines are generally vigorous, and rhythm varied. But there are probably numerous errors of the printer and copyist, as indeed the Cambridge editors allow, 'especially as regards metre,' to use their own words. This makes the selection of this play rather unsuitable for the determination of Shakspeare's metres, and, as Professor Mayor states, it was not purposely so selected. There are a very large number of short lines, especially when ending and beginning speeches. Whether this was intentional, or is to be reckoned among errors, or arose from players' 'cuts,' cannot be determined. Generally they do not produce a bad effect. Long lines, especially real Alexandrines, are not numerous, and perhaps were never intentional."

---

[1] See above, p. 31.

CHAPTER XII.

SHAKESPEARE'S BLANK VERSE—*continued.*

HAMLET.

As Mr Ellis doubts whether *Macbeth* was a good play to choose for the purpose of determining the rhythm used by Shakespeare in his prime, I give the results of a similar study of *Hamlet*, so far as they seem to be of interest in the way of confirming, correcting or adding to the results already obtained.

To speak first of the accent. Excess and defect of accent, the spondee and the pyrrhic, are common alike in all the feet. As examples we may take

I. 2. 82. Togeth|er with | all forms | , moods, shapes | of grief |
          0 1   0   0   2   1   1   1   0 2

III. 2. 225. Thoughts black | , hands apt | , drugs fit | , and time |
           2   2   2   2   2 2   0 2

         agree(ing
         0 1

IV. 5. 190. His means | of death | , his ob|scure fu|neral |
          0   1   0   1   0   0   2   2 0 1

I. 5. 61. Upon | my se|cure hour | thy un|cle stole |
       0 1   0   0   2   1   0 1 0   1

I. 1. 18. Disas|ters in | the sun | ; and the | moist star |
       0 1   0   0   0   2   0   0   2   2

Inversion of accent (trochee) is most commonly found in the 1st foot, sometimes giving the effect of a *choriambus* at the beginning of the verse, or after the middle pause or caesura, of which latter we may take the following as examples

I. 1. 2. Nay, ans|wer me | : stand, and | unfold | yourself |
       1   1 0   1   2   0   0 1   0 1

I. 1. 13. The ri|vals of | my watch | : bid them | make haste |
      0 1 0   0   0   1   2   0   0   2

But we also find it in the other feet without any preceding pause, sometimes giving the effect of an *antispastus*, as

I. 3. 56. The wind | sits in | the shoul|der of | your sail |
0   1   1   0   0   1   0   0   0   1

II. 2. 573. Been struck | so to | the soul |, that pres|ently |
0   1   2   0   0   1   0   2   0   1

I. 5. 166. There are | more things | in heaven | and earth | Hora(tio
0   0   2   1   0   1   0   1   0   1

Than are | dreamt of | in your | philos|ophy |
0   0   2   1   1   0   0   1   0   1

(taking 'your' in a contemptuous sense).

I. 2. 13. In e|qual scale | weighing | delight | and dole |
0   1   0   1   2   0   0   2   0   1

I. 3. 38. Virtue | itself | scapes not | calum|nious strokes |
2   0   0   1   1   0   0   1   0   1

I. 4. 42. Be thy | intents | wicked | or char|ita(ble
1   0   0   1   2   0   0   2   0   1

I. 5. 15. Till the | foul crimes | done in | my days | of na(ture
1   0   2   1   1   0   1   0   0   1

IV. 3. 3. Yet must | not we | put the | strong law | upon (him
0   2   0   1   1   0   1   1   0   1

I. 4. 46. Why thy | canon|ized bones | hearsed | in death | *
2   0   0   1   0   1   2   0   1

II. 1. 81. Pale as | his shirt | ; his knees | knocking | each oth(er
2   0   0   1   0   1   2   0   0   1

III. 2. 55. No! let | the can|died tongue | lick ab|surd pomp |
2   1   0   1   0   1   2   0   1   0

IV. 5. 84. And, as | the world | were now | but to | begin |
1   1   0   1   0   1   1   0   0   2

I. 2. 37. To bus|iness with | the king | more than | the scope |
0   1   0   0   0   1   2   0   0   1

I. 2. 222. And we | did think | it writ | down in | our du(ty
0   1   0   1   0   1   1   0   0   1

I. 3. 64. Of each | new-hatch'd | unfledg'd | comrade | . Beware |
0   1   1   2   1   2   1   0   0   1

(I keep the usual accentuation of *comrade*, as in *Lear* II. 4. 213.)

I. 4. 88. Let's fol|low; 'tis | not fit | thus to | obey (him
0   1   0   1   0   2   2   0   0   1

I. 5. 139. For your | desire | to know | what is | between (us
0   1   0   1   0   1   2   0   0   1

I. 1. 93. Had he | been van|quisher; as | by the same | cov'nant |
0   1   0   1   0   0   1   0   0   1   1   0

(here we might make the 4th foot a pyrrhic, putting *same* into the last foot, which would then have a superfluous syllable).

I. 2. 58. He hath | my lord | wrung from | me my | slow leave |
0   1   0   1   2   1   0   0   2   1

I. 3. 4. But let | me hear | from you | .
0   1   0   1   0   1

Do you | doubt that |
0   0   2   1

I. 4. 65. I do | not set | my life | at a | pin's fee |
0   1   0   1   0   1   0   0   2   1

* In Shakespeare *canónize* regularly has the accent on the 2nd syllable.

II. 1. 86.   But tru|ly I | do fear | it.
$$0 \quad 1 \; 0 \quad 0 \quad 0 \quad 1 \quad 0$$

What | said he |
$$1 \quad 1 \quad 0$$

(the stress seems to lie on *said*, in contrast with the appearance of Hamlet described before, not on *he*).

III. 4. 15.   Have you | forgot | me?
$$0 \quad 0 \quad 0 \; 2 \quad 0$$

No | by the rood | , not so |
$$2 \quad 0 \quad 0 \quad 1 \quad 2 \quad 1$$

We next take examples of irregularity in the number of syllables, and (A) by way of excess;

(*a*) Superfluous syllable at the end (feminine ending).

This, as is well known, is rare in the early plays, such as *Love's Labour's Lost*, where it occurs only twice in the first 50 lines of the 1st Act, and only once in the first 50 of the 2nd Act. On the contrary in the King's speech (*Hamlet* I. 2. 1—39) we find 12 examples, i.e. nearly 1 in 3, and in the same scene (87—102) 10 examples in 16 lines, and in Hamlet's speech in the same scene (146—153) 5 examples in 7 lines, a proportion only exceeded in the un-Shakespearian portions of *Henry VIII*.

Taking Mr Fleay's figures as given in p. 15 of the *New Shakspeare Soc. Trans.* for 1874[1] we obtain the following general averages.

	Blank Verse.	Double Endings.	Proportion.
L. L. L.	579	9	one in 64⅓.
Rom. and Jul.	2111	118	one in less than 18.
Hamlet	2490	508	one in less than 5.
Cymbeline	2585	726	one in little more than 3½.

But Dr Abbott has pointed out (*N. S. Soc.*, ib. p. 76) that though we may trace on the whole a steady increase in the use of the feminine ending, as we pass from the earlier to the later plays, yet such double endings are very unequally distributed through the scenes of the same play. Thus he contrasts *Rich. II.* Act I. Sc. 1, which he calls 'a spirited scene with a sort of trumpet sound about it,' and in which there is free use of the extra syllable (24 in 146 lines), with Act V. Sc. 5 containing

---

[1] Reprinted in his *Shakespeare Manual*, p. 135.

Richard's soliloquy in prison, where the extra syllable occurs only once in 119 lines. And he thus states the occasions on which it is used, ' in moments of passion and excitement, in questions, in quarrel, seldom in quiet dialogue and narrative, and seldom in any serious or pathetic passage.' The phrase ' trumpet sound' does not commend itself to me as applicable here, but otherwise Dr Abbott's remarks agree fairly with my observations in *Hamlet*, except that I should add ' especially in the light and airy conversation of polite society.' Thus to take the extremes of the use of the feminine ending in *Hamlet*, we find it most freely used in

IV. 5. 76—96. The King to the Queen ; average almost one in 2.

v. 2. 237—276. Dialogue between Hamlet and Laertes ; average the same.

I. 3. 91—135. Polonius to Ophelia (omitting Ophelia's replies) ; average one out of $2\frac{1}{2}$.

The average is one in less than 3, in the King's speech to the Ambassadors and Laertes (I. 2. 1—56), and in the King's speech to Hamlet (I. 2. 87—117).

If we examine these scenes, we find that in the conversation between Hamlet and Laertes there is on both sides a straining after excessive courtesy, partly because they are about to enter into a contest of personal prowess, but even more from the wish, on Hamlet's part, to atone for previous rudeness, and, on the part of Laertes, to hide his murderous intention. By the use of the feminine ending the poet endeavours to reproduce the easy tone of ordinary life ; and this no doubt explains its frequency in Fletcher, the poet of society. There is felt to be something formal, stilted, high-flown, poetic, in the regular iambic metre. Three of the other scenes contain speeches by the King. Now the King, we know from Hamlet, is a ' smiling villain ' ; he affects affability and ease ; there is nothing strong or straightforward in his character, but he carries his point by cunning subtilty, ' with witchcraft of his wit.' The same explanation will account for the prevalence of feminine rhythm in the speech of the worldly-wise Polonius.

Consider now the opposite extreme.

I. 1. 112—125.   Horatio's speech, average one in 14.

III. 4. 31—87.   Hamlet's speech to his mother, one in 9.

  ,,   140—216.   ,,   ,,   one in 6.

IV. 4. 32—66.   Hamlet's soliloquy, one in 7.

III. 1. 56—88.   ,,   ,,   one in 7.

I. 5. 10—91.   Ghost's speech, one in less than 7.

II. 2. 473—540.   Old play (The rugged Pyrrhus), one in 6⅓.

III. 3. 73—96.   Hamlet (seeing his uncle praying), one in 5½.

  ,,   36—71.   King's soliloquy, one in 5.

Horatio's speech commencing 'A mote it is to trouble the mind's eye,' is a piece of fine imaginative poetry, standing in strong contrast with his preceding rapid business-like statement about the claim of Fortinbras. In place of the rough, broken rhythm of the former speech, we have here some four or five of the most musically varied lines in Shakespeare, marked by slow movement, long vowels and alliteration. It is only as Horatio descends to earth again, that we have the double ending in l. 124. In Hamlet's speech to his mother, he appears as a stern preacher, obeying the command received from his murdered father. Plainly there is no place here for ease and politeness. The same may be said of the ghost's speech, only that it has an added solemnity. The old play is necessarily regular and formal. Soliloquies, if quietly meditative, or the outpouring of a pleasing emotion, will naturally take the regular poetic form: if agitated, or vehemently argumentative they will be irregular, marked by the use of sudden pauses, feminine ending and trisyllabic feet, as we see in I. 2. 129—160 'O that this too too solid flesh would melt,' etc. This is remarkably shewn in the speech beginning 'To be or not to be.' where we find five double endings in the first 8 lines, these being perplexed and argumentative; but in the next 20 lines there is not a single feminine ending, as these are merely the pathetic expression of a single current of thought. Then in l. 83 follow reflections of a more prosaic turn, and we again have two double endings. It may be noticed that in the soliloquies III. 3. 36—96, six of the twelve double endings consist of the word *heaven* or *prayers*, which are hardly to be distinguished from monosyllables. One other instance may be quoted to illustrate Shakespeare's use of the feminine ending. In I. 1. 165 Horatio says

So have | I heard | and do | in part | believe (it.
But, look | , the morn | in rus|set man|tle clad | ,
Walks o'er | the dew | of yon | high east|ward hill | .

The 1st line is conversational, the two others imaginative without passion, only with a joyful welcome of the calm, bright, healthy dawn after the troubled, spectral night; and we have a corresponding change in the rhythm.

I think Dr Abbott goes too far in saying (*S. G.* § 455) that the extra syllable is very rarely a monosyllable. No doubt it is very rarely an 'emphatic monosyllable,' but pronouns such as *you, it, him, them,* etc. are common enough, e.g.

I. 1. 104. So by | his fa|ther lost | : and this | I take (it

cf. I. 1. 165, 172, I. 5. 119, 121 ;

I. 2. 234. Nay ve|ry pale | .
                          And fixed | his eyes | upon (you

cf. I. 3. 24, 95, I. 5. 129, 138, 180, 183, 185 ;

I. 3. 57. And you | are stayed | for. There | , my bless|ing with (thee
I. 3. 103. Do you | believe | his ten|ders as | you call (them

cf. I. 4. 24 ;

I. 4. 39. Angels | and min|isters | of grace | defend (us

cf. I. 5. 139 ;

I. 4. 84. By heaven | I'll make | a ghost | of him | that lets (me

cf. II. 2. 125 ;

I. 4. 87. Let's fol|low ; 'tis | not meet | thus to | obey (him

cf. I. 5. 113, II. 1. 13, 19, 29 ;

II. 2. 143. This must | not be | and then | I pre|cepts gave (her

We also find *not* in I. 1. 67 ;

In what | partic|ular thought | to work | I know (not.

Sometimes the line ends with two superfluous syllables, more or less slurred, e.g.

I. 2. 57. Have you | your fa|ther's leave ? | What says | Polo(nius

I. 2. 119. I pray | thee stay | with us | ; go not | to Wit(tenberg
      176. My lord | I came | to see | your fa|ther's fu(neral
II. 2. 459. The un|nerved fa|ther falls | . Then sense|less I(lium
II. 2. 91. And ted|iousness | the limbs | and out|ward flour(ishes
II. 2. 70. To give | the assay | of arms | against | your maj(esty

cf. III. 1. 22 ;

II. 2. 539. What's He|cuba | to him | or he | to Hec(uba

(*b*) Superfluous syllable in the middle of the line (feminine
section or caesura).

I think Mr Ellis has succeeded in shewing that the assumption of the ' section' is not essential to the scanning of any line ;
and the fact that there is so little trace of it in Surrey and
Marlowe is not in favour of Dr Guest's idea, that it was still
felt to be obligatory in Shakespeare's time. Shakespeare however would seem to have perceived the gain to the heroic rhythm,
which would arise from making more use of the caesura ; and I
think that the extra syllable which so often precedes the caesura
in his verse, must have been felt by him to be analogous to the
feminine ending. It is a difficult point to prove ; but the
following facts are in accordance with such a supposition.
(1) The large proportion of cases in which an unaccented syllable preceding the caesura is not needed for the metre : in
the first two scenes of *Hamlet* we have 46 lines with such a
syllable, in 21 of which it is superfluous ; (2) the frequent use
of a trochee in the 3rd or 4th foot, when a pause has preceded,
corresponding to the trochee in the 1st foot ; (3) the fact
that short or broken lines often end with a superfluous syllable,
which in them, at any rate, must be regarded as a feminine
ending ; and the further fact that many of the lines, in which
the feminine caesura occurs, are really made up of two broken
lines, e.g.

I. 1. 17. Who hath | relieved | you ?
                               Bernar|do hath | my place |
I. 2. 160. Hail to | your lord|ship.
                               I'm glad | to see | you well |
I. 2. 167. I'm ve|ry glad | to see | you.
                               Good ev|en Sir |
V. 2. 332. To tell | my sto|ry.
                               What war·like noise | is this | .

In such lines it seems a little absurd to keep the un-accented syllable in suspension, as it were, through a lengthened pause, until the latter part of the anapaest is forthcoming. (4) If we compare with the trisyllabic feet, which are produced by treating the extra syllable as metrically effective, those tri-syllabic feet which are unconnected with the caesura, we find many more of the former; thus, in the first two scenes of *Hamlet*, I find 16 of what, I may call, the true or independent trisyllabic feet, and 21 of the apparent trisyllabic feet, which make use of the extra syllable of the caesura. (5) Sometimes we find two superfluous unaccented syllables before the middle pause, which can only be made metrically effective by changing the line into an Alexandrine, as

I. 5. 162. A wor|thy pi|*oneer.* Once more | remove | good friends |
II. 1. 112. I had | not quo|*ted him :* I feared | he did | but tri(fle

(c) True anapaests are found in all the feet; dactyls rarely, except in the 1st foot; still more rarely tribrach, and amphi-brach or bacchius.

II. 1. 25. Ay, or drink|ing, fen|cing, swear|ing, quar|relling |
 0   0   1

III. 1. 154. The observ'd | of all | obser|vers, quite | , quite down |
 0   0   1

V. 1. 241. To o'ertop | old Pel|lion or | the sky|ish head |
 0   0   1

IV. 5. 13. 'Twere good | she were spo|ken with | ; for she | may strew |
 0   0   1

II. 2. 554. Tweaks me | by the nose | , gives me | the lie | i' the throat |
 2   0   0   0   1   1   0   0   2   0   0   1

I. 2. 93. Of imp|ious stub|bornness ; 'tis | unman|ly grief !
 0 0   2   0   0   1

I. 2. 157. With such | dexter|ity to | inces|tuous sheets |
 0 0   0   0   1   0 0   1

I. 1. 86. Did slay | this Fort|inbras, who | by a seal'd | compact |
 0   0   1   0   0   1   0   1

I. 1. 114. A lit|tle ere | the migh|tiest Ju|lius fell |
 0   0   1 0 0   1

The graves | stood ten|antless | and the sheet|ed dead |
 0   1   1   2   0   0   0   1   0   2

II. 1. 107. What, have | you given | him an|y hard words | of late |
 1   0   0   1   0   1 0   1   1   0   1

[Here the 4th foot is bacchius, but we might divide

him any | hard words |
 0   1 0   1   1

giving an amphibrach for the 3rd foot, and a spondee for the fourth.]

I. 1. 83. Thereto | prick'd on | by a | most em|ulate pride |
                      0 0   0   0   1

I. 2. 83. That can | denote | me tru|ly: these | indeed seem |
                                              0   2

[or we might treat this as a case of feminine caesura and divide the last two feet

these in|deed seem |]
    2   0   1   2

I. 4. 31. Carrying | I say | the stamp | of one | defect |
             1 0 0

IV. 4. 40. Bestial | obliv|ion or | some cra|ven scru(ple
           1 0 0   0 0 1

IV. 5. 13. Dangerous | conjec|tures in | ill-breed|ing minds |
            1 0 0

I. 5. 133. I'm sor|ry they | offend | you, hear|tily | ;

Yes, faith | , heartily | .
  2   1   1 0 0

                             There's no | offence | my lord | .

(d) Lines of six feet (Alexandrines) are very rare, except when they are divided between two speakers. What seem to be undivided Alexandrines are sometimes lines with two super-fluous syllables, or they are possibly corrupt, or admit of other explanations, as follows.

I. 2. 2. The mem|ory | be green | , and that | it us | befit(ted.

I incline to omit *that it* with Steevens. It is a cumbrous phrase, apparently inserted to facilitate the construction.

I. 3. 24. Whereof | he is | the head | . Then, if | he says | he loves (you

I think Pope is right in omitting *the.*

I. 5. 13. Are burnt | and purged | away | . But that | I am | forbid |

I should read *I'm* and make the 4th foot a dactyl.

I. 5. 187. God wil|ling, shall | not lack | . Let us | go in | toge(ther

I think Hanmer is right in omitting *together*, which may have been inserted from below.

II. 1. 57. Or then | , or then | , with such | , or such | , and, as | you say |

Pope omits the 2nd *or then.* I think it is better to consider this a line of prose, like I. 5. 176, 7 (As 'well, well, we know,' etc.).

II. 1. 112. I had | not quo|ted him | : I fear'd | he did | but tri(fle
         And meant | to wreck | thee ; but | beshrew | my jeal|ousy |

The former line should, I think, be read with two superfluous syllables at the hemistich: in the latter I should omit *but*, which is not wanted here, and may perhaps have slipt in from the previous line.

II. 2. 564.   Fie up|on't! foh! | About |, my brain | ! Hum, I | have heard |

I have no doubt that the first three words at any rate should be joined to the previous broken line.   They continue in the same strain of self-disgust; while a new start is taken with 'About my brain,' which might well be preceded and followed by a pause.

III. 2. 373.   Conta|gion to | this world | : now could | I drink | hot blood |

The Quarto of 1637 has *the* for *this*, which is both more natural in itself, and has the further advantage of reducing the line to the ordinary number of feet.

IV. 3. 7.   But nev|er the | offence | .   To bear | all smooth | and e(ven

Here we might take *never* as one syllable (*ne'er*), like *ever* and *over*, but I see no objection to supposing that we have here two broken lines, separated by a pause.

IV. 5. 79.   For good | Polon|ius' death | ; and we | have done | but green(ly

I should omit *and* with Pope.   The clause, which it introduces, is not one of the series of sorrows named, but a parenthetical regret, suggested by one of them, viz. the discontent of the people.

IV. 5. 137.   Of your | dear fa|ther's death |, is't writ | in your | revenge |

This seems more like a true Alexandrine than any other line in the Play, but the word *dear* may easily have been inserted, and perhaps it is more in harmony with the lofty tone assumed by the king, to abstain from the use of any coaxing word, until Laertes recedes from his personal threats.

IV. 7. 182.   Unto | that el|ement | : but long | it could | not be |

Here I think we have two superfluous syllables at the hemistich.

I. 2. 90.   That fa|ther lost | lost his |, and the | survi|vor bound |

Both metre and construction lead one to suspect error here, but no satisfactory emendation has been proposed.

v. 2. 68

  —is't | not per|fect con|science
To quit | him with | this arm | ? And is't | not to | be damn'd |

I think Hanmer is right in omitting *and*. If any word were wanted, it should rather be *nay*.

  B. *Syllabic defect.*

  I do not know that I need add anything to what has been said on Fragmentary Lines, except in reference to Mr Ellis's remark, that it seems ludicrous to suppose a ' common section ' to be intended to complete two broken lines. I do not of course suppose it to be actually repeated, but the remembrance of the rhythm to affect and, as it were, justify the following rhythm. At any rate it seems to me a fact that, when we have three broken lines in succession, the 2nd as a rule fits into the 1st, and the 3rd into the 2nd, so that, to the ear, three halves seem to constitute two wholes. Thus in I. 2. 226 foll. I think the effect to the ear is as follows :

  Armed say | you ? Armed | my lord | . From top | to toe | ?
  [From top | to toe] My lord | from head | to foot |
  Then saw | you not | his face | ? O, yes | my lord |
  [O, yes | my lord] he wore | his bea|ver up | .
  What; looked | he frown|ingly | ? A count|enance more |
  In sor|row than | in an|ger. Pale | or red | ?

  Thus arranged we see the reason for the rhythm of the last three words, which are generally printed by themselves, as a short line. Otherwise, to make them rhythmical, we should have to treat *pale* as a monosyllabic first foot.

  Of the few Defective Lines in *Hamlet*, one or two are plainly corrupt, as

  III. 4. 169. And ei|ther ∧ | the devil | or throw | him out |
  IV. 1. 40. And what's | untime|ly done | ∧

and in others it is at any rate probable that a word has been lost, as in

  II. 1. 83. To speak | of hor|rors, | he comes | before (me

where Pope inserts *thus* before *he*.

  II. 1. 91. As he | would draw | it. | Long stayed | he so |

where Pope inserts *time* after *long*.

III. 3. 38. A broth|er's mur|der. | Pray can | I not |

Here Hanmer reads *Pray, alas, I cannot,* but the pause after *murder* may perhaps supply the place of a syllable.

IV. 4. 17. Truly | to speak | and | with no | addit(ion

Pope improves both metre and construction by the insertion of *it* after *speak.*

IV. 4. 65. To hide | the slain | O | from this | time forth |

Pope inserts *then* after *O,* but the exclamation may easily cover the two syllables.

I. 3. 8. Forward | not per|manent | , sweet | not last(ing

Capell inserts *but* after *sweet.* Possibly the pause and the length of the word may be considered to make up for the missing syllable.

I. 1. 50. Stay ! speak, speak ! I charge thee, speak !

Here it would seem that each of the first three words stands for a foot.

III. 4. 177. One word more, good lady.
What shall I do ?

Here it is possible to get the proper number of feet by giving two syllables to *more.*

IV. 7. 60. Will you be ruled by me ?
Ay, my lord.

Walker inserts *good* before *lord,* but we may perhaps disyllabize *ay,* as in IV. 3. 45

For Eng|land. For Eng|land ? A|y Ham|let. Good |

and

II. 1. 36. Wherefore | should you | do this | ? Aÿ | my lord |

Of Fragmentary Lines occurring at the beginning, middle, or end of longer speeches, and not supplemented by other short lines, I find 66, of which 3 consist of one syllable, as 'Swear'; 9 of two, as 'Mark you,' 'Yet I'; 8 of three, as 'Speak to me,' 'I have sworn't,' 'a scullion'; 14 of four, as 'Last night of all'; 12 of five, as 'Thou know'st already'; 13 of six, as 'To hear him so inclined'; 7 of seven, as 'What is the cause, Laertes?'

CHAPTER XIII.

MODERN BLANK VERSE.

TENNYSON AND BROWNING.

WE have seen (p. 14 foll.) that Dr Guest condemns the freedom of Milton's versification as licentious, and that Dr Abbott to some extent shares his view in so far as regards Milton's use of trochees and trisyllabic feet (p. 38 foll.). It may be well therefore to begin with an analysis of the Miltonic rhythm in order to appreciate better the license practised by the poets of our own time, both in respect of pauses and of the substitution of other feet in place of the iamb. I have accordingly taken sections of 200 lines each from the poems of Milton, Tennyson and Browning, with a view to ascertain the comparative frequency of the occurrence of such irregularities. Though it is probable that no two persons would agree precisely as to the pauses and the feet to be found in a passage of some length, yet for the purpose of comparison, this will not make very much difference. As a rule I have followed the printed stopping, except when it appeared to me that this had reference rather to the grammatical construction than to the actual reading of the verse.

The passages selected are Milton (α) *Par. Reg.* I. 1—200, (β) ib. 201—400; Tennyson *Oenone, Gardener's Daughter, Enoch Arden, Lucretius, Gareth, Balin, Sisters, Sir John Oldcastle*; Browning *Aristophanes, Ring and Book* IV. I have analyzed the 1st at length, and contented myself with tabulating the results of the others.

Par. Reg. I. 1—200.

> Lines without any pause, 30, or a little over 1 in 7.

Pauses. Lines with final pause only, 53, or a little over 1 in 4.

> Lines with internal pause only, 71, or a little over 1 in 3.

> Lines with both final and internal pause, 46, or a little under 1 in 4.

> Pause after 1st syllable, 1 in 200[1].

after 1½ syllables[2],	2 in 200 or 1 in 100.
after 2	„	[3], 10, or 1 in 20.
after 3	„	10, or 1 in 20.
after 4	„	28, or 1 in about 7.
after 5	„	15, or 1 in 13⅓.
after 6	„	38, or 1 in about 5¼.
after 7	„	14, or 1 in about 14⅓.
after 8	„	12, or 1 in 16⅔.
after 9	„	1 in 200.

Feminine Ending[4]. 12, or 1 in 16⅔.

Substitution of other feet in place of the iamb.

Pyrrhic.	58 out of 200, or 1 in a little over 3½ lines.
Spondee.	69, or 1 in less than 3.
Trochee.	48, or 1 in 4$\frac{1}{12}$.
	(of which 12 are not initial, or 1 in 16⅔).
Anapaest.	42, or 1 in a little over 5.
Dactyl.	2, or 1 in 100.

[1] Of course a line with two or more internal pauses is reckoned more than once in this list.

[2] By this I mean pause after initial trochee.

[3] By this I mean a pause after the 1st foot when it is iamb, spondee, pyrrhic, dactyl or anapaest; and so, throughout, the even numbers denote the end, the odd the middle of a foot.

[4] In reckoning feminine endings and trisyllabic feet I have given the full number of syllables to doubtful words, such as *power, heaven*.

	Milton		Tennyson								Browning	
	α	β	Oenone	Gard. D.	Arden	Lucretius	Sisters	Gareth	Balin	Oldcastle	Aristoph.	R. and B.
Pauses Final only	53	39	53	51	75	49	48	*		42	53	49
Internal only	71	77	65	59	45	75	57			48	45	45
None	30	19	17	17	19	29	29			11	19	35
After 1st syll.	1	1	2	4	7	8	6	13	11	16	7	15
1½	2	0	5	1	1	6	1	5	6	1	3	1
2	10	16	8	7	5	9	11	13	14	18	3	10
3	10	15	14	14	13	22	12	16	15	19	27	16
4	28	21	23	40	21	31	39	34	29	50	27	23
5	15	12	44	15	19	22	25	12	26	20	30	25
6	38	45	26	32	18	12	30	29	18	25	21	14
7	14	20	19	26	31	23	22	14	27	18	32	15
8	12	18	4	11	3	29	11	17	22	14	5	8
9	1	3	0	7	3	6	16	7	14	5	5	2
Feminine ending	12	10	14	1	8	5	13	6	6	15†	1	0
Substitution Pyrrhic	58	49	66	48	66						31	
Spondee	69	75	45	61	51						80	
Trochee (initial)	36	33	48	33	46	37	26	44	30	34	65	
(not initial)	12	24	2	11	7	6	6	7	7	12	12	6
Anapaest	42	30	25	15	21	45	33	30	24	48	27	88
Dactyl	2	2	1	0	1	3	3	1	1	2	1	2

 * I have left blanks where I thought it was unimportant to ascertain the numbers.

 † Two of which are double, having two superfluous syllables.

Though the preceding table shews that the poets are far from practising a monotonous uniformity, yet I think we may gather from it that Tennyson and Browning are not more observant of the *a-priori* laws of the metrists than Milton is. They have on the whole more lines with final, but without internal pause; somewhat fewer with internal, but without final pause; about the same without any pause at all. As to the forbidden internal pauses, they use the pause after the 1st, 3rd, and 9th syllables more frequently than Milton, and do not differ much from him in their use of the pause after $1\frac{1}{2}$, 2, 8. With regard to the middle pauses, those which divide the feet, coming after the 5th or 7th syllable, are more favoured by the moderns than by Milton, whose commonest pause is after the 6th syllable, and then *longo intervallo* after the 4th. In *Oenone* the pause after the 5th syllable prevails, but taking all the passages together the pause after the 4th seems to be Tennyson's favourite, while Browning seems to prefer the 5th and 7th. This last also abounds in Swinburne. In his *Erechtheus* it comes twice as often as any other pause. Feminine ending is very rare in Browning, but in Tennyson is hardly less frequent than in Milton. Nor is there any marked difference as regards substitution of feet, except that the non-initial trochee is more common in Milton than in the others. In two passages of Tennyson the anapaest is found more often than in Milton; in one passage of Browning it occurs more than twice as often.

My reason for selecting Tennyson and Browning as representatives of Modern English verse is not merely that they stand highest in general estimation at the present time, but that they are so sharply contrasted, the one naturally inclining to a strong and masculine realism, apparently careless of sound, and only too happy to startle and shock and puzzle his readers; the other richly ornate, with an almost feminine refinement, and a natural delight in 'linked sweetness long drawn out,' 'deep-chested music, hollow oes and aes,' such as we find in the *Morte d'Arthur* and *Oenone*. It is thus a matter of great interest to observe the different ways in which novelty of rhythm is sought after by each. One which seems to be

peculiarly Tennysonian is the opposition of the metrical to
the verbal division, by which I mean making the words end
in the middle of the feet, as in

> With ro|sy slen|der fin|gers back|ward drew | .

We might describe this as trochaic or feminine rhythm in
opposition to the markedly iambic or masculine rhythm of

> Puts forth | an arm | and creeps | from pine | to pine | .

Other variations from the normal line will be seen in the lines
cited below. It will be noticed that examples of the double
trochee, which was condemned as a monstrosity in Milton, are
to be found occasionally even in Tennyson and are common
enough in Browning.

Gareth. His horse | thereon | stumbled | ay, for | I saw (it.
      0   1   0   1   2 0   1   0   0   1

What ! shall | the shield | of Mark | stand a|mong these ? |
 2   0   0   1   0   2   2   0   0   2
                 —stood

Beauti|ful a|mong lights, | and wa|ving to (him
 2   0 0 0 0   1   0 1   0 1

White hands and courtesy—

Arden. The lit|tle in|nocent soul | flitted | away. |
     0 1 0 1 0 0   1   2 0   0 1

Down at | the far | end of | an av|enue, |
 1   0   0   2   1   0   0 1 0 1

Just where | the prone | edge of | the wood | began. |
 1   0   1   2   0   0   1   0 1

Take your | own time, | Annie, | take your | own time. |
 1   0   2   1   1 0   1   0   2   1

(a line which, according to my reading, is made up of five
trochees).

> 'Then for | God's sake,' | he ans|wered, 'both | our sakes.' |
>   1   0   2   0   0   1   0   2   0   1
>
> He, not | for his | own self | caring, | but her |
> 1   1   0   1   2   1   0   2 0   2

Balin. I thought | the great | tower would | crash down | on both |
     0   1   0   1   2   0   2   1   0 1

Princess. Strove to | buffet | to land | in vain. | A tree | .
        1   0   2 0   0   1   0   1   0 1

Palpi|tated, | her hand | shook, and | we heard | .
 2 0 1 0   0   1   2   0   0   1

Down the | low tur|ret stairs, | palpi|tating |
 1   0   2   0   1   0   2 0 1 0

(The expressive rhythm of the last line is destroyed by the
scansion suggested in *English Lessons* § 138

> Down the | low tur|ret sta|irs pal|pita(ting.)

Balin. Rolling | back up|on Ba|lin crushed | the man | .
     2 0   2   0 0   1 0   2   0   1

Examples of trisyllabic substitution.

Gareth. Camelot, | a ci|ty of shad|owy pal|aces. |
2   0   0   0 1 0   0   1   0   0   1 0 1

         Southward | they set | their fa|ces. The | birds made |
        2   0   0   1   0   1 0   0   2   1

         Melody | on branch ! and mel|ody in | mid air. |
        2 0 0   0   1   0   2 0 0   0   1 1

Princess. Myriads | of riv|ulets hur|rying thro' | the lawn. |
2 0 0   0   1 0 0   1 0 0   1   0 1

         Fluctua|ted as flow|ers in storm, | some red | some pale |
        2 0 1 0   0   1   0   1   1   2   1   2

Harold. Sanguelac, | Sanguelac, | the ar|row, the ar|row! away ! |
2   0 0   2   0 0   0   1 0   0   1 0   0 1

Gareth. And there | were none | but few | goodlier | than he. |
0   1   0   1   0   2 0   0   1

Oenone. And lis|tened, the | full-flow|ing riv|er of speech. |
0 1   0   0   1   1 0   2 0   0   1

         Rests like | a shad|ow, and | the cica|la sleeps. |
        2   0   0   1 0   0   0 1 0   1

Gareth. The hoof | of his horse | slipt in | the stream, | the stream |
0   1   0 0   1   2   0   0   1   0   1

         Descended—

Arden. Then, af|ter a | long tum|ble about | the Cape |
1   1 0 0   1   2   0 0 1   0   1

Harold v. 2.   —We should have a hand

         To grasp | the world | with, and | a foot | to stamp (it

         Flat. Praise | the Saints. | It is o|ver. No | more blood. |
        2   1   0   1   0 0 1 0   1   0   1

Gareth. Bearing | all down | in thy | precip|itancy. |
1 0   1   1   0 0   0 1 0 0 1

         A yet | warm corpse | and yet | unbur|iable. |
        0   1   1   1   0   1   0 1 00 1

         For thou | hast ev|er ans|wered cour|teously. |
        0   1   0   1 0   1   0   1 0 0 1

         Imming|led with | heaven's az|ure wa|veringly |
        0   1   0   0   1   1 0   1   0 0 1

Guinevere. To whom | the lit|tle nov|ice gar|rulously |
0   1   0   1 0   1   0   1   0 0 1

(Tennyson has a peculiar affection for a final anapaest forming part of a word of four or more syllables.)

Gareth. How he | went down, | said Ga|reth, as | a false knight !
2   0   1   2   0   1   0   1   0   1   1

(If this is the proper scansion, it is a remarkable instance of an anapaest in iambic metre with an accent on the 2nd syllable. Cf. a line from *Hamlet* cited at the bottom of p. 201. In anapaestic metre the accent is often overridden.)

         At times | the sum|mit of | the high cit|y flashed !
        0   1   0   1 0   0   0   0 1 0   2

In the lines which follow the trisyllabic feet are perhaps more naturally described as tribrachs than as anapaests, though in some the final short syllable might form part of the following foot.

Gareth.   Para|bles ! Hear | a par|able of | the knave. |
            2 0   0   1   0   1 0 0   0   0   1

            Down the | long av|enues of | a bound|less wood |
            1   0   1   1 0   0   0 0   1   0   1

            Of thine | obe|dience and | thy love | to me |
            0   1   0 1 0 0   0   0   1   0 1

            Thou art | the king|liest of | all kit|chen-knaves |
            1   0   0   1   0 0 0   1   1   0   1

Oenone.   And shoul|der; from | the vi|olet her | light foot |
            0   1   0   1   0 1 0 0   0   1   1

The feminine ending very often consists of a monosyllable

Gareth.   But where|fore would | ye men | should won| der at (you
Oenone.   Crouch'd faw|ning in | the weed. | Most lov|ing is (she ?

sometimes it is part of a tetrasyllable as

            Have all | his pret|ty young | ones ed|uca(ted.
            In sai|lor fash|ion rough|ly ser|moni(zing.

It is rare to have two superfluous syllables at the end of the line, as

Princess.   And lit|tle-foot|ed Chi|na, touched | on Ma(homet.
              But love | and na|ture, these | are two | more ter(rible.

We find an Alexandrine in *Harold*

From child | to child, | from Pope | to Pope, | from age | to age. |

It has been mentioned that modern poets are fond of placing the pause after the uneven syllables. When the preceding syllable is accented, this very much changes the character of the metre, and in Mr and Mrs Browning has the effect at times of a sharp discord, not always resolved by the succeeding harmony. I give here specimens from Tennyson, italicizing the irregular accent.

Princess.   Till the | sun drop | *dead*, from | the signs. | Her voice |
              0   0   2   1   2   0   0   1   0   1

              Choked, and | her fore|head sank | upon | her hands. |
               2   0   1   0   1   0 1   0   1

              Blackened | about | us, bats | *wheeled*, and | owls whooped. |
              2   0   0   1   0   2   1   0   0   2   1

Gareth.   The La|dy of | the Lake | *stood* : all | her dress |
            0   1 0   0   0   1   1   1   0   1

Wept from | her sides, | as wa|ter flow|ing away. |
2   0   0   1   0   1 0   1 0   0 1

A star | *shot* : 'Lo' | , said Ga|reth, 'the | foe falls.' |
0 1   2   1   0   1 0   0   2   1

An owl | *whoopt* : 'Hark | the vic|tor peal|ing there.' |
0   1   2   1   0   1 0   1 0   1

Guinevere. Clung to | the dead | *earth*, and | the land | was still. |
             2   0   0   2   1   0   0   1   0   1

One reason for the irregularity shewn in the lines I have quoted, is doubtless the simple love of novelty and variety; but no attentive reader can have failed to observe that in most instances there is a special appropriateness of the rhythm to the thought, and that the expressiveness of the rhythm is often much assisted by the selection of vowel and consonant sounds, as in

Princess.   —the river sloped

To plunge | in cat|aract shat|tering on | black blocks |
0   2   0   2 0 0   2   0   0   2   2

A breath of thunder—

Morte d'Arthur. Dry clashed | his har|ness in | the i|cy caves |
And bar|ren chas|ms, and all | to left | and right |
The bare | black cliff | clanged round | him, as | he based |
His feet | on juts | of slip|pery crag, | that rang |
Sharp-smit|ten with | the dint | of arm|ed heels : |
And on | a sud|den, lo ! | the lev|el lake, |
And the | long glo|ries of | the win|ter moon. |

Gareth. Her hand | *dwelt* ling|ering|ly on | the latch. |
       0   1   1   2 0 1 0   0   0   1

Linger | with vac|illa|ting obe|dience |
2 0   0   2 0 1 0   0 1   1

Princess.   —the drum

Beat ; mer|rily blow|ing shrilled | the mar|tial fife, |
2   1 0 0   1 0   2   0   1 00 1

And, in | the blast | and bray | of the | long horn |
0   1   0   1   0   1   0 0   1   1

And ser|pent-throa|ted bug|le, un|dula(ted
0   1   0   1   0   1 0   2   0 1

The banner—

        —as when a boat

Tacks, and | the slack|ened sail | *flaps*, all | her voice |
2   0   0   1   0   1   2   1   0   1

Faltering | and flut|tering in | her throat, | she cried
1 0 0   0   1 0 0   0   0   1   0   1

My brother—

Sometimes the effect of the line, as read, though not the metre itself, might be more exactly given by a reference to the more complex classical measures. Thus

Guinevere. Ready | to spring; | waiting | a chance: | for this |
　　　　　　1　0　　0　　1　　1　0　　0　　1　　0　　1

might be described as made up of two choriambs and an iamb
($-\smile\smile-$ | $-\smile\smile-$ | $\smile-$).

Arden.　　The dead | weight of | the dead | leaf bore | it down |
　　　　　　0　1　　2　　0　　0　1　　1　2　　0　1

bacchius, ionic a minore, cretic ($\smile--$ | $\smile\smile--$ | $-\smile-$).

　　　　Then down | the long | street hav|ing slow|ly sto|len
　　　　1　1　　0　1　　1　1　0　　1　0　1

spondee, bacchius, three trochees ($--$ | $\smile--$ | $-\smile$ | $-\smile$ | $-\smile$).

　　　　And glor|ies of | the broad | belt of | the world |
　　　　0　1　0　0　　0　1　　2　0　　0　1

amphibrach, ionic a minore, anapaest ($\smile-\smile$ | $\smile\smile--$ | $\smile\smile-$).

Oenone.　　A fire | dances | before | her, and | a sound |
　　　　　　0　2　　2　0　　0　1　　0　0　　0　1

iamb, trochee, amphibrach, anapaest ($\smile-$ | $-\smile$ | $\smile-\smile$ | $\smile\smile-$).

The only other point which needs illustration is the un-
stopped line, of which the following may be taken as examples.

Guinevere. And saw the queen who sat between her best
　　　　　　Enid, and lissome Vivien, of her court
　　　　　　The wiliest—
Gareth.　　　　　　　　—what stick ye round
　　　　　　The pasty ?
Sisters.　　　　　　　　　　　—I heard
　　　　　　Wheels, and a noise of welcome at the doors.

I proceed to give examples of similar irregularities from
Browning.

Ring and Book.

IV. 180.　　Tracked her | home to | her house-|top, no|ted too |
　　　　　　1　0　　1　0　　0　0　　1　0　　1　1

IV. 830.　　Help a | case the | Archbish|op would | not help |
　　　　　　2　0　　1　0　　0　1　0　　1　　0　1

IV. 868.　　Bless the | fools ! and | 'tis just | this way | they are blessed |
　　　　　　2　0　　2　0　　0　1　　1　1　　0　0　　1

VI. 942.　　God and | man, and | what du|ty I | owe both |
　　　　　　2　0　　2　0　　0　1　0　1　　1　2

VI. 1048.　　Hating | lies, let | not her | believe | a lie |
　　　　　　2　0　　2　0　　1　0　　1　0　2　　0　1

VI. 1443.　　Matu|tinal, | busy | with book | so soon |
　　　　　　1　0　1　0　　1　0　　0　1　　0　1

VI. 1603.　　Leap to | life of | the pale | elec|tric sword |
　　　　　　2　0　　2　0　　0　1　　0　1　0　　1

VI. 1643. Noted | down in | the book | there, turn | and see |
          1 0   1 0   1   2   1   0   1

VI. 1915. One by | one at | all hon|est forms | of life |
          2 0   2   0   2   1   0   1   0 1

VI. 1952. Foes or | friends, but | indis|solub|ly bound |
          2 0   2   0   0 1 0 1 0   1

VI. 2078. She and | I are | mere stran|gers now : | but priests |
          2 0   2 0   1   2   0   1   0   1
          Should study passion—

IV. 36. One calls | the square | round, t'oth|er the | round square |
        1   1   0   2   2   1 0   0   2   2

IV. 303. It all | comes of | God giv|ing her | a child |
        0 1   1   0   1   1 0   0   0   1

IV. 307. Why, thou | exact | prince, is | it a pearl | or no ? |
        1   0   0 1   1   1 0   0   1   0   1

IV. 869. And the | world wags | still, be|cause fools | are sure |
        0   0   2   1   1   0   1   2   0   1

VI. 917. Would that | prove the | first ly|ing tale | was true? |
        0   1   2   0   1 1 0   1   0   1

VI. 1319. That I | liked, that | was the | best thing | she said |
         2 0   2   2   0 0   2   1   0   1

VI. 1642. I heard | charge, and | bore ques|tion and | told tale |
         0 1   2   0   1   0   0   1   1   1

VI. 1876. And silk | mask in | the pock|et of | the gown |
         0 1   1 0   0   1 0   0   0   1

IV. 880. With that | fine can|dour on|ly forth|coming |
        0   1   2   0   1 0   1   2   0

VI. 820. And the way | to end | dreams is | to break | them, stand, |
        0   0   1   0   2   1   0   0   1   0   2
         Walk, go : | then help | me to | stand, walk | and go. |
         2   2   1   2   0   0   2   1   0 1

VI. 1244.   —Much more if stranger men
         Laugh or | frown,—just | as that | were much | to bear |
        1   0   1   1   1   0   2   0   1   0   1

VI. 1859.   —I saved his wife
         Against | law : a|gainst law | he slays | her now |
        0   1   2   0   1   2   1   1   0   1

VI. 427. Hallo, | there's Gui|do, the | black, mean, | and small |
                    0   0   1   1   1   0   1

VI. 481   —'Lent
         Ended,' | I told | friends 'I | shall go | to Rome' |
        1   0   0   1   1   1   0   1   0   1

VI. 5. And know | it again. | Answer | you? Then | that means |
        0   1   0 0 1   1   0   0   1   1   1

VI. 8. Fronting | you same | three in | this ver|y room |
        1   0   0   1   1   0   1   1   0

VI. 12. Laughter, | no lev|ity, noth|ing indec|orous, lords |
        1   0   1   1 0 0   1   0   0 1 0 0   1

(We have the same pronunciation of 'indecorous' in

    Arist. 135. More de|cent yet | indec|orous | enough | .)

VI. 136. In good | part. Bet|ter late | than nev|er, law ! |
        0   1   1   1 0   1   0   1 0   1

VI. 185. In the | way he | called love. | He is the | fool there |
        1   0   0   2   1   2   2 0 0   2   1

VI. 223.   Oldest | now, great|est once, | in my | birth-town |
             2   0   1   2   0   1   0 0   2   1

                Arez|zo, I rec|ognize | no e|qual there. |
                0 1   0   0   1

VI. 383.   Heads that | wag, eyes | that twink|le mod|ified mirth |
             1   0   1   1   0   1 0   1 0 0   1

VI. 92.   I held | so ; you | deci|ded oth|erwise, |
           Saw no | such per|il, there|fore no | such need |

           To stop | song, loos|en flower | and leave | path : Law, |
           0   1   0   1   1 0   1   0   1   1   2

           Law was | aware | and watch|ing—

VI. 1786.   For a wink | of the owl-|eyes of | you. How | miss then |
              0 0   1   0 0   1   1 1   0   1   2   0

VI. 1800.   I' the quag|mire of | his own | tricks, cheats, | and lies |
              0 0   1   0 0   1   2   1   0   1

VI. 120.   Do I speak | ambig|uously? | the glo|ry, I say, |
            0 0   1   0 1 0 0 1   0   2 0   0 1

           And the beau|ty, I say, | and splen|dour, still | say I, |
           0 0   2 0 0 1   0   2   1   0   1

           Who, a | priest, trained | to live | my whole | life long |
           1   0   2   1   0   1   0   2   1   1

           On beau|ty and splen|dour, sole|ly at | their source, |

           God—have | thus recognized my food—
           2   0   1   1

Sometimes the effect to the ear might be indicated, as
before, by a reference to the more complex classical measures,
e.g.

IV. 216.   Lies to | God, lies | to man, | every | way lies |
             2   0   1   2   0   1   1 0   0   2

cretic, cretic, dactyl, long syllable ($-\cup-$ | $-\cup-$ | $-\cup\cup$ | $-$).

VI. 1783.   You blind | guides, who | must needs | lead eyes | that see |
             0   1   1   0   0   1   1   1   0   1

bacchius, ionic a minore, cretic ($\cup--$ | $\cup\cup--$ | $-\cup-$).

VI. 1083.   —Some paces thence
           An inn | stands ; cross | to it ; | I shall | be there |
           0   1   1   1   0 0   1 0   0   1

bacchius, dactyl, choriamb ($\cup--$ | $-\cup\cup$ | $-\cup\cup-$).

The extreme harshness of many of these lines is almost a
match for anything in Surrey, only what in Surrey is helpless-
ness seems the perversity of strength in Browning. The nearest
approach to it in any modern verse is, I think, to be found in
Aurora Leigh. The quotations are from the 2nd edition, 1857.

        p. 16.   Partic|ular worth | and gen|eral miss|ionariness
               0   1 0 0   1   0   1 0 0   1 0   0 1

(The 3rd syllable in the last word is slurred.)

p. 25. As a | soul from | the bod|y, out | of doors |
　　　　1　0　　2　　0　　0　1　0　1　0　1
p. 27. You clap | hands—' a | fair day'— | you cheer | him on |
　　　　1　　2　　1　　0　　2　1　　0　　1　　0　1
p. 29. 　　　　　　　　　　　　　　　　　　　—mount
　　　Step by | step. Sight | goes fast|er ; that | still ray |
　　　1　0　　1　　2　　0　1　0　　1　　1　1
　　　Goes straight—

But though the Aristophanic vein in Browning is continually tempting him to trample under foot the dignity of verse and to shock the uninitiated reader by colloquial familiarities, "thumps upon the back," such as the poet Cowper resented; yet no one can be more impressive than he is, when he surrenders himself to the pure spirit of poetry, and flows onwards in a stream of glorious music, such as that in which Balaustion pictures Athens overwhelmed by an advance of the sea (*Aristophanes' Apology,* p. 2).

> What if thy watery plural vastitude,
> Rolling unanimous advance, had rushed,
> Might upon might, a moment,—stood, one stare,
> Sea-face to city-face, thy glaucous wave
> Glassing that marbled last magnificence,—
> Till fate's pale tremulous foam-flower tipped the grey,
> And when wave broke and overswarmed and, sucked
> To bounds back, multitudinously ceased,
> And land again breathed unconfused with sea,
> Attiké was, Athenai was not now!

And a little below on the hope of immortality :

> Why should despair be? Since, distinct above
> Man's wickedness and folly, flies the wind
> And floats the cloud, free transport for our soul
> Out of its fleshly durance dim and low,—
> Since disembodied soul anticipates
> (Thought-borne as now, in rapturous unrestraint)
> Above all crowding, crystal silentness,
> Above all noise, a silver solitude :—
> 　　*　　　　*　　　　*　　　　*
> O nothing doubt, Philemon! Greed and strife,
> Hatred and cark and care, what place have they
> In yon blue liberality of heaven?

I hardly know whether it is fancy or not, but to me there is no poetry which has such an instantaneous solemnizing power

as that of Browning.   We seem to be in the company of some
rough rollicking Silenus, and all of a sudden the spirit descends
upon him, the tone of his voice changes, and he pours out
strains of sublimest prophecy.   To use his own figure, a sudden
breeze disperses the smoky haze of the crowded city, and in
a moment we are conscious of the ' crystal silentness' of snow-
crowned Alps towering over our heads.   I will close with the
concluding lines of a poem which has always seemed to me
to have this effect in a remarkable degree, *The strange experience of Karshish, the Arab physician.*

> The very God ! think Abib ; dost thou think ?
> So the All-great were the All-loving too,
> So, through the thunder, comes a human voice
> Saying, ' O heart I made, a heart beats here :
> Face, My hands fashioned, see it in Myself.
> Thou hast no power, nor may'st conceive of Mine ;
> But love I gave thee, with Myself to love,
> And thou must love Me, who have died for thee.'

CHAPTER XIV.

SHELLEY'S METRE[1].

WHATEVER may be our views on the substance of some of Shelley's poetry—and I confess that I am sometimes tempted to characterize it by his own line

'Pinnacled dim in the intense inane'—

still I think we must all recognize in him one who had a natural gift of melody such as is hardly to be found in any other English poet, and a boldness and originality in rhythmical experiments, which makes his versification a very interesting field for metrical study.

I propose therefore, in the present paper, to classify the various metres he has employed; to point out any peculiarities in his way of using them, the licenses he allows himself in diverging from the normal line, and finally to make some observations on what constitutes the beauty and appropriateness of his melody.

We have seen that the great majority, at any rate, of English metres can be explained by the assumption of the ascending and descending disyllabic, commonly known as iamb and trochee, and the ascending and descending trisyllabic, commonly known as anapaest and dactyl. The typical or standard line of each pure metre consists of so many perfectly regular feet with a marked pause at the end of the line, but with no other pause, at least none of such a nature as to clash with the metre by dividing the feet. Since a series of such typical lines would be found intolerably monotonous, the

---

[1] Read before the now defunct Shelley Society.

skill of the versifier is shewn by the manner in which he reconciles freedom with law—i.e., by the amount of variety he is able to introduce without destroying the general rhythmical effect. This result is produced (1) by dropping the final pause and introducing other pauses within the line, so as at times quite to overpower the regular metrical flow; (2) by the insertion of extra-metrical syllables at the end or beginning, or in the interior of the line; (3) by truncation—i.e., by dropping unaccented metrical syllables at the end or beginning or in the interior of the line; (4) by changing the number of syllables in the foot, giving trisyllabic for disyllabic feet and *vice versâ*; (5) by changing the position of the accent in the foot, making it ascend instead of descend, and *vice versâ*; (6) by adding to, or diminishing from the regular number of accents—e.g., by substituting spondee or pyrrhic for iamb.

Before dealing with Shelley's verse, I must add a caution as to the condition in which it has come down to us. There is no difficulty in testing Tennyson's verse, because he is evidently attentive even to the smallest details, and we may accept his printed poems as representing exactly what the poet intended; we are not at liberty to explain away an apparent difficulty or awkwardness by ascribing it to a blunder of the printer. But with Shelley it is just the reverse. The poet wrote at headlong speed and with much inaccuracy. As Mr Forman says (Pref. p. XXXII.), "he was often too completely absorbed in the glorious substance of his poetry to give any attention to subordinate points of form": "although his lines are never unrhythmical, the rhyme is often defective and sometimes the metre as well": p. XI. "unfortunately he did not revise, while at press, more than one half the entire bulk of his poetry." "The largest of the volumes seen through the press by himself is infamously printed": p. XV. "the current texts of Shelley are very corrupt." Again, in p. XXII. he speaks of "the extremely confused state of Shelley's MS. note-books and the difficulty of deciphering and connecting their contents." Shelley himself owns to his carelessness in the preface to the *Revolt of Islam*, where he says, "I must request my readers to regard as an erratum the occurrence of an Alexandrine in the middle of one stanza." In his search for this line, Mr Forman came across two such Alexandrines, and also discovered three instances of seven-foot ballad lines in place of Alexandrines, one stanza which had no Alexandrine, and one stanza of ten lines instead of nine, not to mention peculiarities of rhyming of which I shall speak further on. Some negligences have been corrected by the latest editors from a further examination of Shelley's own MSS., some have been happily emended, but there are many which still need correction.

I proceed now to a general survey of Shelley's metres, beginning with the iambic. I use Moxon's one volume edition of 1853, but have consulted the editions of Forman and Rossetti. The iambic line of one foot only occurs in stanzas consisting of lines of various lengths, as in *The Magnetic Lady* (p. 605),

> And brood on thee, but may not blend
> With thine.

Similarly the two-foot iambic occurs in stanzas mixed with longer lines as in *Mutability* (p. 588):—

> To-mor|row dies |

The three-foot is of more frequent use, especially in alternation with four-foot, as in the chorus from *Hellas*:—

> The world's great age begins anew
> The golden years return.

The four-foot line is the first which constitutes whole poems, both continuous, as *Rosalind and Helen* (which admits frequent trochaic or anapaestic substitution and interchanges four with three and five feet), *Ariel to Miranda*, etc.; and discontinuous or stanzaic, as in *Marianne's Dream* (stanzas varying from six to eight lines), p. 380, *When passion's trance* (five-line st.), p. 600, *Mine eyes were dim* (six-line st.), p. 584.

The five-foot is of course the metre most largely employed by Shelley, whether in continuous (blank or rhymed) or stanzaic poems. Of blank verse there are three varieties: Epic, to which *Alastor* and *Queen Mab* may be referred; Tragic,

as in *The Cenci* and *Prometheus*; and Comic or Burlesque, as in
Swellfoot the Tyrant and *The Cyclops*. The continuous rhyming
five-foot was used by Shelley in some of his greatest poems,
*Julian and Maddalo, Epipsychidion, Mont Blanc, Letter to
Maria Gisborne, Ginevra*, etc. Of the discontinuous or stanzaic
five-foot we may distinguish the following kinds : (*a*) the Terza
Rima, examples of which are *Prince Athanase, The Woodman
and Nightingale, Ode to the West Wind*, and *Triumph of Life*;
(*b*) the four-line stanza, of which the earlier *Mutability* (p. 360)
is an instance; (*c*) six-line stanza, *Marenghi* (p. 444), *Hymn
of Apollo* (p. 516), *Evening* (p. 586); (*d*) eight-line stanza,
Witch of Atlas (p. 529), *Zucca* (p. 603), *Hymn to Mercury*
(p. 645), etc.; (*e*) fourteen-lines (sonnet).

We have also stanzas of five- and six-foot mixed; the most
important being the Spenserian of nine lines, the last line alone
containing six feet. To this belong *The Revolt of Islam* and
Adonais. Another of six lines has six feet in the fourth line,
five feet elsewhere (*Lechlade*, p. 359).

We find seven-foot iambic in a chorus of the *Prometheus*,
p. 204 :—

> I sped | like some | swift cloud | that wings ‖ the wide | air's wil|der-
> nes(ses.

This naturally divides after the fourth foot, giving the effect
of two short lines.

Also in *Stanzas*, p. 363 :—

> Thy lover's eye so glazed and cold ‖ dares not entreat thy stay.

I postpone the consideration of the more complex iambic
stanzas, and go on now to classify Shelley's trochaic measures.
By far the most common of these is the truncated four-foot,
in which the *Euganean Hills* (p. 415) is written. This is
continuous. Examples of stanzaic are *Men of England*, four-
line st. (p. 481), *Music when soft voices die* (p. 583), (and for
the most part) *The Masque of Anarchy* (p. 446). We have
a five-line stanza in *Misery*; a six-line stanza of the complete
trochaic in a chorus of *Prometheus* (p. 220) :—

> Life of | Life ! thy | lips en|kindle |
> With their | love the | breath be|tween them |

Truncated six-line is found in *A Dirge* (p. 602):—

> Orphan | hours the | year is | dead ∧

The *Ode to Heaven* (p. 484) is written in a nine-line stanza.

Two-foot trochaic is found rarely and only as a refrain in poems written in longer metres—e.g., in the *Prometheus* (p. 210) we find a four-line stanza of three feet, alternating complete and truncated, followed by two-foot refrain:—

> In the | world un|known ∧
> Sleeps a | voice un|spoken |
> By thy | step a|lone ∧
> Can its | rest be | broken |
> Child of | Ocean |

A mixture of four and three feet is found in the *World's Wanderers* (four-line st. of 4.4.4.3), and in *Rarely, rarely comest thou* (a six-line st. of 4.3.4.3.4.4).

The anapaestic metre is I think that which is most characteristic of Shelley. Here too the four-foot is far the most common. It is continuous in a *Vision of the Sea* (p. 498), *On the Serchio* (p. 594); discontinuous in *The Sensitive Plant* (p. 490), four-line st. Also in *Death* (p. 360) and *Music* (p. 600), both six-line st.

The four-foot is the only unmixed form of the anapaest used by Shelley. *The Fugitives* (p. 582) is written in five-line st., the first four lines containing two feet, the last one: *The keen stars were twinkling* (p. 637) is in stanzas of four triplets, each triplet containing feminine two-foot, feminine three-foot, and masculine one-foot, e.g.:—

> No leaf | will be sha(ken
> Whilst the dews | of your mel|ody scat(ter
> Delight

Combinations of three-foot and two-foot are found in *Are-thusa* (p. 514), *When the lamp is shattered* (p. 606), *One word is too often profaned* (p. 599). Combinations of four-foot, three-foot, two-foot in the *Ode on Liberty* (p. 483), *The Cloud* (p. 502), also in *Pan* (p. 517).

Combinations of four-foot and two-foot are found in *The Two Spirits* (p. 519); *To-night* (p. 580), which is also affected by internal truncation; *Enchantress*, an unfinished drama (p. 609). In *Autumn* (p. 549) we have a combination of 4.2.1.

The most striking of the Mixed metres is *The Skylark* (p. 504), a five-line stanza, the first four lines being three-foot trochaic, either masculine or feminine, and the fifth line an Alexandrine masc. or fem.

Similes (p. 482) is written in a five-line stanza; the three first stanzas are four-foot trochaic truncated, the fourth and last stanza iambic four-foot.

Trochaic passes into iambic and anapaestic in *The Four Voices of Prom.* Act I. (p. 189), also in *Love's Philosophy* (p. 507).

Iambic and anapaestic are mixed in the very irregular stanzas beginning, "Away, the moor is dark" (p. 363), in *Constantia* (p. 384), in *Lines from the Arabic* (p. 579), *A Dirge* (p. 622), *An Indian Air* (p. 599). In *The Death of Napoleon* (p. 587) the first six lines of the eight-line stanza are anapaestic, the last two iambic.

I now proceed to examine the licenses to be found in Shelley's use of these metres, and we will begin (A) with the variety produced by his use of the pause, and (*a*) with the omission of the final pause. Even Dr Guest would not insist on an actual stop at the end of the line, so I will merely give instances of *Enjambement*, which we may classify as follows:—

(1) *Cases where the end of the line separates the object noun or the subordinate verb from the governing verb.*

Prom. p. 208:
> Oh lift
> ⁀Thine eyes, that I may see his written soul.

Cenci, p. 269 :
> I. know you are my friend, and all I dare
> ⁀Speak to my soul, that will I trust with thee.

But this is not confined to dramatic metres, where we

naturally look for more freedom. It is frequent also in stanzaic metre—e.g., *The Triumph of Life.*

Azure plumes of Iris had
⌣ Built high | over | her wind-|wingèd | pavil(ion

[So I think we must divide, in order to keep the rhyme with the preceding "vermilion." Otherwise I should have been disposed to make "pavilion" a trisyllable with the stress on the first syllable.]

Zucca, p. 604 :

I bore it to a chamber and I planted
⌣ It in a vase full of the lightest mould.

Sometimes we find this close connexion between two distinct stanzas, as in *Liberty* (p. 513), where st. 18 ends—

The solemn harmony

the verb coming in st. 19—

⌣ Paused.

Mercury (p. 652), where st. 40 ends

Not less her subtle swindling baby, who

and 41 begins—

⌣ Lay swathed in his sly smile.

So in *Triumph*, p. 634 :

(The new vision)
With solemn speed and stunning music crost
⌣ The forest ——

We may compare with this the coupling of the end of one paragraph with the beginning of another by means of rhyme, as in p. 556, *air—dare*, and often.

(2) *Preposition separated from its case.*

Prom. p. 238 :

Two visions of strange radiance float upon
⌣ The ocean-like enchantment of strong sound.

Cenci, p. 268 :

I have presented it and backed it with
⌣ My earnest prayers and urgent interest.

p. 289 :

It sleeps over
⌣ A thousand daily acts disgracing men.

p. 290 :   I break upon your rest.   I must speak with
    ⌣ Count Cenci.

p. 291 :   Bernar|do, conduct | you the | Lord Legate to
    ⌣ Your father's chamber.

Alastor, p. 60 :

> (The parasites)
> Starred with ten thousand blossoms flow around
> ⌣ The grey trunks.

(3)   *Adjective or pronoun from its noun.*

Hellas, p. 331 :

> The roar of giant cannon, the earth-quaking
> ⌣ Fall of vast bastions and precipitous towers.

Triumph of L. p. 634 :

> Some upon the new
> ⌣ Embroidery of flowers that did enhance
> ⌣ The grassy vesture of the desert, played.

Adonais, p. 571 :

> A drear
> ⌣ Murmur between their songs is all the woodmen hear.

p. 632 :   She gli|ded along | the riv|er and | did bend (her
    ⌣ Head under the dark boughs.

So even in the purest lyric poetry, as *Skylark*—

> Soothing her love-laden
> ⌣ Soul, in secret hour.

(4)   *Genitive from governing case.*

Prom. p. 227 :

> And the | life-kind|ling shafts | of the | keen sun's
>   1   0   1   2
> ⌣ All-piercing bow.

Triumph, p. 636 :

> The ac|tion and | the shape | without | the grace
> ⌣ Of life.

(5)   *Line ends with conjunction.*

Cenci, p. 280 :

> I see Orsino has talked with you, and
> ⌣ That you conjecture things too horrible.

(6)   *Division between qualifying adverb and word qualified.*

Julian, p. 426 :

> We are even
> ⌣ Now at the point I meant, said Maddalo.

Triumph, p. 636:

Others more

⌣ Humble, like falcons, sat upon the fist.

Islam, p. 170:

An atmosphere which quite

⌣ Arrayed | her in | its beams, | tremulous | and soft | and bright.

(*b*) As we find the chief normal pause disregarded, so we find strong pauses intruded within the feet in such a manner as quite to break the normal rhythm. Thus in the middle of the *first foot*—

Prom. p. 201:

A Worse things unheard, unseen, remain behind.
B Worse?

A In | each hu|man heart | terror | survives |

Alastor, p. 64:

Not a star

⌣ Shone, not a sound was heard; the very winds,
Danger's grim playmates, on that precipice
⌣ Slept, clasped in his embrace.

Prom. p. 190:

I feel

⌣ Faint, like one mingled in entwining love.

p. 198:   Cruel was the power which called
⌣ You, or | aught else | so wretched into light.

p. 204: Beholdst thou not two shapes | from the east | and west |
⌣ Come, as two doves to one beloved nest.

p. 216:   On the race of men
First famine and then toil and then disease,
Strife, wounds and ghastly death unseen before
Fell.

p. 223: Even as a vulture and a snake outspent
Drop, twisted in inextricable fight.

p. 224:   The ponderous hail
Beats on his struggling form, which sinks at length
Prone.

p. 230: Well, my path lately lay through a great city.

W. of Atlas, p. 529:

Her hair

⌣ Dark, the | dim brain | whirls dizzy with delight.

Liberty, p. 507:

(Liberty)

Scattering contagious fire into the sky,
⌣ Gleamed.

Hellas, p. 331:

> Earth and ocean,
> Space, and the isles of life or light that gem.

Cenci, p. 308:

> Dead! The | sweet bond | broken. They come! Let me
> ‿ Kiss those warm lips.

Stop in the middle of the second foot.

Epipsych. p. 558:

> Then I | 'Where?' The | world's e|cho ans|wered 'Where?'

p. 555: Stains the | dead, blank, | cold air | with a | warm shade |

Julian, p. 432:

> making moments *be*
> As mine | seem—each | an im|mortal|ity | .

p. 427:

> "We aspire,
> How vain|ly! to | be strong," | said Mad|dalo | .

Prom. p. 219:

> The coursers fly
> Terri|fied; watch | its course | among | the stars | .

Cenci, p. 307: You do | well, tel|ling me | to trust | in God | .

p. 278: Or I | will—God | can un|derstand | and par(don.

Triumph, p. 630: Of peo|ple, and my | heart sick | of one | sad thought |
0   0   1   1   2   1   1   1

Similarly in four-foot iambic—

p. 407:   A sweet | sleep: so | we trav|elled on |

Stop in the middle of third foot.

p. 425: Meanwhile | the sun | paused, ere | it should | alight
Over the horizon of the mountains——

p. 278: Give us | clothes, fa|ther. Give | us bet|ter food | .

p. 279: My wrongs | were then | less. That | word par|ricide | ,
Although I am resolved, haunts me like fear.

p. 301: Between | the sly, | fierce, wild | regard | of guilt |

p. 272: Thou art | Lucre|tia: I | am Be|atrice.

p. 262: Who art | a tor|turer ! Fa|ther nev|er dream |

[Here the pause comes after the two short syllables of
an anapaest substituted for the third iambic.]

p. 257: To whom | I owe | life, and | these vir|tuous thoughts | .

p. 628: Were or | had been | eyes:—if | thou canst, | forbear |
2   1

p. 631: Of the | young year's | dawn, I | was laid | asleep |
1   1   1   1

Stop in the middle of fourth foot.

p. 277 : How! have | you ven|tured thith|er ? Know | you them ? |
p. 280 :   On whose edge
   Devour|ing dark|ness hov|ers.   Thou | small flame |
p. 304 :   Would that thou hadst been
   Cut out | and thrown | to dogs | first! To | have killed |.
   My father——
p. 308 : Blind light|ning or | the deaf | sea ; not | with man. |
Islam, p. 161 :

   An angel bright as day waving a brand,
   Which flashed | among | the stars, | passed. "Dost | thou
    stand |
   Parleying with me, thou wretch," the king replied.

Stop in the middle of the last foot.

p. 307 : How te|dious, fal se | and cold | seem all | things! I |
   Have met with much injustice in this world.
Prom. p. 223 :
   No pit|y, no | relief, | no res|pite ! Oh |
   That thou wouldst make my enemy my judge.
p. 213 : (A howl)
   Satiates | the lis|tening wind, | contin|uous, vast, |
   Awful, as silence.

[Here the pause comes after the two short syllables of an anapaest substituted for fifth foot.]

(B) I take next the irregularity arising from the addition of extra-metrical syllables, and first at the end of the line, the feminine rhythm. In Orsino's soliloquy (p. 258) it is found in twelve out of twenty-seven lines. This is common in all metres which properly end in an accented syllable, as in four-foot iambic.

   A bright|er Hel|las rears | its moun(tains.

Feminine rhythm is also found in anapaestic metres, as—

Four-foot—

   Over earth | and o|cean with gen|tle mo(tion.

Three-foot—

   And laugh | as I pass | in thun(der.

The less usual forms are (*a*) when the superfluous syllable is a separate word, ordinarily a pronoun, as *it, me, us, you, him, them, her*; also *not*, as in *The Cenci* (p. 254):—

> It is a public matter, and I care (not

art, as in *The Cenci* (p. 304):—

> To me or mine; and what a tyrant thou (art.

too, as in *Faust* (p. 701):—

> My pathos certainly would make you laugh (too.

(*b*) when there are two superfluous syllables instead of one, as

Cenci, p. 266:

> Nor that young imp, whom ye have taught by rote,
> Parri|cide with | his al|phabet, | nor Gia(como.

p. 289:

> But I | was bol|der, for | I chid | Olymp(io.

p. 294:

> Will Gia|como be | there? Orsino? Mar(zio?

Faust, p. 711:

> Until | some leech | diverted with | his grav(ity.

Swellfoot, p. 353:

> This mag|nanim|ity in | your sa|cred maj(esty.

Cyclops, p. 679:

> By Jove | you are. | I bore | you off | from Dar(danus.

(*c*) In Shakespeare we sometimes find a superfluous syllable in the middle of the line. Are we to admit these superfluous syllables in Shelley? Take a line such as that in *The Cenci* (p. 301):—

> To rend and ruin. What say ye now, my Lords?

Here the line is divided between two speakers, and it might be thought that the pause must prevent the superfluous syllable of the former half being joined with the syllables which follow, so as to make up an anapaestic foot. But we have seen that Shelley has no objection to divide the foot by a full stop, and in *A Vision of the Sea* (p. 498) we frequently find the first syllable of the anapaest thus separated from the other syllables—e.g.—

> 'Tis the ter|ror of tem|pest. The rays | of the soul | .
> Leave the wind | to its ech|o. The ves|sel now tossed |

In fact out of thirty-one internal full stops (i.e. stops not at the end of the line) I find that seventeen follow the first syllable of an anapaest, five the second syllable, and nine only come at the end of the foot.

The strongest case for the extra syllable at the hemistich is in the irregular stanzas beginning " Away ! the moor is dark " (p. 363), of which I shall speak further on.

(*d*) The superfluous syllable may appear at the beginning of the line in metres which have the stress on the first syllable of the foot—viz., trochaic and dactylic. I find no proper dactylic metre in Shelley, but the *anacrusis* is very common in his four-foot trochaics, just as initial truncation is in his four-foot iambics. Perhaps it is to break the monotony of the " butterwoman's rate to market," that from the time of Shakespeare and Milton it has been customary to allow these liberties in disyllabic measures of four feet. Thus the *Euganean Hills* has thirty-seven lines beginning with superfluous syllables out of a total of 373—i.e., one-tenth. Three of these thirty-seven have two superfluous syllables, giving the appearance of an anapaestic line, as

> Of the) olive-sandalled Apennine,

where the omission of the first two syllables restores the regular truncated four-foot trochaic. In the other examples one additional syllable gives the effect of a four-foot iambic, as

> Ay) many flowering islands lie.

So also in three-foot, as the *Skylark*, after

> Chorus | hymen|eal |

we have

> What) objects | are the | fountains |

(c) We go on next to consider the license of truncation. This occurs at the end of metres which end in an unaccented syllable, and at the beginning of those which begin with an unaccented syllable. Thus the alternate trochaic lines in the

Ode to a Skylark are generally complete, but we have inter-mixed with them

> All the | earth is | bare ∧
> Teach us | sprite or | bird ∧

On the other hand the anapaestic line not only continually substitutes an iamb for an anapaest, thus dropping one of its unaccented syllables, but at the beginning of the line it may drop both—e.g. :—

> ∧ Leaps | on the back | of my sai|ling rack |

which is just as legitimate as

> May have bro|ken the woof | of my tent's | thin roof |

So in two-foot anapaest (p. 233)—

> ∧ Spec|tres we |
> Of the dead | hours be |

And so the four-foot iambic. Of ninety lines in the *Ariel to Miranda* one-third suffer initial truncation. In *Rosalind and Helen* the proportion is about one-twentieth. This is found also in mixed metres, as *The Magnetic Lady*, which begins—

> ∧ Sleep | sleep on | forget thy | pain |
> My hand is on thy brow.

In *The Ode to Naples* (p. 545)—

> Of some | ether|eal host |
> ∧ Whilst | from all | the coast |

Perhaps the stanzas to *Night* should be regarded as on the whole anapaestic, but in any case many of the lines are iambic, among which we find truncated two-foot.

> ∧ Star-|inwrought.
> ∧ Wouldst | thou me.

Besides this initial truncation, we also meet with medial truncation in some of the more irregular poems—e.g., the one just cited, p. 580—

> Thy broth|er Death | ∧ came | and cried |

which corresponds to

Thy sweet | child Sleep, | the fil|my-eyed |

p. 466 : So good ; and bad | ∧ sane | and mad |

p. 194 : Wail, howl | aloud | ∧ Land | and Sea |

The Earth's | rent heart | shall ans|wer ye |

p. 393 : ∧ Day | and night | ∧ day | and night |

So in the trochaic *Dirge* (p. 602)—

Come and | sigh ∧ | come and | weep ∧

which corresponds to

For the | year is | but a|sleep ∧

(D) It might be considered an extension of this principle, of the insertion or omission of extra-metrical syllables, when Shelley gives in one line a whole foot more, or less, than is required by the metre as shewn in the rest of the poem; but it is perhaps more convenient to defer this for the present, and proceed to the variety caused by increasing or diminishing the number of unaccented syllables within the foot—e.g., by substituting anapaest for iamb, or iamb for anapaest. I find that in five-foot iambic this change takes place rarely in the first foot and most frequently in the fifth foot, the numbers being, out of 165 cases noted, nine in first, thirty-eight in second, forty-three in third, twenty in fourth, and fifty-five in fifth foot. I give the following examples :—

First foot.

Prom. p. 192 :

Of a fal|len pal|ace. Moth|er let | not aught |
0   0   1

p. 220 : The inan|imate winds | enam|oured of | thee ? List |
0   0 1 0 0   1

Second foot.

p. 224 : Prone. And | the ae|real ice | clings o|ver it |
2   0   0 0 1 0 0   1   1   1

Alastor, p. 55 :

That beau|tiful shape. | Does the | dark gate | of death |
0 0   1   1   0   1   0

p. 62 : And mu|sical mo|tions. Calm | he still | pursued |
0 0   1

p. 438 : Aspi|ring like one | who loves | too fair | too far |
0   0   1

p. 298 : As mer|ciful God | spares e|ven the damned. | Speak now |
0 0   1   0   0   1

Third foot.

Cenci, p. 307:

I am | cut off | from the on|ly world | I know |
$\qquad\qquad$ 0 $\qquad$ 0 $\qquad$ 1

Alastor, p. 58:

Of O|cean's moun|tainous waste | to mu|tual war |
$\qquad\qquad$ 0 $\quad$ 0 $\quad\quad$ 1 $\qquad\qquad$ 0 0 $\quad$ 1

Cenci, p. 278:

Under | the pen|ury heaped | on me | by thee |
$\qquad\qquad$ 0 $\;$ 0 $\qquad$ 1

Fourth foot.

Prom. 205:

Or sink | into | the orig|inal gulf | of things |
$\qquad\qquad$ 0 $\quad\;$ 0 1 0 0 $\qquad$ 1

Fifth foot.

Cenci, p. 265:

Then it | was I | whose in|artic|ulate words |
$\qquad\qquad\qquad\qquad\qquad$ 0 $\quad$ 0 $\qquad$ 1

p. 267:$\quad$ Is pen|etra|ted with | the in|solent light |
$\qquad\qquad\qquad\qquad\qquad$ 0 $\quad$ 0 $\qquad$ 1

From thrice|-driven beds | of down | and del|icate food |
$\qquad\qquad$ 0 $\quad$ 0 $\qquad$ 1 $\qquad\qquad\qquad$ 0 0 $\quad$ 1

Alastor, p. 55:

The el|oquent blood | told an | inef|fable tale |
$\qquad\qquad$ 0 $\;$ 0 $\qquad$ 1 $\qquad$ 1 $\;$ 0 $\qquad$ 0 0 $\quad$ 1

Cenci, p. 277:

You hear | but see | not an | impet|uous tor(rent.
$\qquad\qquad\qquad\qquad\qquad\qquad$ 0 0 $\quad$ 1

So in the four-foot iambic

p. 211:$\quad$ Sick with | sweet love | droops, dy|ing away |
$\qquad\qquad\qquad\qquad\qquad\qquad\qquad$ 0 $\quad$ 0 $\;$ 1

The converse (anapaest into iamb) is still more common.
Indeed, anapaestic lines usually have one or more iambs. Thus
in the four feet of *The Sensitive Plant* two are generally
iambs—e.g.—

A sen|sitive plant | in a gar|den grew |

sometimes three—e.g.—

The snow|drop and then | the vi|olet |
$\qquad\qquad$ 0 $\qquad$ 0 $\qquad$ 1

or even four—e.g.—

Into | the rough | woods far | aloof |
Make her | atten|dant an|gels be |

and so in *The Cloud*—

Whom mor|tals call | the moon |

contrasted with

> While I sleep | in the arms | of the blast |

As iamb spreads into anapaest, so trochee into dactyl—
e.g., the *Euganean Hills*.

> Many a | green isle | needs must | be ∧
> 1 0   0
>
> Or the | mariner | worn and | wan ∧
>   1 0 0

p. 447 :
> Like a bad | prayer not | over|loud ∧
> 1   0   0
>
> Whispering | thou art | Law and | God ∧
> 1   0 0

p. 454 :
> Echoing | from the | cave of | fame ∧
> 1 0 0
>
> Those who a|lone thy | towers be|hold ∧
> 1   0   0
>
> On the | beach of a | northern | sea ∧
>   1   0   0
>
> Many|-domed | Padua | proud ∧
>   1 0 0

p. 198 :
> It will | burst in | bloodier | flashes |
>   1 0 0

p. 447 :
> Of the | triumph of | anar|chy ∧
>   1   0   0

p. 200 :
> Drops of | bloody | agony | flow ∧
>   1 0 0

(E) The next variety is that produced by inversion of accent, giving iamb for trochee, etc. All metrists allow that the trochee may take the place of the iamb in the first foot of blank verse, but it is strange how they object to it else-where. Shelley uses it in any part of the line; and even has two trochees together. I will give examples of all positions but the first.

Second foot.

Question, p. 518 :
> And wild | roses | and i|vy ser|pentine |
>   1   0

Prom. p. 242 :
> The un|quiet | repub|lic of | the maze |
> 1 0   0   0

p. 240 :
> And weed|-over|grown con|tinents | of earth |
> 1   0

[In these two the trochee forms part of the same word with the preceding syllable.]

Alastor, p. 52:

When night | makes a | weird sound | of its | own still(ness
                1   0   1   1   0   0

The lone | couch of | his ev|erlas|ting sleep |
             1   0

p. 58 : With fierce | gusts and | precip|ita|ting force |
                       2   0

p. 65 : With bright | flowers, and | the win|try boughs | exhale |
                       1   0

p. 60 : The grey | trunks, and | as game|some in|fants' eyes |
                    2   0

Prom. p. 200:

And beasts | hear the | sea moan | in in|land caves |
   1   0   2   2

Cenci, p. 300:

And art | thou the | accu|ser? If thou ho(pest
           2   0

p. 258 : In all | this there | is much exag|gera(tion.
             1   0

Third foot.

p. 264 : Until | this hour | thus you | have ev|er stood |
                  1   0

p. 266 : Whom in | one night | merci|ful God | cut off |
                               1   0

p. 268 : I who | have white | hairs, and | a tot|tering bo(dy
                 1   0   0   0   1

Will keep | at least | blameless | neutral|ity. |
                        1   0

p. 269 : I am | as one | lost in | a mid|night wood |
                          1   0

p. 273 : Is like | a ghost | shrouded | and fol|ded up |
                             1   0

p. 274 : For thy | decree | yawns like | a hell | between |
                             2   0

p. 275 : To--why | his late | outrage | to Be|atrice |
                              2   0

p. 308 : Dead! The | sweet bond | broken | . They come | . Let me|
            2   0   1   1   2 0

p. 309 : Be as | a mark | stamped on | thine in|nocent brow |
                          2   0   0 0   1

p. 56 : Beneath | the cold | glare of | the des|olate night |
                             2   0   0 0   1

p. 554 : Young Love | should teach | Time in | his own | grey style |
                                     1   0   1   1

p. 632 : Out of | the deep | cavern | with palms | so ten(der
                             1   0

Also in the four-foot line—

p. 388 : A sound | from thee | Rosa|lind dear |
                               1   0

Fourth foot.

p. 244 : Which points | into | the heavens | dreaming | delight |
                                             1   0

p. 277: Are now | no more | as once | parent | and child |
                                       1   0

p. 279: Although | I am | resolved, | haunts me | like fear |
                                      2   0

p. 280: Which as | a dy|ing pulse | rises | and falls |
                                    2 0

       It is | the soul | by which | mine was | arrayed |
                                       1   0

p. 284: Of pub|lic scorn | for acts | blazoned | abroad |
                                     2   0

p. 304: Cut out | and thrown | to dogs | first. To | have killed |
                                        1   0

p. 309: And let | mild pit|ying thoughts | lighten | for thee |
                                         1   0

Faust, p. 711:

       Unheard | of. Then | leave off | teasing | us so |
                                       2   0

Alastor, p. 51:

       Of star|ry ice; | the grey | grass and | bare boughs |
                         1   0   1   1

Prom. p. 187:

       Ah me | alas | Pain, pain | ever | for ev(er
                  2   2   2 0

p. 196: With bit|ter stings | the light | sleep of | revenge |
                                        1   0

p. 240: Which whirl | as the | orb whirls | swifter | than thought |
                     0   0   1   1   2   0

Fifth foot (this is naturally the rarest).

p. 190: I break | upon | your rest | I must | speak with |
       Count Cenci.
                                             1   0

p. 279: What out|rage? *That* | she speaks | not, but | you may |
       Conceive | such half | conjec|tures as | I do |
       From her fixed paleness—
                                                    2   1
                                            2   1

p. 278: I will—| rever|sing na|ture's law |—Trust me, |
       The com|pensa|tion which | thou seek|est here |
       Will be | denied |
                                               2   1

p. 544: And heard | the autum|nal winds | like light | footfalls |
                                                     2   1

p. 260: Check the | aban|doned vil|lain. For | God's sake |
                                              2   1

I now give examples of two or more trochees in the same
line.

p. 300: If thou | hast done | murders | made thy | life's path |
                             2   0   1   0   1   1

p. 201: Worse? in | each hu|man heart | terror | survives |
        2   0   2 0

p. 217: Godlike, | o'er the | clear bil|lows of | sweet sound |
        1   0   1   0   1   1   0   0   1   1

p. 428: Of those | on a | sudden | who were | beguiled |
        1   0   1 0

[but here I am inclined to think that *who* has got out of its place and should come after *those*. It is certainly a harsher line than that which Rossetti would emend by transposing 'plumes' and 'feathers':

> p. 230: Its plumes | are as | feathers | of sun|ny frost |

Another instance of the same kind occurs in p. 265, where a verse might be eked out with a double trochee—

> Fell from | my lips, | who with | totter|ing steps |

but I think the line gains greatly in vigour if we insert *I* before 'who.']

Mt Blanc, p. 367:

> Over | its rocks | ceaseless|ly bursts | and raves |
> 1 0   1   0

Liberty, p. 508:

> The sis|ter-pest, | congre|gator | of slaves |
> 2   0 1 0

Islam, p. 171:

> Not death |—death was | no more | refuge | or rest |
> 2   0   1   0

Epips. p. 561:

> Light it | into | the win|ter of | the tomb |
> 1   0 1 0   0   0

> p. 565: Harmo|nizing | silence | without | a sound |
> 2   0 1 0   1   0

> p. 424: Harmo|nizing | with sol|itude | and sent |
> 2   0 1 0

> p. 64: In thy | devas|tating | omni|potence |
> 2   0 1 0

> p. 632: And as | I looked | the bright | omni|presence |
> 1 0 1   0

> p. 555:   —one intense
> Diffu|sion, one | divine | omni|presence |

[I have put these five together, as it is possible that Shelley may have intended to alter the usual pronunciation of the quadrisyllables, laying the stress in the second syllable of *omnipresence, devastating*, and perhaps on the last of *harmonizing*.]

Cyclops, p. 666:

> And so | we sought | you king. | We were | sailing |
> 1   0   1 0

[Rossetti would insert 'then' after 'we.']

Calderon, p. 687:

> God is | one su|preme es|sence, one | pure es(sence
> 2   0   2 0   1   1   1   1

p. 698 : Only | by not | owning | thyself | subdued |
1 0   1 0

Faust, p. 705 :

Here the | light burns | soft as | the enkind|led air |
1 0   1   1   1 0   0 0 1

p. 710 : So is | the world | drained to | the dregs. | Look here |
1 0   1   0   1   1

It will be noticed that several of these are parallels to Milton's line which has been so fiercely attacked—

Uni|versal | reproach | far worse | to bear |
1 0   1 0

I go on now to give examples of inversion of accent in the trochaic line, not only in the first foot, as in—

The blue | deep thou | wingest |
0   1   2   0

p. 481 : The forced | produce | of your | toil ∧
0   1

p. 447 : The hired | murderers | who did | sing ∧
0   1

p. 454 : The old | laws of | England | they ∧
0   1

p. 455 : Will point | at them | as they | stand ∧
0   1

Shall steam | up like | inspi|ration |
0   1

p. 415 : And sinks | down down | like that | sleep ∧
0   1   1   1

To find | refuge | in dis|tress ∧
0   1

p. 421 : The frail | bark of | this lone | being |
0   1

but also in the second foot as—

p. 450 : Casts to | the fat | dogs that | lie ∧
0   1

Prom. p. 194 :

Trampling | the slant | winds on | high ∧
0   1

p. 612 : Sit by | the fire|side of | sorrow |
0   1

Third foot.

p. 199 : Vomits | smoke in | the bright | air ∧
0   1

p. 451 : Household | dogs when | the wind | roars ∧
0   1

As far as my memory goes, Shelley was the first to use this inversion of the trochee.

Similarly in anapaestic metre we sometimes find a dactyl substituted for an anapaest, as—

Vision of Sea, p. 501 :

Tremulous | with soft in|fluence exten|ding its tide |
1   0   0

(F) We have treated separately of the extension of the unaccented syllables and the inversion of the accent in the foot—but these variations may be combined, as in the use of the dactyl for the iamb. Examples of this are—

In the first foot, where it is most frequent.

p. 272: Misery | has killed | its fa|ther, yet | its fa(ther
      1 0 0

p. 292: Desperate|ly fight|ing. What | does he | confess |
        1 0 0

p. 628: Fallen as | Napo|leon fell | —I felt | my cheek |
      1 0 0

p. 255: Flattering | their se|cret peace | with o|ther's gain |
      1 0 0

p. 53: Many a | wide waste | and tan|gled wil|derness |
      1 0 0   1   1

p. 58: Following | his ea|ger soul | the wan|derer |
      1 0 0

p. 188: Shuddering | through In|dia. Thou | sere|nest air |
      1   0 0   0 0   1

p. 624: Numerous | as gnats | upon | the ev|ening gleam |
      1 0 0

p. 213: Satiates | the list|ening wind |, contin|uous, vast |
      1 0 0   0 0   1

In the second foot (rare).

p. 58: Of wave | ruining | on wave | and blast | on blast |
           2 0 0

In the third foot.

p. 299: That ev|er came | sorrowing | upon | the earth |
                    1 0 0

p. 544: Around | me gleamed | many a | bright se|pulchre |
                    1 0 0

p. 306: And threw | behind | muttering | with hoarse | harsh voice |
                    1 0 0   1   1

p. 53: Of pearl | and thrones | radiant | with chrys|olite |
                    1 0 0

p. 522: Instruments | for plans | nautical | and stat|ical |
      1 0 0   1 0 0

p. 629: Frederic | and Paul | Catharine | and Le|opold |
      1 0 0   1 0 0

p. 635: And oth|ers sat | chattering | like rest|less apes |
                    1 0 0

p. 557: Evil | from good | misery | from hap|piness |
               1 0 0

Also in the four-foot line, e.g.—

p. 409: You might see | the nerves | quivering | within
      0   0   1   1 0 0

(And in p. 410)

In the fourth foot.

p. 298: Guards lead | him not | away. | Cardinal | Camil(lo
1 0 0

p. 213: And call | truth vir|tue love | genius | or joy |
1 0 0

p. 631: Was filled | with ma|gic sounds | woven in|to one |
1 0   0

p. 364: The broad | and burn|ing moon | lingering|ly rose |
1 0 0

(G) The last mode of varying the metre which I specified was the adding to, or taking from, the number of accents in the foot. This, like most of the other licenses which we have been considering, has been condemned by Dr Guest and other metrists, so that it becomes necessary to give a few instances, in order to shew that Shelley at all events practised it. It is however so common that the exception is to find a line which does not contain feet with either no accent or more than one accent. Thus—

p. 255: The dry | fixed eye|-ball, the | pale quiv|ering lip |
1   1   0   0   1   1

has two spondees and one pyrrhic, altogether six instead of five accents.

p. 240: Which whirl | as the | orb whirls | swifter | than thought |
0   1   0 0   1   1   1 0   0   1

one spondee, one trochee, one pyrrhic.

p. 57: At par|ting and | watch, dim | through tears | the path |
0   1 0   0   1   1   0   1   0   1

one spondee and one pyrrhic.

p. 200: Of the | good Ti|tan as | storms tear | the deep |
0   0   1   1 0 0   1   1   0   1

two spondees and two pyrrhics.

P. 258, after normal line—

    Poor la|dy *she* | expects | some hap|py change

follows—

    In his | dark spir|it from | this act |, *I* none |
0 0   1   1 0 0   1   1   2 2

where there are two pyrrhics and three spondees, not a single iamb.

p. 204: Their soft | smiles light | the air | like a | star's fire |
1   1   1   0   1   1

two spondees, one trochee.

p. 302: And, hold|ing his | breath, died | . There re|mains noth(ing
        0   0   1   1   0   0   1   1

two spondees, two pyrrhics.

p. 545: Over | the orac|ular woods | and div|ine sea |
        1 0   0 0 1 0 0   1   0   0 1 1

two anapaests, one trochee, one pyrrhic, one spondee, not a single iamb.

Even when there are three syllables to the foot the accent is sometimes omitted, making a tribrach, e.g.—

p. 253: Bought per|ilous | impu|nity with | your gold |
       1   1 0 0   0 1 0 0   0   0   1

p. 254: Your des|perate and | remorse|less man|hood now |
          0 0 0

p. 273: That faith | no ag|ony shall | obscure | in me |
      1   1   1 1 0 0   0

p. 288: A dark | contin|uance of | the hell | within (him
             0 0 0

p. 289: And Mar|zio be|cause thou | wast on|ly awed |
          0 0 0 1   1

p. 303: Are cen|turies of | high splen|dour laid | in dust |
        0 0 0

p. 59: With the | breeze mur|muring in | the mu|sical woods |
      0   0   1   1   0 0 0   0   1 0 0   1

p. 187: Made mul|titu|dinous with | thy slaves, | whom thou |
           0 0   0

p. 176: And like | the ref|luence of | a migh|ty wave |
             0 0 0

It is much more rare to find two accents in a trisyllabic substitute for an iamb, but the following seem to begin with a cretic.

p. 368: Pile around | it ice | and rock, | broad vales | between |
       1 0 1

p. 369: Slowly rol|ling on | , there man|y a prec|ipice |
       1 0 1

The strong rhythm of the anapaest is more capable of overriding verbal accent and logical emphasis than the more flexible iambic, and its character is in consequence less modified by any collision between the metrical and the natural stress. It is thus not uncommon to find in Shelley a natural cretic forced to act as a metrical anapaest, e.g.—

p. 236: And a thick | hell of hat|reds and hopes | and fears |
           1 0 2

p. 499: The intense | thunder-balls | which are rain|ing from heav(en
             1 0 2

Have shat|tered its mast | and it stands | black and riv(en
                  1   0   2

p. 499 : But sev|en remained. | Six the thun|der had smit(ten
                 1   0   2

p. 501 : Round sea|birds and wrecks | paved with heaven's | azure smile |
                               1   0   2   1 0   2

p. 503 : The volca|noes are dim | and the stars | reel and swim |
                                   1 0   2

p. 517 : Gods and men | we are all | delu|ded thus |
          1   0   2

p. 503 : Till the calm | rivers lakes | and seas |
                   1 0   2

p. 237 : And Love, | Thought and Breath |
                 1   0   2

p. 237 : From the new | world of man |
                1   0   2

p. 214 : Death despair | , love sor(row
          1   0 2   1   2

So too a bacchius or even a molossus is at times pressed into service as an anapaest, e.g.—

p. 583 : The best love|liest and last |
           0   1   2

p. 237 : The powers | that quell death |
                 0   1   2

p. 490 : Which flung | from its bells | a sweet peal | anew |
                                1   1   0 2

p. 501 : With her right | she sustains | her fair in|fant. Death, Fear |
                                      0   1   1

p. 499 : Like dead men | the dead limbs | of their com|rades cast |
           0   1   2   0   1   2

p. 219 : I desire | and their speed | makes night kin(dle
                              1   1

p. 500 : Stand rig|id with hor|ror a loud | long hoarse cry |
                                   1   1   1

even when the anapaest occurs in iambic metre—

p. 633 : And as | a shut li|ly stric|ken by | the wind |
                    0   1   2

unless we suppose the line to begin with an amphibrach.

Sometimes a pyrrhic stands for an anapaest, as

p. 234 : From the chil|drĕn ŏf | a divi|ner day |

p. 490 : And the Nai|ad-like li|ly of | the vale |
                                       0 0

In trochaic metre we find pyrrhics and spondees, as in the *Skylark*—

In the | broad day|light ∧
0 0   1   1

In the | white dawn | clear ∧
0 0   1   1

and

p. 198 : Leave the | bed, low, | cold and | red ∧
                     1   1

p. 447 : With a | pace state|ly and | free ∧
                0 0   1   1   0 0

p. 451 : This de|mand ty|rants would | flee ∧
                 1   1   0   0

p. 452 : Thou art | peace. Nev|er by | thee ∧
                  1   1   0   0

How far should the consciousness of the metre change
the natural pronunciation of the words in such cases as we
have been considering? Hardly at all, I think, in five-foot
iambic verse, a little more in short trochaic, but not much.
It would be absurd, for instance, to read according to strict
metre—

Thou art | peace, nĕv|ēr by | thee

But anapaestic rhythm generally is heard above the natural
emphasis, e.g.—

păved wĭth heāven's | ăzŭre smīle |

though not so far as to destroy the splendid effect of the
molossus—

lŏng hoărse cry |

So far I have only referred to one effect of these metrical
licenses—viz., variety, but no one can have listened to the
lines read, even apart from their context, without feeling that
they often subserve a higher poetical purpose. Take, for
instance, for the use of the trochee—

p. 261 : And lifted up to God, *Father* of all,
          Passionate prayers

—the words 'Father' and 'passionate' gain immensely in
force by the break in the regular rhythm, though the effect
is helped of course by another artifice—if we may call by
that name what is only the action of strong poetic instinct—
I mean *alliteration,* of which I shall shortly speak. I add
a few other examples which may be left to speak for themselves.

p. 56 : Beneath | the cold | glare of | the des|olate night |
                                  2   0

p. 57 : Beauti|ful bird | thou voy|agest to | thine home
              1   0   1   1   0 0   0

p. 256 : Of my | impe|rious step | scorning | surprise |
                          0 0   1   2   0

p. 264 : One look | one smile. | Oh he | has tramp|led me |
                            2   0   0   2

Here the preceding trochee gives wonderful force to the
next accented syllable in *trampled.*

p. 273 : *Never* | to change, | *never* | to pass | away |

p. 300 : Oh thou who tremblest on that giddy verge
  Of life | and death, | *pause* ere | thou ans|werest me | .

p. 309 : Be as | a mark | *stamped on* | thine in|nocent brow |
  1   0   2   0   0 0 1

p. 279 :   Is there made
  Ravage | of thee ? | Oh heart, | I ask | no more |

p. 54 :   ——till meaning on his vacant mind
  Flashed like | strong in|spira|tion—

p. 58 :   A whirlwind swept it on
  With fierce | *gusts and* | precip|ita|ting force |
              2   0

p. 523 : The ripe | corn un|der the un|dula|ting air |
                           0   0 1
  Undu|lates like | an o|cean—
  1 0

Then take the following, as shewing the effect of trisyllabic substitution :—

p. 55 : The el|*oquent blood* | told an | inef|*fable tale* |
  Then yield|ing to | the ir|*resis*|*tible joy* |

p. 58 : Of wave | *ruining* | on wave | and blast | on blast |
  Descending—

contrast the magnificent rhythm of the line thus restored from Shelley's MS. with the old corrupt 'running.'

p. 267 : Is penetrated with the in|solent light | .

The fact that, in general, these licenses are felt to add greatly to the force or beauty of the line, affords I think a ground for suspicion when the result is a weak halting line, like that already quoted.

p. 428 : Of those | on a | sudden | who were | beguiled |

Another contribution to the rhythmical effect comes from the slurring of short syllables or the resolution of long ones. We find syllables ending in *r*, as *fire, desire, retire, empire, poor, hour, fierce, fear,* disyllabized in such lines as

p. 187 : Scorn and | despair | these are |ˈmine emp|ire |
  Cf. 203, 262, 521, 635, 636, 711, 572, 435.

So *däre* with very fine effect in p. 293—

Guilty ? Who dä|res talk | of guilt | my Lord |

But it may be said, " Why not explain this by internal truncation in the second foot, throwing an additional stress on *who* ?" I do not deny that theoretically this is an allowable explanation; but, of two possible explanations, we are bound to take that which is most in accordance with the poet's practice elsewhere. While I know of no instance in which Shelley certainly used internal truncation in five-foot iambic, there are a number of cases in which it appears necessary to disyllabize long syllables followed by *r*, which indeed are very nearly disyllabic in ordinary conversation.

Not only is a long vowel disyllabized before the letter *r*, but also a vowel is interpolated, as in Shakespeare, between a liquid and another consonant, as in p. 488—

Below | far lands | are seen | trembl|ingly |
1   0

On the other hand we have short syllables slurred in such an anapaestic line as—

p. 501 : And o|ver head glor|*ious but dread*|ful to see |

where the third anapaest has strictly four syllables, but *i* is pronounced something like *y*.

p. 499: Is outshi|ning the me|teors, *its bos*|om beats high |
p. 500: ⋀ Black | as a cor|morant *the scream*|ing blast |
p. 501: As of some | *hideous en*|gine whose bra|zen teeth smash |
   0   0
Tremulous | with soft in|*fluence extend*|ing its tide |
1 0 0
p. 215 (*two-foot anap.*):
That the Eter|nal, the Immor|tal
Must unloose | through life's por|tal

These are examples of slurring where one vowel precedes another: we have also examples of slurring where a vowel is followed by a consonant; as in :—

p. 500: Like a rain|bow, and I | *the fallen shower.* | Lo ! the ship |
p. 501: *Swollen with rage* | strength and ef|fort, the whirl | and the
    splash |
p. 500: The wind | has burst out | *through the chasm* | , from the air |

Also in iambic lines :

p. 197:   white fire
Has cloven | to the roots | yon huge | snow-loa|ded ce(dar
   0   0   1

p. 230: Hide that | fair be|ing whom | *we spirits* | call man |
p. 213: Of cat|aracts | from their | *thaw-cloven* | ravines |
p. 171: Eminent | among | these vic'*tims, even* | the fear |

If however anyone prefers to pronounce these syllables fully and call the feet substituted amphibrach or bacchius, I should make no great objection.

There are some cases in which we are compelled to take our choice between an unusual rhythm, and an unusual pronunciation, as in regard to the word 'omnipresence' cited above: thus 'résponse' seems required in—

p. 205: Languish, ere yet the *résponses* are mute
p. 209: Hark! Spirits speak. The liquid *résponses.*
p. 333: Of dying Islam. Voice that art the *rés(ponse*

'contémplatest' in

p. 330: Thou art | as God | whom thou | contém|platest |

'contumēly' (keeping the Latin accent) in

p. 335: Torments | or con tumē|ly or | the sneers |

If we insist on keeping the ordinary pronunciation of the word, the line becomes to my ear either mere prose, or extremely lame verse. I may mention that in two dictionaries (Worcester, and Chambers's Etymological) I find the word marked as I suppose Shelley to have pronounced it, and Ben Jonson has the same pronunciation in *Catiline,* I. 1 (vol. IV. p. 219)

Revenge | the con|tume|ly stuck | upon (you.

ib. IV. 1 (p. 290)
—flies out
In con|tume|lies, makes | a noise |, and stinks |

In p. 560 the stress is on the syllables rhyming with *dead*

And from | her pre|sence life | was ra|dia*ted*
Like light | all oth|er sounds | were pen|etra*ted.*

In p. 255, if the reading is right, we have either two different pronunciations of 'miserable,' or the line ends with a double trochee:

Most mis|erab|le. Why | misér|able? |
No. I am what your theologians call
Hardened—

Possibly Shelley intended the ' no ' of the second line to be taken into the first, and a ' but ' inserted after ' am.'

I have dealt now with the chief metrical variations of Shelley's line. I proceed to speak of irregularities, arising from absence of symmetry in the stanza or poem. I am not sure how far these may be due to carelessness on Shelley's part or on the part of his editors ; how far indeed he was conscious of them, or would have approved them if he had become aware of them. Take for instance the song of Beatrice in *The Cenci*. It consists of two stanzas of eight lines, the first three lines in each being three-foot anapaestic, the fourth in st. 1 is four-foot iamb.

> The clay-|cold corpse | upon | the bier |

to which corresponds in the second st.

> ∧ When | to wake? | never | again |

which we should probably class as truncated iamb. The fifth and sixth lines are iambic three-foot and four-foot, the seventh line in st. 1 should, I think, be read—

> There's a snake | in thy smile | my dear |

so as to correspond with the second st.

> It says | thou and I | must part |

but the eighth line of st. 1 has certainly four feet—

> And bit|ter poi|son within | thy tear |

while the eighth of st. 2 naturally reads with three feet—

> With a light | and a heav·y heart |

In *Death*, p. 383, we have an iambic poem, where the fourth line of st. 1 has four feet with feminine ending—

> They are names | of kin|dred friend | and lo(ver

but the corresponding line of st. 2 has five feet masculine

> Watch the | calm sun|set with | them, and | this spot |

In *Constantia*, p. 382, the first st. is of nine lines, the three others of eleven lines. The sixth line of st. 1 has seven feet :

> Within | thy breath | and on | thy hair | like o|dour it | is wet |

In the other stanzas the sixth line has only four feet.

The three four-line stanzas on a *Faded Violet* (p. 441) have four feet in the last line of the first st.

> Which breathed | of thee | and on|ly thee |

three feet in the other stanzas

> With cold | and si|lent rest |

In *Pan,* p. 517, the first four lines of st. 1 contain two anapaests each—

> From the for|ests and high(lands
> We come | we come |

but the same lines in the other stanzas have three—

> I sang | of the dan|cing stars |
> I sang | of the dae|dal earth |

Lines six to nine in st. 1 and 2 have three anapaests—

> The Sile|ni and Syl|vans and Fauns |

in st. 3 the sixth line has five iambs—

> Singing | how down | the vale | of Mae|nalus |

while the seventh, eighth, and ninth have four anapaests—

> I pursued | a mai|den and clasped | a reed |

The tenth line in st. 1 has three, in st. 2 and 3 four anapaests. The last line in each stanza is anap. 3 + with trochaic or iambic substitution.

The Question (p. 518) has an Alexandrine in the last line of the first st., in the others an ordinary heroic.

In *Witch of Atlas* (p. 538) the fifty-third st. has an Alexandrine instead of heroic in the fourth line. In *Hymn of Apollo* (p. 516), written in five-foot iambic, the third line of the first stanza has only four feet—

> From the | broad moon|light of | the sky |

perhaps some such word as 'nightly' has been omitted before 'sky.'

So perhaps 'silver' should be omitted in the line—

> And a silver shape like his early love doth pass (p. 520)—

as it is the only one in the poem which has more than four feet. Similarly in p. 548 a word seems wanted in the line—

> When the north wind congregates in crowds

—an epithet for 'north-wind' would set this right.

The World's Wanderers (p. 549) is trochaic, with the exception of the first line.

> Tell me | thou star | whose wings | of light |

possibly 'thou' should be omitted.

In *Liberty* (p. 550) the first st. ends with a four-foot anapaest, the others with three-foot.

Some strong language has been used about the *Lament* (p. 596), where the third line has in the first stanza five iambs, and in the second only four—

> Trembling | at that | where I | had stood | before |
> Fresh spring | and sum|mer and win|ter hoar.

It is evident that Shelley cared very little about making his lines symmetrical, so that I should not be disposed to alter the line on that account, but the fact that autumn is the season omitted, while summer, which Shelley himself neglects in his reference to the seasons at the beginning of *Alastor*, and of which Keble says—

> Her bowers are mute, her fountains dry,
> And ever fancy's wing
> Steals from beneath her cloudless sky
> To autumn or to spring,

summer is specified—this leads me to believe that the line was rightly emended

> Fresh spring and summer, autumn and winter hoar.

Possibly the other line may be more pleasing to the ear. I will not dispute it, but I think we do Shelley more honour by ascribing to him the line which gives the best sense.

I have not time here to give a full account of Shelley's more irregular metres, but I will analyse one, which has given me more trouble than any other—viz., the fine wild stanzas in p. 363, beginning—

> Away! the moor is dark beneath the moon.

I take the metre to be iambic, of five, six, or seven feet, breaking at intervals into anapaests. Its rhythm is I think best felt if we divide each line into two sections, and allow of feminine ending to the first section, as in the first two lines of the third stanza:

The cloud | shadows | of mid(night || possess | their own | repose |
For the wea|ry winds | are si(lent || or the moon | is on | the deep |

The first line in the first two stanzas contains five feet, in the third stanza it has six.

The second line in the first two stanzas contains six feet:

ʌ Rap|id clouds | have drunk || the last | pale beams | of even |

[Here I think we should assume initial truncation, the first syllable of 'rapid' representing an iamb; though it would of course be possible to take 'rapid clouds' as constituting an anapaest, or rather a cretic, so as to make a five-foot line.]

Pour bit|ter te|ärs on || its des|ola|ted hearth |

but in the third stanza, as already stated, the first section has a feminine ending, which would permit of its being treated as a seven-foot line

For the wea|ry winds | are si|lent or | the moon | is on | the deep |

The third line has six feet in the first stanza—

Away ! | the gath|ering winds || will call | the dark|ness soon |

To give it the same number of feet in the second stanza, we must suppose initial truncation:

ʌ Watch | the dim | shades as || like ghosts | they go | and come |

in the third stanza it has seven feet—

Some res|pite to | its tur|bulence || unrest|ing o|cean knows |

The fourth line has six feet in the first two stanzas—

And profoun|dest mid|night shroud || the ser|ene lights | of heaven |

[for the stress on the first syllable of 'serene' compare *Prince Athanase*, p. 372—

> Through which | his soul | like ves|per's ser|ene beam |

and note on p. 375—

> Double | the wes|tern plan|et's ser|ene frame |]

in the third stanza it has seven feet—

> Whatev|er moves | or toils | or grieves || hath its | appoin|ted sleep |

The fifth line in the first and third st. has six feet—

> Pause not | the time | is past || every | voice cries | away |
>   1   0   0
> Thou in | the grave | shalt rest || yet till | the phan|toms flee |

but in the second st. seven feet—

> The leaves | of wast|ed au|tumn woods || shall float | around | thy head |

The sixth line is of six feet in every stanza. The two last lines of the third stanza may be read, like the second of the same stanza, as containing six feet with feminine ending of the first section.

> Thy remem|brance and | repen(tance || and deep mu|sings are | not free |
> From the mu|sic of | two voi(ces || and the light | of one | sweet smile |

but perhaps it is better to make them correspond with the last lines of the first and second stanzas by scanning them with seven feet, thus—

> Thy remem|brance and | repen|tance and | deep mu|sings are | not free |

Though the character of the verse is determined by the position of the accent and the number of feet, and it pleases the ear in the first instance by the regular recurrence of the accent and the pause, and then by the apparent unrestraint, the spontaneity which is found to be possible within the bounds of law ; yet the beauty of verses arises not only from the recurrence of the accent and the pause, but also from the recurrence of certain sounds—i.e., from alliteration and rhyme, as well as from the beauty of the separate sounds. There is an extraordinary difference between poets in their sensitiveness to this beauty of sound. Contrast, for instance, these anapaestic lines taken at haphazard from Byron's *Newstead Abbey*—

> On Mars|ton with Ru|pert 'gainst trai|tors conten(ding
> Four broth|ers enriched | with their blood | the bleak field |
> For the rights | of a mon|arch their coun|try defen(ding
> Till death | their attach|ment to loyal|ty sealed |

with the following from *The Sensitive Plant* (p. 490)—

> And the hy|acinth, pur|ple and white | and blue |
> Which flung | from its bells | a sweet peal | anew |
> Of mu|sic so deli|cate soft | and intense |
> It was felt | as an o|dour within | the sense |

What makes the difference between the hard, dry canter of the former and the sweet airy movement of the latter? One difference is the prevalence of doubled consonants, especially of dentals in the one, and of vowels and liquids in the other. It is an effort to pronounce the one, the other flows easily from the lips. Shelley's favourite alliteration in *l* seems to echo the sweet peal of the delicate bells, while Byron's *t*'s and *d*'s are to my mind unmeaning and annoying, and even the *bl* (of *blood* and *bleak*) which Shelley uses with such effect in a later stanza—

> And plants | at whose name | the verse | feels loath |
> Filled the place | with a mon|strous un|dergrowth |
> Prick|ly and pul|pous and blis|tering and blue |
> Liv|id and starred | with a lu|rid dew |

is entirely ineffective in Byron's lines.

I proceed to give other examples of alliteration in Shelley, and first, of *l*. It runs through the beautiful song of the *Prometheus* (p. 220)—

> Life of life thy lips enkindle
> With their love the breath between them.
>
> Child of Light, thy limbs are burning
> Through the vest that seems to hide them.

> p. 54: Till in· the vale of Cashmire, far within
> Its loveliest dell, where odorous plants entwine
> Beneath the hollow rocks a natural bower,
> Beside a sparkling rivulet he stretched
> His languid limbs.

m, p. 52 : And silence, too enamoured of that voice
           Locks its mute music in her rugged cell.

    p. 59 : The ghastly torrent mingles its far roar
           With the breeze murmuring in the musical woods.

w, p. 56 : Their wasting dust, wildly he wandered on
           Day after day, a weary waste of hours

    p. 53 : Many a wide waste and tangled wilderness.

Nor is it only the softer sounds which Shelley knows how to use; we meet *cl* and *cr* in p. 53—

        Frequent with crystal columns and clear shrines
        Of pearl, and thrones radiant with chrysolite.

d, in p. 56 : Where every shade which the foul grave exhales
           Hides its dead eye from the detested day.

b, in p. 53 : With burning smoke or where bitumen lakes
           On black bare pointed islets ever beat
           With sluggish surge.

and of *l, d, g,* in *The Skylark*—

        Like a glow-worm golden
        In a dell of dew.

There is a splendid combination of *b, p, l, g,* and long *i*'s and *o*'s in p. 260—

        Oh, thou bright wine whose purple splendour leaps
        And bubbles gaily in this golden bowl.

There is however a nemesis lying in wait for the love of beauty in sound as in other things, and I think it cannot be denied that Shelley's verse sometimes cloys from over-sweetness, and makes us long for the tonic of Browning's ruggedness. He cannot resist the attraction of such words as ' lorn,' ' silver,' ' solemn,' ' charm,' ' woven,' ' pavilion,' ' lamp,' ' lute,' etc. He sacrifices grammar for the sake of avoiding a disagreeable sound, using—e.g. ' thou ' as an accusative. Several blemishes of the kind have been corrected in Rossetti's and restored in Forman's edition.

But I must turn now to Shelley's use of rhyme. No one has made better use of double rhyme (medial and final), in such a poem as *The Cloud*.

> I sift the snow on the mountains below,
> And their great pines groan aghast,

(notice the alliteration in *s* and *g*)

> And all the night 'tis my pillow white
> While I sleep in the arms of the blast.

But in the use of ordinary rhyme Shelley often shews himself very careless; thus he gives rhymeless lines in rhymed passages, some of which have been ingeniously corrected in Rossetti's edition, but more are left: as in *Athanase* (p. 379), *below* and *wings* have no rhyme; in *Rosalind* (p. 389), there is no rhyme for *loveliness* and *hover*; in *Julian* (p. 428), no rhyme to *spoke*. Sometimes the word itself is repeated as a rhyme, as in p. 389—

> In silence then they took their *way*
> Beneath the forest's *solitude*;
> It was a vast and antique wood
> Through which they took their *way*,
> And the grey shades of evening
> O'er that green wilderness did fling
> Still deeper *solitude*.

Or, if not the actual word, yet a compound, as *motion* is made to rhyme with *emotion*.

The rhymes are often lax, as in most poets—e.g., *ruin* with *pursuing* (pp. 515, 520), *frown* with *disown* (p. 387), *beck* with *black* (p. 531), *and now* with *also* (p. 424). There is however a peculiar negligence in p. 521, where the second half of *empire* is disyllabized in one line, and the last part of it, the final -*er*, is made to rhyme with the entire word *fire*—

> When lamp|-like Spain | who now | resumes | her *fire*
> On free|dom's hearth | grew dim | with em|*pire*.

Compare p. 635, where the line

> Under | the crown | which girt | with em|pïre |

rhymes with

> Of king|ly mant|les, some | across | the tire |

So, in *Hymn to Mercury* (p. 645)—

> She gave | to light | a babe | all babes | excel(ling,

where the last syllable is superfluous, rhymes with

> A shep|herd of | thin dreams | a cow | stealing |

which has no superfluous syllable[1].

There is what might seem a similar instance in p. 539, where the line which one would naturally scan,

> Or char|iotee|ring ghast|ly al|liga(tors

is made to rhyme with 'floors' and 'doors.' But I suppose Shelley must have pronounced it *alligatórs*.

I have not made any study of long complicated rhyme systems, but, as far as my own feeling goes, rhymes lose their effect when they are separated by more than ten lines, as *sky* and *high* in *Rosalind and Helen*, p. 389.

I will bring to an end this very imperfect and fragmentary view of Shelley's metre by a few more general remarks on its development. In early poems we see marks of the influence of former poets, of Southey throughout *Queen Mab*, but also of Pope in such lines as (p. 32)—

> Guides the fierce whirlwind, in the tempest roars,
> Cheers in the day, breathes in the balmy groves,
> Strengthens in health and poisons in disease.

Here and there we meet the genuine Shelley, as in p. 47—

> Low through the lone cathedral's roofless aisles
> The melancholy winds a death-dirge sung.

Alastor is full of reminiscences of Wordsworth. We meet such phrases as 'natural piety,' 'the deep heart of man,' 'a woe too deep for tears.' Compare too the concluding lines—

> But pale despair and cold tranquillity,
> Nature's vast frame, the web of human things,
> Birth and the grave, which are not as they were.

---

[1] Curiously Campion has two instances of a similar license in one short poem (*Golden Treasury*, c. 1):

> Of Nep|tune's em|pire let | us *sing* |
> At whose command the waves obey;
> To whom the rivers tribute pay,
> Down the | high moun|tains *slid(ing*

and in the next verse:

> The Tri|tons dan|cing in | a *ring* |
> ·   ·   ·   ·   ·
> Like the | great thun|der *sound(ing.*

Milton's *Lycidas* is the model in parts of the *Ode to Liberty*
(p. 510) and *Adonais*; and Shakespeare's *Othello* and *Macbeth*
in *The Cenci*. There is also an echo of *The Merchant of Venice*
in Beatrice's speech (*Cenci*, p. 308), "Plead with swift frost,"
etc. The Odes to *Liberty*, to *Naples*, etc. were I suppose
suggested by Coleridge's odes, and probably *Rosalind and
Helen* by *Christabel*. Shelley's use of the anapaest seems to
be quite his own. His iambic verse in much of *The Cenci* and
the *Adonais*, has, I think, all the stateliness of Milton with
perhaps more of flexibility and sensibility. If I had to select
a single passage which in my opinion exhibits Shelley at his
highest in metre, as in every other poetical quality, it would
be the description by Beatrice of the scene where her father
is to be murdered. I never read it without thinking of
Cassandra in the *Agamemnon*. There is the same intensity
of imagination in the two cases: in the one calling up all
the past horrors of the house of the Atridae before the bodily
eye; in the other finding the doom of the lost soul written
on the natural features of the landscape. But there is a
marked contrast between the quality of the imagination at
work in the two cases, between the strong masculine grip of
fact and reality in the former and the diffusion of a sort of
electric atmosphere which seems to characterize the latter;
between what we might call the imagination of form and the
imagination of colour. Hence we are not surprised to find
that the foreboding of Beatrice turns out to be no genuine
prophecy of actual fact, but a mere subjective hallucination.
I think the same contrast might be shewn at length in the
Prometheus of the two poets.

I add one or two emendations which have occurred to me
in reading through Shelley's poems. In *Marianne's Dream*
(p. 379) the line 'And o'er the vast cope of bending heaven'
would run more easily if the superfluous 'and' were omitted.
In *Calderon* (p. 695) the second of the following lines—

> And thenceforth shall so firm an amity
> 'Twixt thou and me be, that neither fortune
> (nor time nor heaven can divide us).

should surely have 'as' inserted before 'that.' In p. 288 it should be '*reverend*' not '*reverent* brow.' In p. 332 'And seems—he is—*Mahommed*' not '*Mahomet*.'

In p. 337 I do not see the sense of saying

> *Where* fairer Tempes bloom, there sleep
> Young Cyclads on a sunnier deep.

The Cyclads are not in Thessaly. I believe Shelley wrote 'here.' In *Julian*, p. 424, it is more natural to read '*The* day had been cheerful but cold,' instead of '*this* day.' In p. 434 we find the lines—

> No thought on my dead memory—Alas! Love,
> Fear me not, against thee I'd not move

To scan these lines we should have to treat 'love' as a feminine ending of the former, and suppose it to rhyme with the masculine ending of the latter: we should also have to disyllabize 'fear' in the latter, or to read 'I would' in full. These harshnesses are avoided if we transfer 'love' to the beginning of the latter line, but then we lose the rhyme. Still that is not unexampled in Shelley's verse, and it is on the whole, I think, the best solution of the difficulty; though I would not deny that Shelley himself may have intended the rhyme under some confused impression that 'love' belonged to the former line.

In p. 513 can it be right to speak of Art '*diving* on fiery wings to Nature's throne'? I think Shelley wrote 'rising' or 'soaring.' In the *Hymn of Pan*, would it not be more natural to say 'From the forests and highlands *they* come, *they* come; listening to *my* sweet pipings,' instead of '*we* come'? compare the last verse:

> And all that did then attend and follow,
> Were silent with love, as you now, Apollo,
> With envy of my sweet pipings.

In *Prometheus*, p. 211, we should, I think, read

> Or when some star, of many one,

instead of 'many a one.' It is a reminiscence of Wordsworth's Ode. In p. 212 it does not seem to me that the emendation 'than' for 'which' improves the line,

> Ay, many more which we may well divine.

The question put is: Are there more spirits? to which the answer is: Yes, many which we may divine, but cannot speak of now. In p. 209, 'around the crags' is, I think, more poetical, more suited to the airy spiritual voices than Rossetti's 'among.' In p. 240 I should be inclined to insert 'the' after 'laughed' in the line

> Round which death laughed, sepulchred emblems
> Of dead destruction—

As I am here dealing with the *Prometheus*, I will end my paper with an observation which may be new to some of my readers, that the three queer names of snakes mentioned in it— *seps*, p. 222; *dipsas*, p. 229; and *amphisbaena*, p. 231—are taken from Lucan. Was Shelley reading the *Pharsalia*, when he composed it?

CHAPTER XV.

THE HEXAMETER AND PENTAMETER.

Im Hexameter steigt des Springquells flüssige Säule :
Im Pentameter drauf fällt sie melodisch herab.

SCHILLER.

In the Hexameter rises the fountain's silvery column ;
In the Pentameter aye falling in melody back.

COLERIDGE.

THE first introduction of the Hexameter into English poetry, as into the poetry of other nations, was due to the Renaissance. Those who had learnt to appreciate the power and beauty of the metre of Homer and Virgil became impatient of the restrictions of alliteration and rhyme, as well as of the general slovenliness of English versification which marks the interval between Chaucer and Surrey. Thus Ascham, writing in 1568 of the change in the Latin metres commenced by Ennius and perfected by Virgil, says (*Schoolmaster*, p. 176 f. ed. Mayor): 'This matter maketh me gladly remember my sweete tyme spent at Cambridge and the pleasant talke which I had oft with M. Cheke and M. Watson of this fault, not only in the olde Latin Poets, but also in our new English Rymers at this day. They wished, as Virgil and Horace were not wedded to follow the faultes of former fathers...but by right imitation of the perfit Grecians had brought Poetrie to perfitness also in the Latin tong, that we Englishmen likewise would acknowledge and understand rightfully our rude beggarly ryming, brought first into Italie by Gothes and Hunnes, whan all good verses and all good learning were destroyed by them, and after caryed into France and Germanie, and at last received into England by men of excellent wit indeede, but of small learning and less judgement in that behalfe.' 'The noble Lord Th. Earle of Surrey, first of all English men, in translating the fourth booke of Virgil, and Gonsalvo Periz, that excellent learned man and secretarie to kyng Philip of Spaine, in translating the *Ulysses* of Homer out of Greeke into Spanish, have both by good judgement avoyded the fault of ryming, yet neither of them hath fullie hitte perfit and trew versifying. In deede they observe just number and even feete: but here is the fault, that their feete be feete without joyntes, that is to say, not distinct by trew quantitie of sillables. And so such feete be but numme feete, and be even as unfitte for a verse to turn and runne roundly withall, as feete of brasse or wood be unwieldie to go well withall[1].' 'The spying of this fault now is not the curiositie of English eyes, but even the good judgement also of the best that write in these dayes in Italie; and namelie of that worthie Senese Felice Figliucci, who writyng upon Aristotle's Ethickes...amongest other things doth most earnestlie invey agaynst the rude ryming of verses in that tong: and whan soever he expresseth Aristotle's preceptes with any example out of Homer or Euripides, he translateth them, not after the rymes of Petrarke, but into soch kinde of perfite verse, with like feete and quantitie of sillables, as he found them before in the Greke tonge: exhorting earnestlie all the Italian nation to leave of their rude barbariousnesse in ryming and folow diligently the excellent Greke and Latin examples in trew versifying.' 'This I write...to exhorte the goodlie wittes of England, which, apte by nature and willing by desire, geve themselves to Poetrie, that they, rightly understanding the barbarous bringing in of rymes, would labour, as Virgil and Horace did in Latin, to make perfit also this point of learning in our English tong[2].' Again, in p. 71, speaking of translations of Homer, he says, 'it was not made at the first more naturallie in Greke by Homere, nor after turned more aptelie into Latin by Horace, than it was a good while ago in Cambridge translated into English, both plainlie for the sense and roundlie for

---

[1] *Schoolmaster*, p. 181.　　　　[2] *Ib.* p. 185.

the verse, by one of the best scholars that ever S. John's College bred, Mr Watson, myne old frend, sometime Bishop of Lincoln. Therefore for their sake that have lust to see how our English tong, in avoidyng barbarous ryming, may as well receive right quantitie of sillables and trewe order of versifying ...as either Greke or Latin, if a cunning man have it in handling, I will set forth that one verse in all three tonges, for an example to good wittes that shall delite in like learned exercise.

HOMERUS :

πολλῶν δ' ἀνθρώπων ἴδεν ἄστεα καὶ νόον ἔγνω.

HORATIUS :

Qui mores hominum multorum vidit et urbes.

M. WATSON :

All travellers do gladly report great praise of Ulysses,
For that he knew many men's maners, and saw many cities[1].'

These lines of Watson's are also praised in Webbe's *Discourse of English Poetrie*, 1586 (quoted in the notes to Ascham, p. 259): 'There is one famous Distichon, which is common in the mouthes of all men, that was made by one Master Watson, fellowe of S. John's Colledge in Cambrydge about 40 yeeres past, which, for sweetnes and gallantnes thereof in all respects, doth match and surpasse the Latine coppy of Horace.' It would seem therefore that the earliest English hexameter was written before the middle of the 16th century. And Ascham himself in the *Toxophilus*, published in 1544, gives the following specimens of his own writing :

'Twang' quoth the bow, and 'twang' quoth the string, and quickly the shaft flew.
Up to the pappe his string did he pull, his shaft to the hard iron.
What thing wants quiet and merie rest, endures but a small while.

So little ground had Gabriel Harvey, who himself refers to Watson's lines[2], for his claim to have been the first inventor of the English hexameter. The earliest notice we have of Harvey's

---

[1] Watson is said to have translated the first book of the *Odyssey*, but it is no longer in existence.

[2] See Ascham, p. 260.

hexameters is in Spenser's letter written in 1579, where he says, 'I like your late English Hexameters so exceedingly well, that I also enure my pen sometimes in that kind; which I find indeed, as I have heard you often defend in word, neither so hard nor so harsh, that it will not easily and fairly yield itself to our mother tongue.'

However, it was no doubt mainly owing to Harvey's authority and influence, that the hexameter enjoyed a considerable vogue during the reign of Elizabeth. Before giving specimens of his work and that of his followers, I will first mention the names of some of the foreign versifiers who led the way in this enterprize. Dr Karl Elze, in his Programm on *Der Englische Hexameter* (Dessau, 1867), says that Italy first set the fashion with Leon Baptista Alberti (1404—1484); that it was taken up in France by Etienne Jodelle (1532—1573), Etienne Pasquier (1529—1615), and Antoine de Baïf (1532—1589); and in Germany about the same time by Kolross, Birck, and Gesner. Spain followed in the person of Villegas (1596—1669)[1].

I return now to Harvey, whose verses afterwards met with deserved ridicule from Greene and Nash. His *Encomium Lauri* begins as follows:

> What may I | call this | tree? A | Laurell? | O bonny Laurell: |
> Needs to thy | bow will I | bow this | knee, and | vayle my bo|netto |.

His *Speculum Tuscanismi* thus:

> Since Gala|teo came | in, and | Tusca|nism gan | usurp; |
> Vanitie a|bove all : | Villanie | next her: | Stateliness | empress: |
> No Man | but Mi|nion, Stowte | Lowte, Plaine | Swayne, quoth a | Lording:|
> No words | bŭt valo|roŭs, no | deeds but | womanish | only. |

A somewhat better example is

> Virtue | sendeth a | man to re|nown, fame | lendeth a|bundance |
> Fame with a|bundance | maketh a | man thrice | blessed and | happy |.

We have two elegiac couplets from Spenser, who seems to have soon wearied of the experiment:

---

[1] Specimens of Jodelle, Pasquier and Villegas will be found in Southey, Appendix to *Vision of Judgement.*

See ye the | blindfol|dĕd prĕtty | God, that | featherèd | archer, |
Ōf lov|ērs mise|rīes ‖ whīch măketh | hīs bloŏdy | game ? |
Wot ye why | hīs mo|thĕr with a | veil hath | coverèd | hīs face ? |
Trust me, | lest he my | love ‖ happily | chance to be|hold. |

Sir Philip Sidney is far better in

First shall | fertile | grounds not | yield in|crease of a | good seed, |
First the | rivers shall | cease to re|pay their | floods to the | ocean, |
First shall | virtue be | vice, and | beauty be | counted a | blemish, |
Ere that I | leave with | song of | praise her | praise to so|lémnize. |

But he is also responsible for the following:

Lady re|served by the | heaven to | dŏ păstŏrs' | companies | honour[1], |
Joining | yoūr sweet | voice to the | rural | muse of a | desert, |
Here you | fully do | find this | strange ope|ration | ŏf love, |
How to the | woods Love | runs, as | well as | rides to the | palace, |
Neither he | bears rever|ēnce to a | prince nor pi|tȳ to a | beggar. |

     *   *   *   *

But, O | happy be | you, which | safe from | fīry re|flection |
Of Phœ|būs vio|lēnce, in | shade of | sweet Cypa|rissus, |
Or pleas|ănt myr|tĕll, may | teach the un|fortunate | Echo |
In these | woods to re|sound the re|nowned | name of a | goddess. |

     *   *   *   *

Self-lost | in wan|drīng, banish|ĕd that | place we do | come from. |

     *   *   *   *

Ōpprest | with rui|nŏus con|ceits by the | help of an | outcry. |

Worst of all is 'the learned Mr Stanyhurst' in his translation of Virgil, published at Leyden in 1582, in which it is difficult to find anything intelligible for quotation. The following is a favourable specimen,

Now do they | raise ghast|lȳ light|nīngs, now | grisly re|boundings |
Ōf ruff|-raff roar|ing, mens | hearts with | tĕrror a|grizing, |
With pell|-mell ramp|ing, with | thwick-thwack | sturdily | thundering|.

Webbe in his *Discourse of English Poetrie*, 1586, gives a translation of the First Eclogue of Virgil, from which I take the following:

That same | city so | brave, which | Rome was | wont to be | callèd, |
Fool, did I | think to be | like this of | ours, where | we to the | pastures |
Wonted | were to re|move from | dams our | yŏung prĕtty | cattle | .

---

[1] Or should we make the 4th foot a trochee, adding 'do' to the 3rd? This would give a line without a caesura.

Our last quotation shall be from Abraham Fraunce, Fellow of St John's College, Cambridge, who translated Watson's Latin poem *Amyntas* in 1591. Mr Courthope (*Hist. of Eng. Poetry*, vol. II. p. 299) speaks of it as 'the only example of the style possessing the slightest pretensions to elegance,' and quotes the following passage 'as shewing a sense of grace and beauty.'

Hollow | caves, ragg'd | rocks, waste | hills, green | watery | fountains |
Fŏr pity | sweetly re|ply, and | answers | make to my | mourning. |
Strong oak | tall pine|tree, green | laurel, | beautiful | ivy |
Shake their | leaves for | grief and | bend their | boughs to my | groaning. |
Only that | one, in | whom my | joys are | only re|posed, |
Yields no | lovely re|ply, no | answer | makes to my | mourning |

The discords of these early hexameters were not unperceived by contemporary critics, nor even, in some cases, by the authors themselves. Thus Ascham writes (*Schoolmaster*, p. 178), '*Carmen Hexametrum* doth rather trotte and hoble than run smoothly in our English tong.' Spenser in his letter to Harvey says, 'The only or chiefest hardness is in the accent, which sometime gapeth and as it were yawneth ill-favouredly; coming short of that it should, and sometime exceeding the measure of the number; as in "carpenter," the middle syllable being used short in speech, when it shall be read long in verse, seemeth like a lame gosling, that draweth one leg after her; and "heaven," being used short as one syllable, when it is in verse stretched out with a diastole, is like a lame dog that holds up one leg. But it is to be won with custom, and rough words must be subdued with use. For why, a God's name, may not we, as *well as*[1] the Greeks, have the kingdom of our own language, and measure our accents by the sound, reserving the quantity of the verse?' Harvey in reply maintains that the common pronunciation should be adhered to in verse; but quantity seems to be the ruling principle in many of the examples given above.

Nash is perhaps the most severe of the critics. In his answer to Harvey's *Four Letters*, he writes: 'The hexameter verse I grant to be a gentlemen of an ancient house—so is many an English beggar—yet this clime of ours he cannot

---

[1] Printed 'else' in the editions.

thrive in : our speech is too craggy for him to set his plough in : he goes twitching and hopping in our language, like a man running upon quagmires, up the hill in one syllable, and down the dale in another, retaining no part of that stately smooth gait which he vaunts himself with among the Greeks and Latins.' With special reference to Stanihurst he writes in 1589, that his 'heroical poetry recalled to life whatever hissed barbarism hath been buried this hundred year, and revived by his ragged quill such carterly variety as no hodge ploughman in a country but would have held as the extreme of clownery': and again in 1592, 'Master Stanihurst, though otherwise learned, trod a foul, lumbering, boisterous, wallowing measure in his translation of Virgil[1].'

The extraordinary development of the English iambic in the hands of such masters as Spenser, Shakespeare, and Milton, drove out all thought of the hexameter, and we hear no more of it till 1737, when an anonymous translation of two of the Eclogues of Virgil appeared, shewing no improvement on the older experiments.   Take as an example,

Thē cĭty | called Ro|mā, Meli|baeus I | simply i|magined |
Oūr cĭty | rēsemb|lĭng, whither | oft we | swains are ac|customed |
Oūr ten|dēr proge|nȳ of | ewes to | drive to the | market. |

Then about the year 1760 Goldsmith, in an essay on Versification, undertakes the defence of the hexameter. 'It is generally supposed,' he says, 'that the genius of the English language will not admit of Greek or Latin measure; but this, we apprehend, is a mistake owing to the prejudice of education.' 'Sir Philip Sidney is said to have miscarried in his essays; but his miscarriage was no more than that of failing in an attempt to introduce a new fashion...We have seen several late specimens of English hexameters and sapphics, so happily composed, that by attaching them to the idea of ancient

---

[1] In Schipper's *Englische Metrik*, p. 445 *n.*, there is a tentative bibliography of English Hexameter Verse.   In it we find the names of John Dickenson, who brought out his *Shepherd's Complaint* (a poem of no special interest) in 1596, and Thomas Edwards, the author of *Cephalus and Procris*, which appeared in 1595.   The latter however is in heroics, not, as stated, in hexameters.

measure, we found them in all respects as melodious and agreeable to the ear as the works of Virgil and Anacreon or Horace.'

I am unable to think of any English poem to which Goldsmith can be here alluding.   In Germany, it is true, there had
been a new birth of the hexameter in 1748, the year in which
Klopstock brought out the first three cantos of the *Messiah* ;
and this was followed by the Vossian translation of the *Odyssey*
in 1781, and by Goethe's *Hermann und Dorothea*, in which the
German hexameter reached its culminating point, in the year
1797.   Nor was it long before an echo was awakened in
England.   Before the end of the century Coleridge and William
Taylor of Norwich began to translate from the German, and
also to produce original hexameters.   It will suffice to quote a
few lines from Taylor's versification of Ossian, published in the
Monthly Magazine for June 1796 :

Thou who | rollst in the | firmament | round as the | shield of my | fathers |
Whence is thy | girdle of | glory, O | Sun, and thy | light ever|lasting ? |
Forth thou | com'st jn thy | awful | beauty ; the | stars at thy | rising |
Haste to their | azure pa|vilions ; the | moon sinks | pale in the | waters.

Coleridge is rougher at first, but achieves a more perfect and
varied harmony in his later pieces.   In *Mahomet* he seems to
be trying a prentice hand :

Prophet and | priest, who | scatter'd a|broad both | evil and | blessing, |
Huge wăsteful | empires | founded, and | hallowed | slow perse|cution |
Soul-wither|ing, but | crushed the | blasphemous | rites of the | Pagan |

In his translation from Stolberg, assigned to the same year
(1799) by J. D. Campbell, he attains a higher level :

Travelling the | vale with mine | eyes—green | meadows and | lake with
      grĕen | island |
Dark in its | basin of | rock, and the | bare stream | flowing in | brightness, |
Thrilled with thy | beauty and | love in the | wooded | slope of the |
      mountain, |
Here, great | mother, I | lie, thy | child with his | head on thy | bosom |

Still better is his translation of Schiller's lines, and indeed in
my opinion far superior to the original, which I quote for the
purpose of comparison :

Schwindelnd | trägt er dich | fort auf | rastlos | strömenden | Wogen :
Hinter dir | siehst du, du | siehst || vor dir nur | Himmel und | Meer. |

Strongly it | bears us a|long in | swelling and | limitless | billows, |
Nothing be|fore and | nothing be|hind, but the | sky and the | ocean. |

Before going on to consider the further development of the English hexameter, it may be well here to point out in what respects it differs from the ancient hexameter, 'Dactylic Hexameter Catalectic,' in which the last dactyl loses its final syllable, so as to give a line consisting of five dactyls and a trochee; but, as the final syllable of a verse was indifferently long or short, the final trochee might always be a spondee. Of the five dactyls which remain, the fifth must, as a rule, remain a dactyl; the first four may be indifferently dactyls or spondees. Sometimes a spondee is used in the fifth foot; but then, to give weight to the exceptional rhythm, the two last feet are generally contained in a single word, and the fourth foot is in most cases a dactyl. In the fragments of Ennius we find one or two verses without a single dactyl. The only instance in later writers seems to be one from Catullus:

> Si te lenirem nobis neu conarere.

But, to make a verse, it is not enough to place side by side six feet of the kind mentioned, as in the line of Ennius,

> Sparsis hastis longis campus splendet et horret.

For the beauty and harmony of the verse *caesura* is necessary; i.e., in some part or parts of the verse, the end of a word must coincide with the middle of a foot. The best and most common caesura in the dactylic hexameter is where the division occurs after the fifth half-foot, as in

> Tityre | tu patu|lae || recu|bans sub | tegmine | fagi, |

where there are also two subordinate caesuras after *tu* and *recubans*. But the caesura in the third foot is sufficient by itself to produce a perfectly harmonious verse, as in

> Illius | immen|sae || ru|perunt | horrea | messes. |

To avoid monotony the best poets seek variety of rhythm by other caesuras. Next in power to the caesura after the fifth half-foot, comes that after the seventh half-foot; but to give a proper verse, this caesura must be combined with others, as in

Quid faci|at lae|tas sege|tes || quo | sidere | terram |[1].

It is unnecessary to go into further minutiae here. The main differences between the rules for the Latin and the English metre are: (1) the substitution of accent for quantity, (2) the substitution of the trochee for the spondee.   As to the former we have seen that there was a diversity of opinion and practice in the Elizabethan age; and even in the Victorian age some have advocated the return to the principle of quantity, as Cayley in the *Transactions of the Philological Society*, 1862, Pt. I. p. 67 foll.   I quote a specimen of his quantitative line, marking the syllables in which quantity is at variance with the natural accent:

Ah me! great mournīng for Achaean land is appointed:
These were glad tidīngs for Priamus and for his household,
And his o|thēr Tro|jāns would at | heart be dearly delighted,
Could they but be apprised of this contention between you.

The same is done by Spedding, quoted in Matthew Arnold's book *On Translating Homer*, pp. 150, 154,

Verses | so modu|lāte, so | tuned, so | varied in | accent, |
Rich with un|expec|tēd chan|gēs, smooth | stately so|norous, |
Rolling e|vēr for|wārd, tide|līke with | thunder in | endless |
Prōces|sīon, com|plēx mĕlo|diēs, pause, | quantity, | accent; |
After | Virgili|ān prece|dēnt and | practice in | order. |

          *   *   *

Softly com|ēth slum|bēr clos|īng th' o'er|wearied | eyelid |

See also below on Mr Stone.

But the vast preponderance of opinion is in favour of the accent as the determining principle of the rhythm of the English hexameter, while not denying the influence of quantity in subordination to the former.   It is a fault, as Arnold says (p. 83), to force the quantity and abuse the accent by shortening long syllables and lengthening short ones; but it is a far worse fault to require the removal of the accent from its natural place to an unnatural one, in order to make the line

---

[1] Abbreviated from H. A. J. Munro's account of Latin Prosody, given at the end of the *Public School Grammar*.

scan. While it is advisable to construct all verses so that by reading them naturally—that is, according to the sense and legitimate accent—the reader gets the right rhythm; it is still more imperative to keep intact the accent in the hexameter, avoiding such a rhythm as that in Spenser's line

Wot ye why | hĭs mo|thĕr with a | veil hath | coverèd | hĭs face ? |

where 'not only is the reader causelessly required to make havoc with the natural accentuation, in order to make it run as a hexameter, but also, in nine cases out of ten, he will be utterly at a loss how to perform the process required, and the line will remain a mere monster for him.' We have examples of both faults in the lines above quoted from Coleridge's *Mahomet*, which begin 'Huge wăsteful' and 'Soul-witherĭng.' Other examples from later poets will be found below.

The second point of difference between the Latin and the English hexameter arises from the fact of the comparative rarity of the accentual spondee. This is however not unfrequently employed with good effect in Kingsley's *Andromeda*, e.g.

Such in her | stature and | eyes and the | broād whīte | light of her |
    forehead, |
Stately she | came from her | place, and she | spoke in the | midst of the |
    people : |
'Pure are my | hands from | blōod : mōst | pūre thĭs | heart in my |
    bosom. |
Yĕt ōne | fault I re|member this | dăy, ōne | word I have | spoken.' |

The want of inflexions and the prevalence of monosyllables are two other causes which differentiate the English hexameter not only from the Latin, but from the German also. The want of inflexions controls the order of the words; the prevalence of monosyllables tends to make the close of the word coincide with the close of the foot. The latter difficulty has perhaps been exaggerated by foreign critics, such as Dr Elze, the connexion between article and noun, pronoun and verb, preposition and noun, being so intimate as almost to melt them into one.

I go on now to give examples of the theory and practice of the writers of English hexameters during the 19th century. Southey, who claims to lead the way,

'I first adventure, follow me who list.'

but who only followed in the wake of W. Taylor and Coleridge, says, in the Preface to his *Vision of Judgement* (published in 1821), that he had been long of opinion 'that an English metre might be constructed in imitation of the ancient hexameter, which would be perfectly consistent with the character of our language, and capable of great richness, variety, and strength.' As a pattern he quotes a verse of the Psalms, originally pointed out by Harris of Salisbury as a natural and perfect hexameter,

Why do the | heathen | rage and the | people i|magine a | vain thing ? | [1]

Beside the change of the spondee into the trochee, Southey says that, in order to avoid monotony, he has taken the liberty ' of using any foot of two or three syllables at the beginning of the line ; and sometimes, though less frequently, in the 2nd, 3rd, or 4th place.' Speaking of the Elizabethan hexameter, he says it was a failure, because ' Sidney and his followers wished to subject the English pronunciation to the rules of Latin prosody,' and that, while it is 'difficult to reconcile the public to a new tune in verse, it is plainly impossible to reconcile them to a new pronunciation. There was the further obstacle of unusual and violent elisions ; and moreover, the easy and natural order of our speech was distorted by the frequent use of forced inversions, which are utterly improper in an uninflected language.'

Southey has some very beautiful verses, such as

Fade, like the | hopes of | youth, till the | beauty of | earth is de|parted. |
Dark and dis|tinct they | rose. The | clouds had | gathered a|bove them, |
High in the | middle | aīr, hūge | purple | pillowy | masses, |
While in the west be|yond was the | lāst pāle | tint of the | twilight. |

[1] Dr Guest's criticism of this line is on a par with his other judgments on things rhythmical. 'Properly read,' he says, 'the accent should be on *and* and *thing* '!

Two other excellent hexameters have been discovered in the Authorized Version :

God is gone | up with a | shout, the | Lord with the | sound of the | trumpet. |
How art thou | fallen from | heaven, O | Lucifer | son of the | Morning | .

To which Mr Reginald Haines in an article in *N. and Q.* for June 29, 1901, adds several other examples.

But I do not think his licenses have always a good effect. Compare for the initial pyrrhic[1]:

'Tĭs ă | dēep dŭll | sound, that is | heavy and | mournful at | all times, |
Fŏr ĭt | tells of mor|tality | always. But | heavier | this day |
Fell on the | conscious | ear its | deeper and | mournfuller | import | .

Still less satisfactory is the pyrrhic in the 2nd foot, with initial iambic, as in

    —Here, | lost in their | promise |
And prīme, | wĕre thĕ | children of | art, who should | else have de|livered /
    *   *   *   *
Nŏr leāst | fŏr thĕ | hope and the | strength that I | gathered in | boyhood |

and what appear to be amphibrachs in the 1st foot, as

Thăt nōt fŏr | lawless de|sires nor | goaded by | desperate | fortunes |
    *   *   *   *
And Shākespeăre | who in our | hearts for him|self hath cre|ated an |
  empire | .

In the following we seem to have iambs in other feet beside the 1st :

Hear heaven | yĕ ān|gĕls heār |, souls of the | good and the | wicked |

and possibly a molossus and cretic in these :

Armed the | chemist's | hānd : wĕll thēn | mīght Elĕu|sinian | Ceres |
And my | feēt mĕthoūght | sunk, and I | fell pre|cipitate, | starting |

Southey is also faulty in the management of the caesura, which is altogether wanting in

And the | regions of | Paradise | sphere within | sphere inter|circled |
So by the | unseen | comforted | raised I my | head in o|bedience |

and in elision, or slurring, as in

Hĭs reverend | form up|rose, heaven|wărd his | face was di|rected |
In the | Orĭent and | Occident | known from | Tagus to | Tigris |[2]

---

[1] In the lines which follow I mark what seems to me the true accentuation, where it is opposed to the metre, not feeling sure how they would have been pronounced by Southey.

[2] There is one line of Southey's which I was at first unable to scan. It is thus given in the one-volume edition of his works

  Tier over | tier, they | took ʌ | place a|loft in the | distance |

but on looking in the ten-volume edition I found the missing syllable supplied by *their*.

Coleridge is more moderate in the licenses he claims (p. 615 n.), viz. the use of cretic, instead of the dactyl (provided that the accent on the 1st syllable is stronger than that on the third), and anacrusis at the beginning of the line. This license would cover Southey's initial amphibrach. As examples we may take from the *Hymn to the Earth*:

Fŏrth yĕ swēet | sounds from my | harp, and my | voice shall | float on your | surges |
Was it not | well with thee | then, when | first thy | lap was un|girdled, |
Thy) lap to the | genial | Heaven the | day that he | woo'd thee and | won thee |

Southey was followed by Hookham Frere who, in 1824, sent a friend some English hexameters 'of the right sort without false quantities,' of which I subjoin a specimen:

Malta, sovereign isle, the destined seat and asylum
Of) chivalry, honour, and arms, the nursing mother of heroes,
Mirror of ancient days, monumental trophy, recording
All that of old was felt or feared or achieved or attempted,
When proud Europe's strength, restored with the slumber of ages,
Roused, and awoke to behold the triumphant impious empire
Throned in the East :—

In 1830 he tried the same metre in translating a chorus of the *Frogs* beginning,

Now may the powers of earth give a safe and speedy departure
To the) Bard at his second birth, with a prosperous happy revival,
And may the city fatigued with wars and long revolution,
At) length be brought to return to just and wise resolutions,
Long in peace to remain. Let restless Cleophon hasten
Far from amongst us here : since wars are his only diversion,
Thrace, his native land, will afford him wars in abundance.

Frere introduces these lines with the following remarks: ' The reader may perhaps observe an irregularity in the second line—what the grammarians call an anacrusis, i.e. unaccented syllables prefixed to the first *ictus*. This would be inadmissible in the regular classical hexameter; but the irregularity is so little offensive to the ear, that the writer, in other attempts to construct English hexameters, has found himself, in more than one instance, falling into it. He has therefore preferred to leave it as it stands, an instance of the liberty which may be deemed allowable in adapting to the English language this difficult but by no means impracticable metre.'

In 1841 Longfellow published his translation of Tegner's poem on the *Children of the Lord's Supper*, written in Swedish hexameters; in the preface to which he says, 'The translation is literal, perhaps to a fault....I have preserved even the measure, that inexorable hexameter, in which it must be confessed the motions of the English Muse are not unlike those of a prisoner dancing in his chains.' As, in 1847, he produced a more important poem in the same metre, viz. the well-known *Evangeline*, and again at a later date the *Courtship of Miles Standish*, we may suppose that further experience modified his earlier doubts as to the employment of this line. The following passage from *Evangeline* may serve to illustrate his rhythm, which is, I think, both smoother and, at the same time, more varied than Southey's.

Then came the | labourers | home from the | field, and se|renely the | sun sank |
Down to his | rest, and | twilight pre|vailed. A|non from the | valley !
Softly the | Angelus | sounded, and | over the | roofs of the | village |
Columns of | pale blue | smoke, like | clouds of | incense as|cending |
Rose from a | hundred | hearths, the | homes of | peace and con|tentment. |

He is not however free from faults of accentuation and disregard of quantity, as in

Lay in a fruitful | văllĕy. Vāst | meadows | stretched to the | eastward |
Yet under | Benedict's | roof hŏspi|tality | seemed more a|bundant |
Thăt thĕ | dying | heard it and | started | up from their | pillows |
Thăt thĕ | angel of | death might | see the | sign and pass | over |
Then through those | realms of | shade in | multiplied | rĕvĕrbĕr|ations |
Afterwards | whĕn āll wăs | finished the | teacher re|entered the | chancel |
Enter | not with a | lie on life's | journey ; the | multitude | hears you |
Beautiful, | and in his | hand a | lily ; on | life's rōaring | billows | .

Caesura also is sometimes wanting, as in

Such as the | peasants of | Normandy | built in the | reign of the | Henries |
Numberless | noisy | weathercocks | rattled and | sang of mu|tation |

In the same year, 1847, appeared *English Hexameter Translations*, chiefly by Whewell, Julius Hare, Sir John Herschel, and Hawtrey. About one-fourth of the volume consists of Elegiacs. In the preface it is said, that the poems, having been written by several persons at various times, will probably shew discrepancies in the versification. 'It is believed, however, that these are slight; for all the pieces are executed with the intention that the lines being read according to the natural and ordinary pronunciation, shall run into accentual hexameters or pentameters....Such verses may be no less acceptable to the English, than they have long been to the German poetical ear, and may be found suited in our language, as well as in its sister speech, to the most earnest and elevated kinds of poetry.' The longest piece (occupying 140 pages out of 275) is Whewell's translation of *Hermann and Dorothea*, which cannot, I think, be considered a great success. The reader is never beguiled into forgetting that it is a translation from the German. It contains several examples of initial pyrrhic or iamb, as

Fŏr thĕ | rest held | still their | way, and | hastily | passed on |
Fŏr sŏ | Fear with her | abject | chill creeps | into the | bosom, |
Ănd dārk | Care, which to | me far | worse than the | evil it|self is. |
Ănd thĕ | careful | dame brought | forth of the | generous | liquor |
Ĭn thĕ | rich cut | flask, on the | bright clear | circle of | metal, |
Wĭth thĕ | goblets | green, the | genuine | glass of the | Rhine wine. |
Wĭth kēen | look full-|fixed on his | brow the | minister | scanned him |

Sometimes the accentuation is wrong in the other feet:

For we | two made our | choice not | ĭn dăys | ŏf re|joicing |
Which, be|fŏre sūn|rĭse is | felt, had | woke me from | slumber |
Then comes | eve and | frŏm āll | sides and in | every | corner |
Mother in | vain it | wĭll then | bĕ that | wealthy pos|sessions |

Far better than this is Hawtrey's translation from the Third Iliad, which Matthew Arnold praises as 'the most successful attempt hitherto made at rendering Homer into English':

Clearly the | rest I be|hold of the | dark-eyed | sons of A|chaia ; |
Known to me | well are the | faces of | all ; their | names I re|member; |
Two, two | only re|main, whom I | see not a|mong the com|manders, |
Castor | fleet in the | car, Poly|deukes | brave with the | cestus,
Own dear | brethren of | mine ; one | parent | loved us as | infants. |
Are they not | here in the | host, from the | shores of | loved Lake|daimon? |

Or, though they | came with the | rest in | ships that | bound through
    the | waters,
Dare they not | enter the | fight or | stand in the | council of | Heroes, |
All for | fear of the | shame and the | taunts my | crime has a|wakened ? |
So said | she ;—long | since they in | Earth's soft | arms were re|posing, |
There in their | own dear | land, their | Father|land, Lake|daimon. | [1]

Lancelot Shadwell brought out his translation of the Iliad three years before the appearance of *Evangeline*. The rhythm, as seen in the following lines, is not bad, but his taste is atrocious, as shewn in the selection of such forms as Luky, Ily, Fthia to represent the Greek Λυκίη, Ἴλιον, Φθίη.

First on the mules and the dogs fell thickly the murderous shower ;
Next on themselves the destructive darts, wide-wastefully wounding,
Light[2]; and the funeral piles were daily and nightly rekindled.
Nine days long through the camp ranged fiercely the shafts of Apollo.

In the year 1848 appeared Clough's *Bothie of Tober-na-Vuolich*, a serio-comic poem which, harsh and rugged as it occasionally is, still shews, I am disposed to think, a freedom and a mastery over the resources of the English hexameter, such as is not to be found in any other example of the metre. Compared with Hawtrey's and Kingsley's more correct and musical measures, Clough's measure is like that of Horace's Epistles compared to the Aeneid, only that Clough often rises out of the conversational tone into real passion and emotion. Dr Elze has, I think, a little misunderstood this, when he treats the *Bothie* as a burlesque, and asks, Where is the humour in a trochaic line, like

At the | last I | told him | all, I | could not | help it ? |

But there is no intention to be humorous here : it is intentional negligence, like that shewn in Shakespeare's use of the feminine rhythm, see above on *Hamlet* (p. 196 foll.).

---

[1] Arnold changes 'Lakedaimon' into 'Lacedaemon' 'in obedience to my own rule that every thing *odd* should be avoided in rendering Homer, the most natural and least odd of poets.' He also changes, without remark, the order of words in the last line but one, reading 'they long since,' I suppose, in order to emphasize the contrast between 'she' and 'they'; but this gives a less harmonious third foot.

[2] An attempt to reproduce the rhythm of the Greek,

βάλλ'· αἰεὶ δὲ πυραὶ νεκύων καίοντο θαμειαί.

It is interesting to read Clough's own estimate of the hexameter, written for an American magazine in 1853 (*Life*, I. p. 396 f.). He speaks there of Longfellow as having attuned the ears of his countrymen on both sides of the Atlantic to the flow and cadence of this hitherto unacceptable measure. It was in fact the reading of *Evangeline* which induced him to try the hexameter himself (vol. I. 136). While allowing the excellence of Hawtrey's translation, he holds that Homer's rounded line and Virgil's smooth verse were both of them 'totally unlike those lengthy, straggling, irregular, uncertain slips of *prose mesurée*, which we find it so hard to measure, so easy to read in half a dozen ways, without any assurance of the right. Is

> Conticuere omnes intentique ora tenebant

the same thing as

> Hab' ich den Markt und die Strasse doch nicht so einsam gesehen?

Is the following a metrical sequence :—

> Thus in the ancient time the smooth Virgilian verses
> Fell on the listening ear of the Roman princes and people.
> Ut belli signum Laurenti Turnus ab arce?

'There is one line, one example of the smooth Virgilian verse, which perhaps Mr Longfellow would have allowed himself to use

> Spargens humida mella soporiferumque papaver ;

yet even this most exceptionable form, with its special aim at expressing by an adaptation of sound to sense the

> Scattering of | liquid | honey and | sopo|riferous | poppy,

is a model of condensation, brevity, smoothness, and *netteté*, compared with that sprawling bit of rhythmical prose into which I have turned it.'

As specimens of his own verse we may take the following :

Scarcely with | warmer | hearts and | clearer | feeling of | manhood, |
Even in | tournay and | foray and | fray and | regular | battle, |
Where the | life and the | strength came | out in the | tug and the | tussle |

    ·   ·   ·   ·   ·

Ín the | gránd old | tímes of | bóws and | bílls and | cláymore |
At the old | Flodden | field or | Bannockburn | or Cul|loden |

    ·   ·   ·   ·   ·

Better a | cowslip with | earth than a | prize car|nation with|out it. |
'That I al|low,' said | Adam.　But | he with the | bit in his | teeth, scarce |
Breathed a brief | moment, and | hurried ex|ultingly | on with his | rider, |
Far over | hillock and | runnel and | bramble, a|way in the | champaign, |
Snorting de|fiance and | force, the | white foam | flecking his | flanks, the |
Rein hanging | loose to his | neck and | head pro|jecting be|fore him : |
Oh, if they | knew and con|sidered, un|happy ones; | Oh, could they | see, could |
But for a | moment dis|cern, how the | blood of true | gallantry | kindles, |
How the old | knightly re|ligion, the | chivalry | semi-quix|otic |
Stirs in the | veins of a | man at | seeing some | delicate | woman |
Serving him, | toiling for | him and the | world—　.

I add one specimen from *Amours de Voyage*, p. 337

Tibur is | beautiful | too, and the | orchard | slopes and the | Anio |
Falling, | falling | yet, to the | ancient | lyrical | cadence ; |
Tibur and | Anio's | tide ; and | cool from Lu|cretilis | ever, |
With the Di|gentian | stream and | with the Ban|dusian | fountain, |
Folded in | Sabine re|cesses, the | valley and | villa of | Horace.

It will be noticed that one of the above lines and, I think, a very fine one, is made up of six trochees, but such a line is seldom satisfactory, considered by itself: compare that condemned by Dr Elze,

At the | last I | told him | all.　I | could not | help it |

which however, if read slowly with the proper pauses, expresses very well the feeling of utter surrender which belongs to the passage.

Another example is in p. 216, which is also unbroken by caesura,

Boudoir, | toilette, | carriage, | drawing-|room and | ball-room. |

In other lines *enjambement* is very marked, though not quite to the same extent as in *Amours de Voyage*, p. 311

—I know I
Yet shall | one time | feel the | strong cord | tighten a|bout me, |
Feel it, re|lentless, up|bear me from | spots I would | rest in; and | though the |
Rope sway | wildly, I | faint, crags | wound me, from | crag unto | crag re- |
bounding, or |, wide in the | void, I | die ten | deaths; ere the | end I |
Yet shall | plant firm | foot on the | broad lofty | spaces I | quit, shall |
Feel under|neath me a|gain the | great massy | strengths of ab|straction |

So in p. 319 we have a line ending in the middle of 'collapse,' in 340 in the middle of 'enfolded.' Misplaced accent and disregard of quantity are illustrated in two lines of the above, and still more in the lines which follow, where I mark the quantities, as I suppose Clough to have read them.

Two length|wāys in the | midst for | keeper and | gillie and | peasant |
Feudal | tenures | mercantile | lords, cŏmpe|tition and | bishops |
Bŭt ă nĕw | thĭng was | in me and | longing de|licious pos|sessed me |
Hither to | hideous | close, mŏdĕrn-|florid | mŏdern-fīne|lady |
Dishes and | fishes, bĭrd, | beast and | sesquipe|dalian | blackguard |
Thirdly, a | Cambridge | man I | knew, Smĭth, a | senior wrangler | [1]
Pass slŏwly | o'er them, ye | days of Oc|tober, ye | soft, mĭsty | mornings |
Scarce by a | channel deep-|cut, răging | up and | răging | onward |
Doubtless some|whĕre in some | neighbourhood | have, and are | careful
  to | keep, some |

The first foot is frequently an iamb, sometimes an amphibrach, or trochee with anacrusis : compare

Ye Gods | what do I | want with this | rubbish of | ages de|parted ? |
At last, | dearest Lou|isa, 1 | take up my | pen to ad|dress you |
And surely | seldom have | Scotch and | English more | thoroughly |
  mingled |
However | so it must | be, and | after due | pause of | silence |
The Nea|politan | army, and | thus ex|plains the pro|ceeding |
Would) mix in it|self with | me, and | change me, I | felt myself | changing |

In one line we have to admit anacrusis of two syllables, or to treat it as anapaestic with feminine ending :

With a) mathe|matical | score hangs | out at | Inver|ary |

I have observed two instances of final truncation ; one of which may be excused as a quotation :

—The lions
Roaring | after their | prey do | seek their | meat from | God ∧ |

The other, I think, must be a wrong reading : I should suggest the addition of 'him' after 'resist.'

Laid her | hand on her | lap : Phĭlip | took it ; she | did not re|sist ∧
So he re|tained her | fingers, the | knitting bȇing | stopped, but e|motion |

----

[1] Or perhaps this should be scanned

Thirdly a | Cambridge | mān I knew, | Smith, a | senior | wrangler | .

It will be noticed that in the last line 'being' is treated as a short monosyllable. We find the same thing in pp. 209, 262.

But while the | healths were bêing | drunk was | much tribu|lation and |
    trouble |

Carrying | off and at | once for | fear of bêing | seen, in the | bosom |
Locking-up | ãs in a | cupboard the | pleasure that | any man | gives them | .

Similarly with other participles, as in p. 265

But I keep | sayîng in my | mind, this | long time | slowly with | trouble |
Eying through | eddyîng grĕen | waters the | green-tinting | floor under|neath
    them |

The following instances of slurring are even harsher :

It was by | accident | purely I | lit on the place, | I was re|turning |

whether we assign 'place' to the 4th or 5th foot.

Ye un|happy sta|tuĕttes and | miser|ãble | trinkets |
See thy | children's | children, and | dĕmocracy up|on New-|zealand !
O mister | Philip may it | never hereafter | seem to be | different! |
Permeates | far and | pierces to the | very | cellars | lying in |
Narrow, | high, back-|lane and | court and | alley of | alleys |

In two of these lines the final foot is either slurred or a dactyl. For other examples see *Amours*, p. 302

Would to | heaven the old | Goths had | made a | cleaner | sweep of it |
O my | tolerant | soul be | still, but you | talk of bar|barians |
Each has to | eat for him|self, di|gest for him|self and in | general |
It is no | play but a | business.. | Off go | teach and be | paid for it |
Georgy de|clares it ab|surd, but Mam|ma is a|larmed, and in|sists he has |
Taken up | strange o|pinions—

The last license I will instance is the absence of caesura, as in

Poor ala|baster | chimney-piece | ornaments | under glăss | cases |
Highland | peasants gave | courteous | answer to | flattering | nobles |

The stimulus which led to the writing of the *Bothie* came, as we have seen, from America. Its appearance in turn seems to have led Longfellow to employ in his later poem of *Miles Standish* a rougher metre than that of *Evangeline,* and Bret Harte's comic *Stagedriver's Story* was probably modelled upon the *Bothie.* I quote a few lines

Half-way | down the | Grade I | felt, Sir, a | thrilling and | creaking, |
Then a | lurch to one | side, as we | hung on the | bank of the | cañon, |
Then looking | up the | road, I | saw in the | distance be|hind me |
The) off hind | wheel of the | coach, just | loosed from its | axle and |
    following. |
One glance a|lone I | gave, then | gathered to|gether my | ribbons, |
Shouted, and | flung them out|spread on the | straining | necks of my |
    cattle ; |
Screamed at the | top of my | voice, and | lashed the | air in my | fury, |
While down the | Geiger | Grade on | three whĕels the | vehicle | thundered. |

It is curious that Clough, after his great success in the accentual hexameter, should have been tempted to try a 'meta-phrase' from the *Odyssey*, constructed upon the ancient principle of quantity, 'so far as in our forward-rushing, consonant-crushing, Anglo-savage enunciation, long and short can in any kind be detected—quantity attended to in the first instance, and care also bestowed, in the second, to have the natural accents very frequently laid upon syllables which the metrical reading depresses.' For my own part I find these later hexameters of the author of the *Bothie* melancholy reading, as melancholy as the *Bothie* itself is delightful : compare *Iliad* I. (vol. II. p. 465)

To re|press I | came if | practic|able your | anger, |
Out of | heaven,—the | goddess, the | white-armed | Hera, de|sired me, |
Solici|tŏus for the | good of the | one a|like and the | other. |
Ābstain | frŏm vio|lēnce, put | back the | sword in the | scabbard, |
Let op|probrious | words, if | neces|sāry re|quite him. |

Actaeon (ib. p. 467)

Artemis, | Arcadi|ān wood-|rover, a|lone, hunt-|weary |
Unto a | dell cen|trīng many | streamlets | hĕr foot un|erring |
Hād gui|dĕd. Plata|nūs with | fig-tree | shaded a | hollow, |
Shaded a | water|fāll, where | pellu|cīd, yet a|bundant, |
Streams from | perpetu|āl full-|flowing | sources a | current. |

The Lectures *On Translating Homer*, by Matthew Arnold, appeared in 1861. He maintains there (p. 77) that the metre which gives the best chance of preserving the general effect of Homer is the hexameter, which, 'whether alone or with the pentameter, possesses a movement, an expression, which no metre hitherto in common use among us possesses.' After praising Hawtrey's translation as the best which we have of any part of Homer, he goes on to speak of Clough's pastoral as in two respects more like the *Iliad* than any other English poem; viz. 'in the rapidity of its movement, and the plainness and directness of its style.' 'Mr Clough's hexameters are excessively, needlessly rough; still...his composition produces a sense in the reader, which Homer's composition also produces... the sense of having, within short limits of time, a large portion of human life presented to him, instead of a small portion.' 'His poem...has some admirable Homeric qualities; out-of-door freshness, life, naturalness, buoyant rapidity' (p. 178). On the other hand, of Longfellow he says (p. 82), 'the merit of the manner and movement of *Evangeline*, when they are at their best, is to be tenderly elegant; and their fault, when they are at their worst, is to be lumbering; but Homer's defect is not lumberingness, neither is tender elegance his excellence. The lumbering effect of most English hexameters is caused by their being much too dactylic; the translator must learn to use spondees freely. Mr Clough has done this, but he has not sufficiently observed another rule...and that is, to have no lines which will not *read themselves*.'

In his own verse Arnold frequently uses the liberty for which he pleads in p. 151, of beginning the line with an iamb instead of a trochee; not, I think, with entire success. Compare p. 95:

In the | plain there were | kindled a | thousand | fires : by | each one |
Thĕre sāt | fifty | men in the | ruddy | light of the | fire. | [1]
By their | chariots | stood the | steeds and | champed the white | barley |

and p. 97:

Ănd wĭth | pity the | son of | Saturn | saw them be|wailing |
Ănd hĕ | shook his | head and | thus ad|dressed his own | bosom : |
Ah, un|happy | pair, to | Peleus | why did we | give you, |
Tŏ ă | mortal? but | ye are with|out old | age, and im|mortal. |
Was it that | ye, with | man, might | have your | thousands of | sorrows ?
For than | man, in|deed, there | breathes no | wretcheder | creature |
Ŏf āll | living | things, that on | earth are | breathing and | moving | .

---

[1] Mr Spedding having suggested that this line must have been intended to be scanned with initial trochee, 'Thēre sāt,' Arnold declares (p. 251) that he means it to have the usual pronunciation, giving a rhythm which may be compared with Virgil's 'Velóces jaculo.'

I prefer much the lines in which he adopts a more usual rhythm, such as

In the | bloody | dust, be|neath the | feet of their | foemen. |
Why dost thou | prophesy | so my | death to me, | Xanthus? It | needs not.
I of my|self know | well, that | here I am | destined to | perish, |
Far from my | father and | mother | dear : for | all that I | will not |
Stay this | hand from | fight, till the | Trojans are | utterly | routed. |

The only fault which I find here is the absence of the accent on 'that' in the last line but one.

Kingsley's *Andromeda*, composed in 1852, may, I think, be regarded as the most perfect example of the English hexameter. In a poem of more than 450 lines, I have not noticed any discord arising from false quantity or false accentuation. He indulges in none of the licenses of which we have seen instances in other hexameters; and yet he knows how to preserve his verse from monotony by means of his skilful use of the caesura and varied combinations of dactyl, trochee and spondee[1]. The following lines may be given as a specimen of his work. In the notes which follow I have pointed out the number of dactyls and the position of caesuras in each line.

1. Slowly she | went by the | ledge ; and the | maid was a|lone in the | darkness, |
2. Watching the | pulse of the | ōars dīe | down, as her | ōwn dīed | with them. |
3. Tearless, | dumb with a|maze she | stood, as a | storm-stūnned | nest-ling |
4. Fallen from | bough or from | cāve līes | dumb, which the | home-going | herdsman |
5. Fancies a | stone, till he | catches the | light of its | terrified | eyeball. |
6. So through the | lōng lōng | hours the | māid stōod | helpless and | hopeless, |
7. Wīde-ēyed, | downward | gazing in | vain at the | blāck, blānk | dark-ness. |
8. Feebly at | last she be|gan, while | wīld thōughts | bubbled with|in her : |
9. "Guiltless I | am : why | thus, then? Are | gods more | ruthless than | mortals? |

---

[1] Kingsley's theory of the hexameter, if it may be so called, is given in his *Life*, vol. I. pp. 338—349.

10. "Have they no | mercy for | yōuth ? nŏ | love for the | souls who have | loved them ? |

11. "Even as | I loved | thēe, drēad | sea, as I | played by thy | margin, |

12. "Blessing thy | wave as it | cooled me, thy | wind as it | breathed on my | forehead." |

1. Has five dactyls. The principal caesura is after the accented syllable in the 3rd foot, which may be described as 3rd foot masculine. There is a secondary caesura after 'slowly' (1st foot feminine), also after 'alone' (5th foot masculine). For the sake of brevity these will be denoted as 3 m., 1 f., 5 m. 2. Three dactyls. Caes. after 'down' (4 m.). 3. Two dactyls. Caes. after 'stood' (4 m.); close of word and foot (for which I use the word *closure*) after 'tearless' (1 cl.). 4. Four dactyls. Caes. after 'dumb' (4 m.), secondary after 'cave' (3 m.). 5. Five dactyls. Caes. after 'stone' (2 m.), secondary after 'light' (4 m.). 6. Two dactyls. Caes. after 'hours' (3 m.), closure after 'stood' (cl. 4). 7. Two dactyls. Caes. after 'vain' (4 m.), secondary after 'black' (5 m.); cl. after 'wide-eyed' (cl. 1). 8. Three dactyls. Caes. after 'began' (3 m.), secondary after 'feebly' (1 f.); cl. after 'thoughts' (cl. 4). 9. Three dactyls. Caes. after 'am' (2 m.) and 'then' (3 f.). 10. Four dactyls. Caes. after 'youth' (3 m.), secondary after 'souls' (5 m.). 11. Three dactyls. Caes. after 'thee' (3 m.), and 'sea' (4 m.). 12. Five dactyls. Caes. after 'me' (3 f.), secondary after 'wave' (2 m.) and 'wind' (4 m.).

It will be remembered that Arnold speaks of the lumbering effect of most English hexameters as being due to the excessive use of the dactyl. This is true, when the dactyl is clogged with false accents and false quantities, and woolly with harsh elisions, but not in the case of Kingsley's clean-cut measure. Arrowy swiftness is rather the quality of such lines as

Fearing the | stars of the | sky, and the | roll of the | blue salt | water |
Bounding from | billow to | billow, and | sweeping the | crests like a | sea-
    gull |

Tennyson's satire which follows is pointless for verses like these. But it is, I think, fully justified as a criticism on the quantitative hexameter.

These lame hexameters the strong-winged music of Homer !
   No, but a most burlesque barbarous experiment.
When was a harsher sound ever heard, ye Muses, in England ?
   When did a frog coarser croak upon our Helicon ?
Hexameters no worse than daring Germany gave us :
   Barbarous experiment, barbarous hexameters.

In 1866 Sir John Herschel brought out a translation of the
Iliad in hexameters, from which I quote the following lines.
The metre is correct, but with no special interest.

How could I face the Trojans and long-robed matrons of Troia,
If, like a dastard, I shrank aloof and avoided the battle ?
Nor could my soul endure it ; for aye have I learnt to be foremost,
Valiantly ever to dare and fight in the van of the Trojans,
Winning renown for myself and my father's glory upholding.

C. S. Calverley in 1868 wrote an interesting paper in opposition to the theory that 'there could be no true translation of
a Greek or Roman poet which did not reproduce his metre,'
and shewed, as Clough had done before, that these metrical
imitations are far from giving the effect of their originals. He
has however not shrunk from trying his own hand at the
hexameter, but, to my thinking, with only qualified success.
Thus the lines from Lucretius which follow seem to me to be
tame and characterless, as compared with the intensity of
Munro's prose translation, and rhythmically to be monotonous
and inharmonious, as compared with the ringing melody of
Kingsley's verse.

Statues of youth and of beauty may not gleam golden around him,
(Each in his right hand bearing a great lamp lustrously burning,
Whence to the midnight revel a light may be furnishèd always) ;
Silver may not shine softly, nor gold blaze bright, in his mansion,
Nor to the noise of the tabret his halls gold-cornicèd echo :—
Yet still he, with his fellow, reposed on the velvety greensward,
Near to a rippling stream, by a tall tree canopied over,
Shall, though they lack great riches, enjoy all bodily pleasure.
Chiefliest then, when above them a fair sky smiles, and the young year
Flings with a bounteous hand over each green meadow the wild-flowers :—
Not more quickly depart from his bosom fiery fevers,
Who beneath crimson hangings and pictures cunningly broidered
Tosses about, than from him who must lie in beggarly raiment.

It will be noticed that, out of 13 lines, nine have caesura 3 f. There is a similar monotony in the translation from the *Iliad*.

These were the words of the King, and the old man feared and obeyed
    him :
Voiceless he went by the shore of the great dull-echoing ocean,
Thither he got him apart, that ancient man ; and a long prayer
Prayed to Apollo, his Lord, son of golden-ringleted Leto :
    " Lord of the silver bow, thou whose arm girds Chryse and Cilla—
Cilla beloved of the Gods—and in might sways Tenedos, hearken !
Oh ! if, in days gone by, I have built from floor unto cornice,
Smintheus, a fair shrīne for thee ; or burned in the flames of the altar
Fat flĕsh of bulls and of goats ; then do this thing that I ask thee :
Hurl on the Greeks thy shafts, that thy servant's tears be avengèd."

Here all the lines have caesura 3 m.   I have marked two long syllables which are made short.

In 1886 T. Ashe published an hexameter poem of domestic life, in which there is much beauty, but the rhythm is impoverished by the paucity of dactyls and the predominance of the penthemimeral caesura (3 m.).   Compare :

On the | hillside | grew the | pines in | silence to|gether |
. Grand trunks straight and tall, that flushed blood-red in the sunset;
Yet the sun, in splendour flashing down from its zenith,
Could not pierce the dense and twisted screen of the branches :
They, that rocked in storm and madly howled in the winter,
Now were calm and still, or only swayed in a whisper.

Perhaps there is more of variety in the lines which follow : ·

Much is | changed and | únchanged | ín the | village of | Orton, |
New-cut | names, new | mounds be|side the | tower or the | chancel ; |
Some, long | sad, are | happy ; | some are | sad, who were | merry. |
Bells of | joy, of | dole, have | thrilled the | air of the | valley. |
Feet, now | many a | day tired | óf the | stones and the | plodding, |
Rest at | last and | ache not, be|neath the | green of the | hillocks ; |
Feet of | small new-|comers | roam in the | grass of the | meadows. |

The latest hexameters known to me are the lines entitled *After Defeat*, by Mr William Watson, published in 1899, the *Translations of the Iliad* contained in *A Reading of Life*, by George Meredith, published in 1901, and those by Mr William Johnson Stone, appended to an Essay *On the Use of Classical*

Metres in English, which appeared in 1899. Of the first the following may be taken as a specimen:

Pray, what | chorus is | this? At the | tragedy's | end what | chorus? |
Surely be|wails it the | brave, the un|happily | starred, the a|bandoned |
Sole unto | fate, by | yonder in|vincible | kin of the | vanquished? |
Surely sa|lutes it the | fallen, not | mocks the an|tagonist | prostrate? |

of the second the following:

Nay, as a | pillar re|mains im|movable, | fixed on the | tombstone |
Haply of | some dead | man, or it | may be a | woman there-|under; |
Even like | hard stood they | there, at|tached to the | glorious | war-car, |
Earthward | bowed with their | heads; and of | them so la|menting in-|
    cessant |
Ran the hot | tear-drops | downward | on to the | earth from their | eyelids, |
Mourning their | chario|teer; ăll their | lustrous | manes dŭsty-|clotted |
Right side and | left of the | yoke-ring | tossed to the | breadth of the |
    yoke-bow |

Mr Stone, while allowing the legitimacy of the accentual hexameter, and confessing that Southey's metre 'has borne fruit, some of it well worth producing,' insists that it has no right to be compared with the classical hexameter, and is quite unfit to represent Homer. What he really delights in is the quantitative hexameter. For examples of this he refers to Stanyhurst's *Virgil,* from which he quotes

And the go|dēsse Ju|nō full | freight with | poysonèd | envye |
With thun|drīng light|nĭngs my | carcase | strongly be|blasted |

He also quotes from Clough's *Actaeon,* and from Spedding. Of the metre of the last he says 'I am confident that he has a perfect right to claim that it is exactly like Virgil's in effect. But he is also right in saying that Virgilian hexameters are almost impossible in English.' Mr Stone would therefore go back straight to the fountain-head and model our metre not on the Latin but on the Greek. 'I believe that our language is singularly like ancient Greek in intonation.' He explains this by saying that 'the ordinary unemphatic English accent' may be defined like the Greek accent, as 'a raising of pitch and nothing more.' There is something pathetic in the combined earnestness and hopelessness with which he urges this and other points. 'I know I shall be looked upon as insane.' 'It is, I know, too much to expect that I have carried any one with me so far as this.' He refers to 'the unfortunate fact that the opinions expressed are such as no one else thinks or believes,' and confesses that his 'appeals are made without any sort of confidence to unsympathetic readers.' 'But I shall really be rewarded...if I have induced any one to agree with me that there is no other way...but to bind ourselves with a strict prosody, and to conform to the rules of the metre we are engaged with.'...'No one need agree with me on any single point of prosody, but a strict prosody there must be, if the attempt is to have any sure basis at all.' He then gives various rules of quantity, which 'do not aim at any sort of completeness,' but 'are simply points which have occasioned me difficulty, and which I have had to decide for myself. There may be many things which have not occurred to me, and many of my conclusions to which exception will be taken.'

Mr Stone does not seem to be quite consistent on the subject of quantity. In p. 4 he says 'English words have a distinct quantity, to any one who will attend to it, and if pronounced accurately'; (p. 10) 'In my opinion there are only three monosyllables with open vowels that may be scanned short, and they only because they are proclitics...*a*, *to*, and *the*. Yet all writers have made use of the extraordinary license of allowing such words to be common or even short. Even Tennyson has *my* and *be* short'; (p. 13) 'Most of us are still under the impression that we may scan a vowel long or short as we will'; (p. 50) 'If readers cannot have the ordinary accent emphasizing the metre, they pine at least for unquestionably long syllables. This desire is quite unreasonable, because the gradations of quantity are infinite and there are syllables which may be long or short at will'; yet (p. 20) 'even for quantitative verse the intention of the writer must never be in doubt, nor, I maintain, is it, if rules of prosody be strictly observed.' In p. 43 he speaks of 'the extreme difficulty of writing such (quantitative) verse, and the bar it would be to any freedom of thought....A beginner would find his path as thickly strewn with thorns as that of a boy learning Latin verses. He would make false quantities far more ghastly, and his tongue would

refuse, quite rightly, to shift the accent on to the long syllable.
...But practice and severe correction will in the end, I believe,
make the rules of metre very little more galling than the rules
of rhyme, and the feeling of victory even more enchanting. The
quantity of the word will be felt at once.'

We now turn to the examples by which Mr Stone illustrates
his theory of the hexameter. A poet might make quantity his
guiding principle without causing any great difficulty to the
ordinary English reader, provided that, like Tennyson in his
classical metres, he took care not to oppose accent to quantity ;
but Mr Stone will have none of such cowardly compromises: he
rejoices in the 'combative accent' (pp. 9, 24). Of former experiments he selects for special praise Clough's Pentameters in
the lines which follow :

> Towns hamlets leaving, towns by thee, bridges across thee,
>   Pass to palāce gardēn, pass to citīes populōus.
> Murmuring once, dimplīng, 'mid woodlands wandering idly,
>   Now with mighty vĕssēls loaded, a mighty rĭvēr.

and his *Actaeon*, of which we may take as a specimen

>   —swiftly revealing
> Hĕr mai|dēnly bŏ|sōm and | all her | beauty be|neath it, |
> Tō thĕ rĭ|vēr wătĕr | over|flowing | tō re|ceive her | [1]
> Yielded her | ambrosi|āl na|kēdness.

The following are his directions for reading his own hexameters. ' What do I require of my readers ? I ask them to
read my verses slowly, with the natural accent unimpaired, and
with such stress as they think right on the long syllables by
way of ictus. This will probably at first fail to give them any
idea of the rhythm....I would ask them then to combine voice-
duration with voice-stress on such syllables, to exaggerate the
length. Finally in very stubborn cases, if this plan fails, I ask
them to read them as a schoolboy reads Virgil, with voice-
pitch, voice-stress, and voice-duration all concentrated on the
long syllable. Thence they may work back to the first process,
that of emphasizing the rhythm by stress only.' ' The under-
lying principle of my rhythm is, I think, compensation. You

---

[1] I suppose Clough must have scanned it thus, as he makes the first syllable
of ' river ' short in the preceding quotation.

are required to balance the accent and the quantity, the accentual variety being based on quantitative uniformity.'

In the lines which follow I begin by marking the stress, as I suppose it to have been intended by the author; and then add other lines on which the reader may exercise his own ingenuity.

Unyoked | frŏm thĕ wăg|gōns, drĭvĕn | off to the | bindweed | pastures |
By the rush|ĭng swirl|ĭng rĭvĕr, | and the wo|mĕn set a|bout it |
Then with an|ointing of | oil they | washed, and | on the ri|vēr-bank |
Took their | meal, the lin|ĕn dry|ĭng there | ĭn the sun | hard by. |
White-armed | Nausica|ā lead|ĭng the mea|sūre to the | players |
As the ăr|rōw-scătter|ĭng gŏddĕss | Artemis | hunts on a | hill-side | [1]
Glorying | in the răp|ĭd-foŏt|ĕd | hinds and | hardy-foŏt|ēd boars |
None so | tall, but | shē stands | leader a|mong them heăd | ānd brow. |

Then they shouted aloud, and great Odysseus was awakened,
And sitting up pondered in his heart and doubted in his mind :
'Ah me, in what country, to what manner of men am I come?
Is this people a race cruel, savage, impious, unjust?'
So saying did great Odysseus quit his homely dwelling-place,
From the thick undergrowth with his huge hand breaking a branch off'
So went he, as in his might trusting a hill-bred lion :
And to him on this wise perplexed seemed it the better way
Standing apart to address words of supplication, honied words[2].

I conclude with a few words on the pentameter, consisting of two dactylic penthemimers, i.e. of two sections, each containing two dactyls followed by a long syllable. To my mind this

---

[1] I think this must be the scansion intended, as Mr Stone (p. 9) dilates on the blunder of "making a vowel followed by a doubled consonant long by position." "Why should the first syllable of 'hitting' be longer than 'hit'? The doubling of a letter in English has no other purpose than the marking of the preceding vowel as short."

[2] While I am opposed to Mr Stone's general principle, I have found much that is interesting and instructive in his incidental remarks. I observe that he attributes to me on more than one occasion an opinion from which I entirely dissent, that "the ancients were like children, who, as soon as they get a rhythm into their heads, love to emphasize it; and that the classical metres are more elementary than ours" (pp. 6, 49). He has apparently misunderstood my paragraph on the routine scansion (p. 6 above) where I quote Ruskin on his own childish scanning, and afterwards refer to the traditional language of the poets about the Muse singing, as bearing witness to a time long anterior, in which metre was still a kind of sing-song.

is far less suited to the English language than the hexameter, mainly because it is difficult to prevent the long syllable, which closes the two sections of the line, from being also a monosyllable. Thus Coleridge's line, which stands at the head of this chapter, is spoilt by the sort of snap with which it closes in the word 'back.' Tennyson improves on this at the expense of the first line in his corrected couplet:

> Up springs hexameter with might as a fountain ariseth:
> Lightly the fountain falls, lightly the pentameter.

I think the elegiacs which please me most are Whewell's on the death of his wife, which are given in the Appendix to the *Memoir*, p. 537 f.

> Solemn and sad folds round me the darkening eve of the sabbath:
> Solemn as often of old, sad with a fresh-fallen grief.
>
> Blessed beyond all blessings that life can embrace in its circle,
> Blessed the gift was when Providence gave thee to me,
> Gave thee gentle and kindly and wise, calm, clear-seeing, thoughtful,
> Thee to me, as I was, vehement, passionate, blind:
> Gave me to see in thee, and wonder I never had seen it,
> Wisdom that shines in the heart clearer than intellect's light.
>
> Vainly till then had I roved the land from mansion to mansion:
> Pleasure and kindness I found, found not the love that I sought.
> Vainly had I explored the long-flowing river of Science,
> Back to its fountain-heads, down to its glittering sea.
>
> Thus we parted, diverse how far our paths and our portions!
> She to the Saviour's embrace, I to the wearisome world.
> I to the wearisome world to toil all lonely and helpless:
> Yet not lonely quite, her since I bear in my heart:
> Yet not helpless quite, for thy companionship, dear one,
> Still shall lend me its help, guiding and raising me still.
>
> There in the beautiful land, the land of the lake and the mountain,
> There where the loveliest lake lies in the loveliest vale.

With these may be compared Clough's elegiacs in the *Amours de Voyage*—

19—2

Is it illusion? or does there a spirit from perfecter ages,
   Here, even yet, amid loss, change, and corruption, abide?
Does there a spirit we know not, though seek, though we find, com-
      prehend not,
   Here to entice and confuse, tempt and evade us, abide?
Lives in the exquisite grace of the column disjointed and single,
   Haunts the rude masses of brick garlanded gaily with vine,
E'en in the turret fantastic surviving that springs from the ruin,
   E'en in the people itself? is it illusion or no?

Sometimes Clough is very careless of quantity and accent, as in the commencing lines of Canto I.

Over the great wīndy waters and over the clear-crēsted summits,
   Unto the sun and the sky [and] unto the perfecter earth,
Come let us go—to a land wherein gods of the old time wandered,
   Where every breath even now changes to ether divine.
Come let us go, though with|al a voīce | whisper, the | world that we
      live in,
   Whithersoever we turn, still is the same nārrow crib ;
'Tis but to prove limitation, and measure a cord, that we travel ;
   Let who would 'scape and be free, go to his chamber and think;
'Tis but to change ídle fancies for memories wilfully falser ;
   'Tis 'but to go and have been.'—Come, little bark, let us go.

It will be observed that the word which I have bracketed in the 2nd line is extra-metrical. I do not know whether this is owing to any accidental carelessness, or whether Clough really meant to substitute a spondee, trochee, or dactyl, for the monosyllable at the close of the 1st section of the pentameter. I am inclined to think such a measure would be more suited to the English ear than the regular Latin metre[1]. We might then describe the English elegiac metre as consisting of six trochees with dactylic or spondaic substitution, the pentameter line always closing with two dactyls and a truncated trochee. The lines quoted by Schipper (vol. II. p. 450), as a specimen of elegiacs, from Swinburne's *Hesperia* might at first sight seem to follow this rule.

Out of the | golden re|mote wild | west, where the | sea without | shore is, |
   Full of the | sunset, and | sad, if at | all, with the | fullness of | joy. ʌ

---

[1] I am glad to find that this view is shared by Mr Haines in *N. and Q.* cited above, as well as by Dr Abbott.

But the lines which follow shew that the metre is not dactylic, but anapaestic, thus[1]:

Ăs ă wīnd | sets in | with the au|tumn that blows | from the re|gion of sto(ries,

∧ Blows | from a per|fume of songs | and of mem|'ries belov'd | from a boy |

∧ Blows | from the capes | of the past | oversea | to the bays | of the pres(ent

∧ Filled | as with shad|ow of sound | with the pulse | of invis|ible feet | .

We have however a real example of the truncated or cata-lectic hexameter in the late Lord Bowen's translation of Virgil, published in 1887, of which the following lines may be taken as a specimen :

Death's dark gates stand open, alike through the day and the night,
But to retrace thy steps and emerge to the sunlight above,
This is the toil and the trouble. A few whom Jupiter's love
Favours, or whose bright valour has raised them thence to the skies,
Born of the gods, have succeeded:—
Still, if such thy desire, and if thus thy spirit inclines
Twice to adventure the Stygian lake, twice look on the dark
Tartarus, and it delights thee on quest so wild to embark,
Learn what first to perform :—

I will close with some fine elegiacs by Mr William Watson taken from the poem entitled *Hymn to the Sea* (1899)

Man with inviolate caverns, impregnable holds in his nature,
    Depths no storm can pierce, pierced with a shaft of the sun :
Man that is galled with his confines, and burdened yet more with his
    vastness,
    Born too great for his ends, never at peace with his goal :
            *   *   *   *
Nought, when the harpers are harping, untimely reminds him of durance;
    None, as he sits at the feast, whispers Captivity's name;
But would he parley with Silence, withdrawn for a while unattended,
    Forth to the beckoning world 'scape for an hour and be free,

Lo, his adventurous fancy coercing at once and provoking,
    Rise the unscalable walls built with a word at the prime ;
Lo, immobile as statues, with pitiless faces of iron,
    Armed at each obstinate gate stand the impassable guards.

[1] See above, on Metrical Metamorphosis, ch. VI. pp. 84 foll.

APPENDIX A.

M. Gaston Paris, Mr H. Nicol, and Prof. Paul Meyer on the Old French Decasyllabic Metre.

Extract from M. Gaston Paris's edition of *La Vie de Saint Alexis,* poème du XIe siècle (Paris, 1872), p. 131 :—

"Le vers a dix syllabes au *minimum ;* il peut en avoir onze ou douze si l'hémistiche[1] et le vers ont une terminaison féminine. Il y a donc quatre types: 1° vers de dix syllabes, masculins à l'hémistiche et à la rime: ‖ *Ja máis* | *n'iert téls* ‖ *com fút* | *as an|ceisórs* ‖; 2° vers de onze syllabes, masculins à l'hémistiche, féminins à la rime: ‖ *Sor toz* | *ses pérs* ‖ *l'amát* | *li em|perédrè* ‖; 3° vers de onze syllabes, féminins à l'hémistiche, masculins à la rime: ‖ *Enfánt* | *nos dónè* ‖ *qui séit* | *a ton* | *talént* ‖; 4° vers de douze syllabes, féminins à l'hémistiche et à la rime: ‖ *Donc li* | *remémbrèt* ‖ *de son* | *seinór* | *celéstè* ‖. Le vers est donc un *décasyllabe,* pouvant avoir une syllabe de plus, nécessairement atone, après la quatrième et après là dixième... Le décasyllabe apparaît pour la première fois dans le poème de Boèce, où il a exactement le même caractère que dans le nôtre ; c'est aussi le vers du *Roland* et de la plupart des anciennes chansons de geste. Le vers est toujours très-exactement fait, et toutes les syllabes comptent:...pour savoir ...la juste mesure il faut tenir compte des cas où se produit l'*élision.*"

"I have marked the feet and hemistiche ; and put an acute over the accented words and syllables, a grave over the extra unaccented syllable. M. Paris does not state—it being generally known—that the second syllable of the second and fifth feet must be accented. Words ending in a syllable with unaccented *e* have the accent on the one before it ; all others on the last. The accents in the other feet (always disyllabic) are not fixed ; the cesura is always after the second foot.

---

[1] "Cette dénomination est admise, bien qu'à la rigueur elle soit inexacte."

"The poem on Boethius is of the tenth century, and is the oldest Provençal work of which a fragment has been preserved; here are two lines (from Bartsch's *Chrestomathie Provençale*, 2ᵉ édition, Elberfeld, 1868, p. 1):

> Pro non | es gáigrè ||, si pe|nedén | za 'n prén ||.
> No cre|dét déu || lo nós|tre cre|ator ||.

There are no feminine rhymes; in the first example the *e* of *en* is elided after the preceding *a*.

"The *Chanson de Roland* is eleventh century, rather later than the *Alexis*, and its versification is just the same (Th. Müller's edition of the Oxford MS., Göttingen, 1863, p. 1, 2):

> Cárles | li réis ||, nóstre em|peré|re mágnè ||.
> Il en | apélèt || e ses | dúx e | ses cúntès ||.
> Blancan|dríns fút || des plus | sáives | païéns ||.
> De vas|selágè || fut | a|séz che|valér ||.

The first of these has the unaccented *e* of *nostre* elided before the following vowel, as usual." [H. N.]

[Prof. Paul Meyer of Paris has most kindly sent me the following remarks in reference to some queries made as to the above.

"The short paragraph of G. Paris, with H. Nicol's additions, does not profess to give a complete idea of the French decasyllabic verse, but is correct, so far as it goes. In French versification there is no fixed place for the accent except at the end of the line and, in long verses, about the middle of the line. There are three distinct forms of the decasyllabic verse, (1) that in which the accents fall on the 4th and 10th syllables, (2) that in which they fall on the 5th and 10th, (3) that in which they fall on the 6th and 10th. These forms are never found combined in one poem, as they are in the Italian, where the hendecasyllable may have the middle accent on the 4th or on the 6th syllable indifferently in the same poem. The Alexandrine verse has always the accent on the 6th and 12th syllables. In lines under ten syllables no accent has a fixed place but the one which marks the end of the verse, always admitting an unaccented syllable after it (the feminine rime). Very ancient French poetry does however admit generally an accent on the

4th syllable in octosyllabic verse (see G. Paris in *Romania* I.
294). But this accent on the 4th syllable of the octosyllabic
verse does not require a pause after it, as would be the case in
longer verses.

"That Shakespeare's verse has its origin in the French decasyllabic verse was proved long ago by Zarncke, the Leipzig professor, in his essay *Ueber den fünffüssigen Iambus mit besonderer
Rücksicht auf seine Behandlung durch Lessing, Schiller und
Goethe* (Leipzig, 1865)."]

It may be of interest to some of my readers if I insert
here a short abstract of Zarncke's essay, which is now out of
print, and of which, as far as I know, the copy which has come
into my hands, since the preceding chapters were written, is
the only one to be seen in England. At any rate it is not in
the British Museum or in the Cambridge University Library.
It is of importance as giving the views of one of the most
competent of German metrists on the origin of the heroic line,
together with a specimen of his metrical analysis as applied
to the poetry of Lessing and Schiller. The German title adds
und Goethe, but the metre of the last is only just touched on in
the concluding pages (88—93).

Zarncke begins by lamenting the indifference shewn by
German scholars in regard to the metres employed by their
greatest poets. Germans have done much to illustrate the
metres of the ancients, but Koberstein, he says, is almost the
only historian of literature who has paid any attention to their
own verse. To judge aright of the blank verse of Lessing,
Schiller and Goethe we must have some knowledge of the
previous history of the 5-foot iambic. The earliest specimen of
this is a Provençal poem on Boethius belonging to the first half
of the 10th century. We have no ground for tracing the metre
back either to the Greek 5-foot iambic or 5-foot trochaic with
anacrusis, nor to the Latin hendecasyllabic, which is quite
opposed to it in rhythm. We can say no more of it than that
it was in all probability the ordinary metre of the Romance
epic and spread from France into other countries[1]. The best

---

[1] See however my Preface, p. viii.

account of it is that by Diez in his *Altröm. Sprachdenkmalen*, Bonn, 1846. The oldest form has always the masculine ending, the caesura after the 2nd foot, and a decided pause both at the caesura and at the end of the line. Very frequently the caesura is feminine (i.e. the 1st section ends with a superfluous syllable) and the initial unaccented syllable of the 2nd section is omitted.

Thus we obtain the following scheme ⌣−⌣−(⌣)‖(⌣)−⌣−⌣− giving rise to four different kinds of verse, according as the caesura is masculine or feminine, and the 2nd section complete or truncated[1].

> Enfánts | en díes ‖ forén | omé | felló |
> Qu'el é|ra cóms ‖ ∧ mólt | onráz | e ríx |
> Nos jó|ve óm|ne ‖ quandiús | que nós | estám |
> Donz fó | Boé|cis ‖ ∧ córps | ag bó | e pró |

In the *Alexius* and *Song of Roland*, dating from the 11th century, we meet with examples of feminine ending, as

> Faités | la guér|re ‖ cum vós | l'avéz | emprí|se

though this is rarely found in conjunction with feminine caesura or sectional truncation, sufficient variety being produced by the superfluous syllable at the end.

In other poems of the same date we find the caesura, masculine and feminine, after the 3rd foot. From about the middle of the 12th century, the 5-foot verse gave place to the 4-foot and 6-foot (Alexandrine), but was still retained for lyric poetry, undergoing however two changes: (1) the caesura, which occurs regularly after the 4th syllable, was treated simply as a metrical, not a logical pause, (2) the preceding accent was often thrown back or inverted, making the 2nd foot a trochee, as

> Bona | dómna ‖ per cui | planc e | sospir |

Diez calls this the 'lyrical' caesura, in contrast to the earlier 'epic' caesura.

Later on, all the accents, except the last, became liable to inversion, as

> Bélha | dómna ‖ válham | vóstra | valórs |

---

[1] For the sake of brevity I have used here my own symbols and terminology.

thus giving the following scheme

$$\cup - \mid \cup - \parallel \cup - \mid \cup - \mid \cup - \mid \cup$$
$$- \cup \mid - \cup \parallel - \cup \mid - \cup \mid$$

From 1500 the feminine caesura disappears altogether owing to the growing weakness of the final *e*. The more regular form of the 5-foot iambic became known as the *vers commun* and was employed by Ronsard for epic and by Jodelle for tragedy. By the end of the 16th century, however, there was a reaction in favour of the Alexandrine, the stiff monotony of the rhyming 5-foot with its fixed pauses after the 4th and 10th syllables being felt to be unsuitable for the more animated styles of poetry[1].

The Italian hendecasyllabic metre had been developed out of the Provençal lyric poetry long before it was made famous by Dante. It differs from the French in the constant feminine ending (*a*), the freedom of the caesura which may be either masculine or feminine, and either after the 2nd or 3rd foot (*b*), the use of *enjambement*, i.e. the absence of a final pause, so as to allow one verse to run on into another (*c*), the transposition of the accent in any foot except the last, but especially in the 4th foot (*d*), as

Le Don|ne i | Cavalier ‖ l' árme | gli amo|re

This freedom of rhythm is accompanied by greater freedom in the rhyme, so as to connect together not merely two consecutive lines but whole stanzas.

In England the 5-foot iambic has played a more important part than in any other country. Introduced probably by Chaucer from France at the beginning of the 15th century, by the middle of the 16th it succeeded in throwing off the fetters of rhyme, and became the blank verse of the English drama and epic. The use of the feminine ending and of transposition of accent was however more restricted than in Italy.

In Germany we find examples of the 5-foot iambic closing a four-foot stanza as early as the 12th century[2]. It was

---

[1] See Ebert, *Entwicklungsgeschichte der französischen Tragödie*, Gotha, 1856.
[2] See Lachmann's Preface to his edition of *Wolfram*, p. xxviii.

probably borrowed from the Provençal, but is much freer as to
the use of the caesura, which sometimes disappears altogether.
This freedom continued in spite of the growing influence of
French poetry during the 16th century, till Martin Opitz (d.
1639) laid down the law that there must always be a caesura
after the 4th syllable. Gottsched, writing in 1737, is very
severe on those who break this law, and 'place the caesura any-
where or nowhere,' probably said in reference to such poems
as Bodmer's translations from Thomson. The Anglicized form
however continued to grow in popularity; thus J. H. Schlegel
(1757) announces his intention to adopt the licenses allowed in
English, and while distinguishing three caesuras (after the 4th,
5th and 6th syllables) says it is not necessary for every line to
have the caesura. Wieland (1762) was the first to substitute
anapaests and trochees for the iamb. Klopstock in the Preface
to his *Salomo* says he has interspersed 6-foot and hendecasyllabic
lines among the regular 5-foot, that he substitutes anapaest for
iamb wherever he finds it convenient, and that he often ends
a line with an ionic, 3rd paean or pyrrhic. Herder wrote in
favour of the use of the English metre for the drama in 1768,
and Lessing employed it in his *Nathan* in 1778. He intersperses
freely 6-foot and 4-foot lines, makes the superfluous syllable of
the 'feminine ending' equal in weight to the preceding accented
syllable, elides short final *e* before a vowel or *h*, sometimes
before a consonant as *ohn' dieses, nehm' sich,* and even at the
end of the line, as *und bring' | Ihn her.* More important are
the changes he introduced in regard to the length of his periods
and the use of the caesura. At first, as still in France, each
5-foot line was complete in itself, but the Italians and still more
the English had led the way in connecting lines by *enjambement* and building them up into long periods. In *Nathan* we
meet with periods extending over as many as 27 lines. These
are artfully combined with shorter periods, and the verses are
marked by the antagonism between the sense (logic) and metre,
and by the boldness of the *enjambement.* Thus the end of the
line comes between subject and predicate, as in *Babylon | Ist von
Jerusalem—sagt | Der Patriarch;* between adjective or article
and noun, as *die strengsten | Entschlüsse—mein | Gewissen—*

der | Bescheidne Ritter—ich im | Begriff war; between preposition and noun, as *durch | Das Feuer—von | Euch;* and other closely related words as, *Pilger zu | Geleiten—so | Unendlich viel —zu stürmen und | Zu schirmen—er wandelt wieder auf | Und ab—ganz | Gewiss—will | Ihm danken—sagt wie | Gefällt euch.* Besides this, Lessing takes pains to break the rhythm of the individual line by a pause shortly after the beginning or before the end, as

> —wie ? weil
> Es ganz natürlich ; ganz alltäglich klänge.

> —Ist
> Ein alter Eindruck ein verlorner ? Wirkt
> Das Nehmliche nicht mehr das Nehmliche ?

> Um lieber etwas noch unglaublichers
> Zu glauben—

Sometimes the latter section of a preceding line joins with the earlier section of the following line to make a perfect 5-foot, as

> —Dass doch
> Die Einfalt immer Recht behält ! Ihr dürft
> Mir doch auch wohl vertrauen—

The line is also frequently broken by being divided between different persons. It is only at the end of the period that the antagonism of logic and metre is reconciled.

The caesura is needed to give variety to a line which is complete in itself, but may be dispensed with in a line so much varied as Lessing's. We are not therefore surprised to meet with lines of his which have no caesura or pause of any kind.

Schiller at first wrote his plays in prose, but in 1786 began to employ the 5-foot iambic as modified by Lessing, thus

> Ich drück' an meine Seele dich. Ich fühle
> Die deinige allmächtig an mir schlagen.
> O jetzt ist alles wieder gut. In dieser
> Umarmung ist mein krankes Herz genesen.

He often uses 4-foot and 6-foot lines and occasionally 7-foot. He is even bolder than Lessing in his use of the monosyllable in feminine ending, as *Freúnd mehr, warúm nicht.* Elision is rare, except where a monosyllabic pronoun follows the verb, when

it occurs even at the end of a line, as *was wollt' | Ich denn.*
In length of period and *enjambement* he follows Lessing. As
examples of the latter we may take *du bist | Gerettet—ich | Ver-
gesse—er | Verachtet es—mein ganzes | Verdienst—im linken
Flügel des | Palastes.* He neglects the caesura and divides the
line between different speakers. In *Wallenstein* (1798) we find
further freedom in the length of the line, varying from 7-foot
to 1-foot, and in the use of anapaests and trochees, the former
in all the feet but especially in the last, the latter only in the
1st foot. Slurring is also employed. As examples of harshness
in the use of feminine ending and of *enjambement* may be cited
*vorm | Feind liegt—zu | Mir drang—Kein | Wórt mehr—; es war
der drei | Und zwanzigste des Mai's—wenn der Nachtisch auf-|
gesetzt—eh' die Glücks-|Gestalt mir wieder wegflieht.* The lines
however preserve their individuality better than in Lessing, and
are less often divided between different speakers.

In *Marie Stuart* and *Jungfrau von Orleans* anapaestic substitution is very frequent, but *enjambement* and feminine ending
are less used; rhyme is more common, the verbal and metrical
accents are often opposed. In Schiller's two last dramas *Braut
von Messina* and *Wilhelm Tell* the characteristic feature is the
extended use of the trochee, not merely at the beginning but in
the middle of the line, as

Und du | bist falsch | wie sie! | zwínge | mich nicht | .

The duke Carl August complains of this license in a letter
to Goethe. In other respects however these latest plays are
more regular than the earlier[1].

---

[1] Those who are interested in the historical development of English Metres
will find it worth their while to read a paper by Prof. W. P. Ker on the
Analogies between English and Spanish Verse, printed for the Philological
Society in 1899.

APPENDIX B.

Technical Terms of Greek and Latin Metres[1].

THE following are all the combinations of long and short
syllables, which are called feet, and which have distinctive
names :

Of two Syllables:

Pyrrhichius	⌣ ⌣
Iambus	⌣ –
Trochaeus	
or	– ⌣
Choreus	
Spondaeus	– –

Of three Syllables:

Tribrachys	⌣ ⌣ ⌣
Dactylus	– ⌣ ⌣
Anapaestus	⌣ ⌣ –
Amphibrachys	⌣ – ⌣
Creticus	– ⌣ –
Bacchīus	⌣ – –
Antibacchīus	– – ⌣
Molossus	– – –

Of four Syllables:

Proceleusmaticus	⌣ ⌣ ⌣ ⌣
Paeon primus	– ⌣ ⌣ ⌣
—— *secundus*	⌣ – ⌣ ⌣
—— *tertius*	⌣ ⌣ – ⌣
—— *quartus*	⌣ ⌣ ⌣ –
Ionicus a minore	⌣ ⌣ – –
—— *a majore*	– – ⌣ ⌣

[1] Adapted from Donaldson's *Latin Grammar*.

Diiambus	◡ – ◡ –
Ditrochaeus	– ◡ – ◡
Choriambus (i.e. Trochaeus + iambus) }	– ◡ ◡ –
Antispastus	◡ – – ◡
Epitritus primus	◡ – – –
—— *secundus*	– ◡ – –
—— *tertius*	– – ◡ –
—— *quartus*	– – – ◡
Dispondaeus	– – – –

There are only two kinds of proper feet or distinct and primitive rhythms.

(a) The equal rhythms, in which one long syllable is opposed to two short, so that the ratio is $\frac{1}{1}$; these are

Dactylus, 'the dactyl,' – ◡ ◡; as *mŭnĕră*;
Anapaestus, 'the anapæst,' ◡ ◡ –; as *lăpĭdēs*.

(b) The double rhythms, in which a long and a short syllable are opposed, so that the ratio is $\frac{2}{1}$; these are

Trochaeus, 'the trochee,' – ◡; as *mūsă*;
Iambus, 'the iambus,' ◡ –; as *ămās*.

To these may be added the representative feet; i.e. the *spondaeus* or 'spondee,' which represents the equal rhythm by two long syllables, as *dīcūnt*, and the *tribrachys* or 'tribrach,' which represents the double rhythm by three short syllables, as *brĕvĭbŭs*.

Each simple foot has two parts, one of which is said to have the *ictus* (stress) upon it and is called *arsis*, the other part is called *thesis*. In Dactylic and Trochaic verse the arsis is on the first part of each foot. In Anapaestic and Iambic on the last.

It is essential to the harmony of a line that some one or more of its feet should be divided between two different words. This division is called *caesura* or 'cutting.' There are two kinds of *caesura*—the *masculine, strong,* or *monosyllabic caesura*, when only the first syllable of the foot is in the preceding word; and the *feminine, weak,* or *trochaic caesura,* where the first two syllables of a dactyl are in the preceding word, and the remaining short syllable in the word which follows. Thus in the following line we have *strong caesuras* in the second and fourth feet, and *weak caesura* in the third place:

Formosam | resonare | doces | Amaryllida silvas.

If a word is so placed in a verse as to coincide with a metrical foot, we have a *diaeresis,* which is the opposite of the *caesura;* thus there is a *diaeresis* in the first and fifth feet of the following line of Virgil:

Lumina | labentem caelo quae | ducitis | annum.

Half a foot is technically called a *hemimer* (ἡμιμερές), and *caesuras,* which take place in the middle of the second, third, fourth and fifth feet respectively, are called *trihemimeral, penthemimeral, hephthemimeral* and *ennehemimeral caesuras.*

The term 'metre' besides its general sense has a special sense denoting a certain portion of a metrical line. In Dactylic verse one foot constitutes a metre of this kind, the dactylic hexameter having six feet; in Trochaic, Iambic and Anapaestic two feet constitute a metre; thus Iambic dimeter has four feet, as *inar|sit aes|tuo|sius |.*

If a metre terminates in a *hemimer,* it is called *catalectic* or 'interrupted'; if it is completed, it is called *acatalectic* or 'uninterrupted.'

If the supposed or prescribed metre is redundant by a *hemimer,* the term *hypercatalectic* is applied. Two catalectic forms are so common that they are often called feet; these are the *choriambus* or dactylic trihemimer; as *ēxtŭlĕ|rās ||,* which may be termed the dactylic dimeter catalectic; and the *creticus* or trochaic trihemimer; as *ēffĕ|rūnt ||,* which may be termed the trochaic monometer catalectic.

INDEX.

For EU product safety concerns, contact us at Calle de José Abascal, 56–1°,
28003 Madrid, Spain or eugpsr@cambridge.org.

www.ingramcontent.com/pod-product-compliance
Ingram Content Group UK Ltd.
Pitfield, Milton Keynes, MK11 3LW, UK
UKHW042150130625
459647UK00011B/1268